Shakespeare and His

Shakespeare and His Authors

Critical Perspectives on the Authorship Question

Edited by William Leahy

continuum

Continuum International Publishing Group

The Tower Building   80 Maiden Lane
11 York Road   Suite 704
London SE1 7NX   New York NY 10038

www.continuumbooks.com

British Library Cataloguing-in-Publication Data
A catalogue record for this book is available from the British Library.

ISBN: 978-0-8264-3684-9 (hardback)
          978-0-8264-2611-6 (paperback)

Library of Congress Cataloging-in-Publication Data
A catalog record for this book is available from the Library of Congress.

Typeset by Newgen Imaging Systems Pvt Ltd, Chennai, India
Printed and bound in Great Britain by CPI Antony Rowe, Chippenham, Wiltshire

Contents

Acknowledgements

Nicholas Royle's essay in this collection, 'The Distraction of "Freud": Literature, Psychoanalysis and the Bacon–Shakespeare Controversy', first appeared in the *Oxford Literary Review*, 12, (1990) 101–39. I would like to thank both the editors and publishers for their kind permission to reproduce it here. Some of the material included in the essay by Graham Holderness, 'Shakespearean Selves', first appeared in 'Author! Author!: Shakespeare and Biography', *Shakespeare* 5.1, (2009) 122–33. I am grateful to the editors and to Routledge/Taylor and Francis for permission to reproduce the material.

Notes on Contributors

Andrew Bennett is Professor of English at the University of Bristol. His books include *Ignorance: Literature and Agnoiology* (2009), *Wordsworth Writing* (2007), *The Author* (2005), *Romantic Poets and the Culture of Posterity* (1999) and *Keats, Narrative and Audience: The Posthumous Life of Writing* (1994). With Nicholas Royle he has published *An Introduction to Literature, Criticism and Theory* (4th edition, 2009) and *Still Lives: Elizabeth Bowen and the Dissolution of the Novel* (1995).

Dominic Dromgoole is Artistic Director of the Globe Theatre, London and the author of *Will and Me: How Shakespeare Took Over My Life* (2006).

Sean Gaston is Reader in English at Brunel University, West London. He is the author of *Derrida and Disinterest* (2005), *The Impossible Mourning of Jacques Derrida* (2006), *Starting With Derrida: Plato, Aristotle and Hegel* (2007) and *Derrida, Literature and War: Absence and the Chance of Meeting* (2009).

Graham Holderness is Professor of English at the University of Hertford-shire. His books include: *D.H. Lawrence: History, Ideology and Fiction* (1982), *Shakespeare's History* (1985), *The Shakespeare Myth* (1988), *Shakespeare: The Histories* (2000), *Anglo-Saxon Verse* (2000), *Cultural Shakespeare: Essays in the Shakespeare Myth* (2001), *Visual Shakespeare: Essays in Film and Television* (2002) and *Textual Shakespeare: Writing and the Word* (2003). His novel *The Prince of Denmark* was published in 2002. He is editor of *Critical Survey*, and a Fellow of the English Association.

William Leahy is the Head of the School of Arts at Brunel University, West London. He has published widely on Shakespeare's History plays and is the author of *Elizabethan Triumphal Processions* (2005).

Willy Maley is Professor of Renaissance Studies at the University of Glasgow. He is the author of *A Spenser Chronology* (1994), *Salvaging Spenser: Colonialism, Culture and Identity* (1997) and *Nation, State and Empire in English Renaissance Literature: Shakespeare to Milton* (2003). He has also edited seven collections of essays, the latest of which are, with Andrew Murphy, *Shakespeare and Scotland* (2004); with Alex Benchimol, *Spheres of Influence: Intellectual and*

Cultural Publics from Shakespeare to Habermas (2007) and with Philip Schwyzer, *Shakespeare and Wales* (2009).

Nicholas Royle is Professor of English at the University of Sussex. His books include *Telepathy and Literature* (1991), *E. M. Forster* (1999), *The Uncanny* (2003), *How to Read Shakespeare* (2005), *In Memory of Jacques Derrida* (2009) and (with Andrew Bennett) *An Introduction to Literature, Criticism and Theory* (4th edition, 2009). He is co-editor of the *Oxford Literary Review*.

William D. Rubinstein is Professor of History at the University of Aberystwyth. He has published widely on many topics, including modern British elites in *Who Were the Rich?* (2009), modern Jewish history in *Genocide* (2004) and *Israel, the Jews, and the West: The Fall and Rise of Antisemitism* (2008) and on fundamentalism in *The End of Ideology and the Rise of Religion* (2009). In recent years he has become interested in the Shakespeare authorship question, and is the co-author, with Brenda James, of *The Truth Will Out* (2005).

Mark Rylance is an actor and was the first Artistic Director of the Globe Theatre, London, a post he held for ten years. He is also a theatre director and playwright and is author of the play, *The Big Secret Live – I Am Shakespeare – Webcam Daytime Chat-Room Show* (2007).

Sandra G. L. Schruijer is Professor of Organization Sciences at the Utrecht School of Governance, University of Utrecht, and Professor of Organizational Psychology at TiasNimbas Business School, Tilburg University, both in The Netherlands. She has published widely on the psychology of inter-organizational relations, organizational boundaries and group negotiation. Sandra is editor of the *Journal of Community and Applied Social Psychology*.

Introduction: The Life of the Author

William Leahy

'It is not what we don't know that troubles us', said Mark Twain, 'it is what we know but isn't so'. Although it is unknown whether Twain was thinking of Shakespeare when this was said, with a single sentence he defines the parameters of the Shakespeare authorship controversy. For those who will not countenance any 'problem' with the authorship of Shakespeare's plays and poems – most people who have an opinion on the matter and certainly the vast majority of academics – there is nothing that 'we don't know'. In this sense, there is nothing to trouble us because everything that needs to be known in attributing all the plays and poems written by 'William Shakespeare' to the man who was born and bred in Stratford-upon-Avon and who became a successful actor and playwright in London is known; no problem therefore exists. To those who do perceive there to be a problem with such attribution, the difficulty lies precisely in that certainty, in the knowledge that everything that needs to be known is known. This just 'isn't so' they believe. Twain is an interesting and pertinent example to use here, given that he was indeed a 'doubter' and in a brilliantly satirical and semi-autobiographical work entitled *Is Shakespeare Dead?* (1909) outlined the case for the 'problem' with Shakespeare as the author before subsequently putting forward his own argument that Francis Bacon was the true author of the plays and poems. Twain's central difficultly in accepting Shakespeare as the author is a fairly typical one, in that he felt he simply could not match the known biography of the 'man from Stratford' with that of the author of a totality of works which seem to encompass experiences, ideas, relationships, knowledge – *life*, essentially – far removed from that possible for a glover's son from a country town. Some call an attitude such as Twain's snobbery; others, sociology.

Twain's comment is important in another sense, in that it is founded in a clear perception of 'we' and 'you', an evident and all-encompassing 'us' and 'them'. There are those who know we know (us) and those who know we do not know (them). Such has been the delineating reality of the Shakespeare authorship controversy, consisting as it traditionally has of 'Two Households both alike in dignity,' constantly 'From ancient grudge' on the verge of breaking 'to new mutiny' (*Romeo and Juliet*, prologue). However, although these two sides are indeed both 'alike in dignity', they are certainly not alike in terms of power. Those who believe there to be *no* problem with Shakespeare as the author of the works traditionally attributed to him – Stratfordians – as well as being very much in the majority, can count just about all academics, and certainly professional literary scholars, among their number. Those who perceive a problem with the traditional attribution – non-Stratfordians – are, generally speaking either non-academics or are not literary scholars in terms of professional status. This has led to a situation whereby Stratfordians have found themselves able to characterize non-Stratfordians as 'amateurs', and damn them with the pejorative value inherent in that term. This despite the fact that many of the acknowledged great Shakespearean scholars of the past, such as E. K. Chambers, for example, were not professional academics but were, indeed, amateurs. This being the case, the authorship question gives rise to all sorts of interesting and relevant negotiations associated with authority and social roles within our culture and the ways in which these roles are changing and being challenged in the twenty-first century. This collection of essays is, to some extent, testament to these very developments.

That the Shakespeare authorship question is an 'academic taboo' is a truism which needs little in the way of evidence to support it. To my knowledge, only three professional literary academics have written about this subject at any length, and two of those three have done so in a spirit of great scepticism. The first literary scholar to do so was Samuel Schoenbaum in his seminal *Shakespeare's Lives*, his approach clear in the designation of his analysis of the authorship question as 'Deviations' (1970; 1991: 385–481). Schoenbaum's thesis is clear in the final sentences he writes on the subject:

> Away from the Academy, whether in the lounge bar of a cruise ship or in the shadow of the Moorish wall in Gibraltar or on an Intourist bus on the road to Sevastopol, the professor of English (once his identity has been guessed by fellow-holiday-makers) will be asked, as certainly as day follows night, 'Did Shakespeare *really* write those plays?' He will do well to nod assent and avoid explanation, for nothing he says will erase suspicions fostered for over a century by amateurs who have yielded to the dark power of the anti-Stratfordian obsession. One thought perhaps offers a

crumb of redeeming comfort: the energy absorbed by the mania might otherwise have gone into politics. (450–51)

The second major consideration of the subject by a professional Shakespearean scholar, Jonathan Bate's best-selling *The Genius of Shakespeare*, which devoted a chapter to the authorship controversy (1997: 65–100), repeats the air of ridicule that defines Schoenbaum's views. Almost thirty years later, Bate begins his chapter by professing empathy with those who doubt Shakespeare, but proceeds to dismiss alternative theories as wrong-headed and foolish. Finally, there is Nicholas Royle's long essay, which appeared in 1990 and which is reproduced in this collection; 'The distraction of "Freud": Literature, Psychoanalysis and the Bacon–Shakespeare controversy' (1990a: 101–38). This essay is not specifically about the authorship question but is much more a contemplation on Freud and Derrida. Perhaps this explains why Royle is not in the business of summoning the question up in order to call its very *raison d'être* into question, as seems to be the case with Schoenbaum and Bate.

That so few professional academics are interested in the Shakespeare authorship question, particularly Shakespearean scholars, is surprising in the sense that the questioning of the authorship of the plays attributed to William Shakespeare has existed – contrary to received knowledge – since 1592; the very beginning, according to orthodox chronology, of Shakespeare's writing career. The received knowledge holds rather that the authorship question began with Delia Bacon in the 1850s, with her positing her namesake Francis Bacon (no relation) as the true author. Bate is typical in his view of this (some of which he emphasises for effect); '*No one in Shakespeare's lifetime or the first two hundred years after his death expressed the slightest doubt about his authorship. . . .* That nobody raised the question for two hundred years proves that there is no intrinsic reason why there should be a Shakespeare Authorship Controversy' (73). If this were true, it would explain, at least to some extent, why there has been so little interest shown by professional academics in the authorship question. If it were true, then the conclusion Bate reaches would seem correct and serious doubt regarding the claims made by non-Stratfordians would be perfectly justifiable. However, the truth of Bate's initial statement regarding the questioning of Shakespeare's authorship in his own lifetime is questionable. For, it seems that at least two examples of such questioning exist.

Robert Greene's *Groats-worth of Wit* (1592) is one of the most researched and written about pieces of 'Shakespeareana' in existence. It is widely regarded as evidence that Shakespeare was in London at the time, and evidence too that his burgeoning career as a playwright was underway. Though now generally accepted as having been written by Henry Chettle, who then passed it off as Greene's work due to its controversial nature, *Groats-worth of Wit* is still considered to be proof that Shakespeare was establishing himself as a playwright in London in 1592. The oft-quoted evidence is the following passage taken from the text, wherein the author warns three un-named playwrights (none of whom are Shakespeare) about an actor referred to as 'Shake-scene':

> Yes, trust them not: for there is an vpstart Crow, beautified with our feathers, that with his *Tygers hart wrapt in a Players hyde*, supposes he is as well able to bombast out a blanke verse as the best of you: and being an absolute *Iohannes fac totum*, is in his owne conceit the onely Shake-scene in a countrey. O that I might intreate your rare wits to be imploied in more profitable courses: & let those Apes imitate your past excellence, and neuer more acquaint them with your admired inuentions. I know the best husband of you all will neuer proue an Usurer, and the kindest of them all will neuer seeke you a kind nurse: yet whilest you may, seeke you better Maisters; for it is pittie men of such rare wits, should be subiect to the pleasure of such rude groomes. (Greene 1592)

This passage is accepted by scholars as being directed at Shakespeare, as evidence that this young playwright was ruffling the feathers of his older, more educated fellow writers. Furthermore, Jonathan Bate, like the vast majority of critics, believes that this passage demonstrates that Shakespeare was becoming an important literary figure by 1592 (1997: 16), not just because of the reference to 'Shake-scene', but because the line '*Tygers hart wrapt in a Players hyde*' is a reference to his *3 Henry VI*. Bate writes: 'For Greene, then, Shakespeare's is a double offence: as an actor he gains credit for mouthing fine lines which really belong to the university wits, and as an upstart writer he is now imitating their style. Even borrowing their phrases, in his own plays' (16). However, in her interpretation of the *Groats-worth of Wit*, Diana Price has shown that significant weaknesses and gaps exist in this kind of conventional reading (2001). According to Price, orthodox criticism of this passage tends to look at it in isolation from the rest of the text, and if, she argues, the entire *Groats-worth of Wit* is considered, a very different reading becomes valid: 'When missing pieces . . . are reinstated, the salvo levelled at Shake-scene turns out to be an attack against an untrustworthy actor who is also a moneylender and … a paymaster of playwrights' (Price 47). This seems to fit what we know of William Shakespeare, as he is on record as an actor, as a theatre shareholder/broker and, in this very same year as a moneylender. The *Groats-worth of Wit* is often quoted as the first appearance on record of Shakespeare in London, but it is worth remembering that his first appearance in the capital city on record sees him lending the sum of £7 to one John Clayton (Savage 1929, 4:151–2). Given this, Price's conclusion is that in the *Groats-worth of Wit*, 'Shake-scene is resented, not as a promising dramatist who threatens the *status quo*, but as a paymaster, callous usurer, and actor who ... thinks he can pass off their words [the three professional playwrights] as his own' (50). Price interprets the phrase 'upstart crow' not as meaning an 'upstart writer' as Bate does, but by revealing that Aesop's crow 'was a proud strutter who borrowed from the feathers of others, [and] Horace's crow was a plagiarist' (48), that a direct reference is being made to Shakespeare's practice of literary theft. In this context, the phrase 'beautified with our feathers' takes on an obvious meaning and certainly gives rise, despite the generally held view, to the perception of a contemporary authorship question. The author of the *Groats-worth of Wit* is clearly stating that this actor 'Shake-scene' is stealing the writing of his colleagues and putting his own name to it. Such a realization is supported when one considers, as Diana Price does, an epigram composed by Ben Jonson entitled 'On Poet-Ape':

> Poor POET-APE, that would be thought our chief,
>   Whose works are e'en the frippery of wit,
> From brokage is become so bold a thief,
>   As we, the robb'd, leave rage, and pity it.
> At first he made low shifts, would pick and glean,
>   Buy the reversion of old plays ; now grown
> To a little wealth, and credit in the scene,
>   He takes up all, makes each man's wit his own:
> And, told of this, he slights it. Tut, such crimes
>   The sluggish gaping auditor devours;
> He marks not whose 'twas first: and after-times
>   May judge it to be his, as well as ours.
> Fool! as if half eyes will not know a fleece
>   From locks of wool, or shreds from the whole piece?
>
> (Jonson 1875, 8: 44–5)

Jonson, in a poem that seems to repeat almost exactly the accusations articulated by Greene, referred to callous actors as 'poet-apes' and here accuses one of firstly 'procuring plays with lapsed copyrights . . . [and then has] passed off someone else's work as his own; sold plays that were not his to sell; or adapted or vulgarized someone's work for popular consumption' (Price 93). Jonson, it is believed, wrote this epigram some time between 1595 and 1612. If it is directed at Shakespeare (and the evidence is strong; see Price 91–5), it would be the only piece that Jonson wrote relating to Shakespeare during the Stratford man's lifetime. As well as this, it is further evidence of an authorship problem related to Shakespeare at his moment of operation. It is, along with the Greene text, evidence of a Shakespeare authorship question that is over 400 years old and that was taking place around Shakespeare as he was establishing himself in the theatre.

One aim of this current collection, following on from the above, is as a corrective to the silence over the years; not in any way in order to suggest that someone other than Shakespeare wrote the plays attributed to him, but rather to demonstrate that the Shakespeare authorship controversy is a historical, social and cultural phenomenon worthy of research and analysis in academia. It has been in existence since Shakespeare's lifetime; it generates masses of intellectual and historical analysis; it interests millions of people all over the world; it relates to all sorts of notions of identity, power, authority, ownership, cultural superiority and the transmission of conventional, dominant knowledge(s). In short, it has all the characteristics of an academic subject; all of the properties of an area of knowledge that should generate academic research, analysis and argumentation. This collection represents the first serious attempt at such an endeavour.

* * *

In one sense, the belief, articulated by Jonathan Bate (and many others) that the Shakespeare authorship question is indeed only about 200 years old holds some truth. Our notion of the author as the originator, register and arbiter of what s/he writes is a relatively recent development and Andrew Bennett's opening essay 'On not Knowing Shakespeare (and on Shakespeare not Knowing): Romanticism, the Authorship Question, and English Literature' shows how the authorship question is inherent in the dominant, romantic conception of the author that our culture prioritizes. The important determiner of this entire view of Shakespeare as author is closely tied to the romantic idea of genius, a concept which, bordering on the theological, demands a figurehead shed of definite attributes but who can be re-made in the image of any culture's values. The focus on subjectivity is a theme continued in Willy Maley's 'Malfolio: Foul Papers on the Shakespeare Authorship Question'; Shakespeare still being viewed, according to Maley 'As if a man were author of himself / And knew no other kin'

(*Coriolanus*, 5.3.33–4). Setting this idea in the greater context of Derrida's engagement with literature and, more specifically in his belief that 'everything is in Shakespeare', Maley ponders whether it is ever possible to 'get outside' Shakespeare (and thus the authorship question) given that he is so entwined inside notions of self and constructions of authorship itself. Much of what interests Maley about both Derrida and the 'proper name' is revisited later in the collection in the essays of Royle and Gaston.

William Rubinstein, as a historian, considers more closely these issues regarding the sometimes contradictory methodologies of historical and literary endeavour and ponders the Shakespeare authorship controversy as a purely historical phenomenon. Rubinstein believes that the question of the authorship of Shakespeare's works is simply a historio-graphical issue, similar to any other question about the past which historians debate and discuss, and decided by the evidence. He finds that rational debate about the authorship question by English Literature academics – who are not historians and who often reject historio-graphical discussion which goes beyond the 'text' – has always been impossible. To some extent, this attitude is justified by the number of eccentric theories about the authorship question which have arisen over the past 150 years. But overall, Rubinstein argues that this attitude represents a denial of legitimate questions about the authorship controversy.

Nicholas Royle's essay 'The Distraction of "Freud": Literature, Psychoanalysis and the Bacon–Shakespeare Controversy', first appeared in 1990 and forms part of his ongoing interest in Derrida and Freud. Royle takes as his starting point Freud's conversion to a belief that Edward de Vere, the seventeenth Earl of Oxford was responsible for the works attributed to Shakespeare, and the continuing discomfort Freudian scholars demonstrate with this belief. Royle reads this event through the works of Derrida in a complex and playful analysis that sees Freud's conversion, like his belief in telepathy, as a 'distraction' and as based on the difficulties surrounding the 'proper name'. As Royle states:

[M]y hypothesis [is] in four parts: i) that *Signsponge* (1984) (and Derrida's other work on the signature and proper name) appears to offer a way of identifying Shakespeare as author, a way which at the same time tampers with traditional scholarly distinctions between 'internal' and 'external evidence', questioning the very idea of signing and appropriation (by the author, by the reader, in the name of the author, and so on); ii) that *Hamlet* can be read not only as a text signed, on the 'inside', by Shakespeare, but also as a text which is specifically *about* the idea and act of signing; iii) that the logic of this reading can be extended to other 'Shakespeare' texts; and iv) that, finally, all of this can be linked up with the question of psychoanalysis, and above all with the proper name(s) of 'Freud'. (106)

In what is in many ways a 'response' to the reading of Royle's essay, in 'No Biography: Shakespeare Author', Sean Gaston explores the quasi-theological need to describe the author of the works of Shakespeare as either 'uniquely no one' or 'someone unique'. Gaston argues that the urge for no biography (for the unparalleled creation in the wake of a Christ-like absence of biography, and the impossible and violent legacy of the genius of being no one) is as strong as the urge for the restitution of the biography (which exposes the frail fault line between researching and searching, between an institutional attribution and an antiquarian enthusiasm, between an apparent secularism and the full conviction of belief). When it comes to Shakespeare, Gaston says, academia cannot avoid the passion of original discovery and the theology of the etymon. The chapter ends by examining Nicholas Royle's (and to some extent Maley's) case for Shakespeare as author by tracing the disseminated proper name(s) 'shake', 'spear', 'nick', 'william' through the works and through Royle's essay itself.

The starting point for Graham Holderness, in his chapter 'Shakespearean Selves', is the dominant school of thought in the 1980s, where Shakespeare criticism derived largely from the work of Marx, Darwin and Freud. In comparison, the Shakespeare authorship question is, he says based on much older notions of the self and of being. In this older (romantic) approach, the author is sovereign, the originator and shaper of the writing, the driving imaginative force, the controlling artistic authority. The writer is cause, writing the effect. In the 1980s, the Shakespeare authorship question was not really a question at all; the writer was an effect of the writing. Now, Holderness feels, we have got the author back from the dead. His emotional experience predicates the writing, it causes it to be. But that remains an inferential relationship impossible to prove or demonstrate. So the critic has recourse to his imagination, and creates a narrative consistent with the documentary facts, and with the emotional truths embedded both in the writing, and in the heart of the critic. Holderness focuses in on the example of a specific biography of Shakespeare, Stephen Greenblatt's *Will in the World: How Shakespeare Became Shakespeare* (2004), and shows that Greenblatt posits a Shakespearean 'self' that drove the writings while accepting that this 'self' is obscure and impenetrable. Greenblatt accepts that the channel of causation from self to work is hard to map; but presupposes that some such transference must have occurred. Holderness shows how

Greenblatt puts much of his own personal experience into his biography of Shakespeare.

William Leahy's chapter 'Shakinomics; or, the Shakespeare Authorship Question and the Undermining of Traditional Authority', is concerned with the reasons why academia has traditionally ignored the authorship question and marginalized the issues it brings up concerning identity, ownership and social/cultural authority. Using the work of Michel de Certeau, Leahy shows how the orthodox view of the Shakespeare biography functions as a powerful 'theoretical' truth and how this explains both a stagnation in terms of Shakespearean biographical research and the ongoing 'stand off' between Stratfordians and non-Stratfordians. Using a contemporary model from the business world, Leahy suggests a way to end this stand off that could be beneficial for all concerned and see a reanimation of the biographical impulse in Shakespeare studies.

Sandra Schruijer's contribution 'Fighting over Shakespeare's Authorship: Identity, Power and Academic Debate', is very much founded in and is an analysis of this 'stand off' using conflict theory parameters. Schruijer adopts a social–psychological perspective in trying to understand the Shakespeare authorship debate, especially its fierce and destructive nature. She constructs the debate as a relational conflict rather than as a task conflict, and mobilizing social–psychological perspectives characterizes the debate as one involving the protagonists' various social identities and varying power positions. Schruijer tellingly illustrates her arguments with examples from personal experience as well as findings from a survey among non-Stratfordians.

The collection ends with two interviews on the authorship controversy with two individuals very much on the front line of Shakespeare in performance. Mark Rylance, the famous Shakespearean actor, is a non-Stratfordian, and was so for the duration of his ten years as the Artistic Director of the Globe between 1996 and 2005. Dominic Dromgoole, his successor as Artistic Director at the Globe is a solid Stratfordian, though is not as dismissive of the authorship question as many of his fellow directors and performers. Both provide insight into the 'everydayness' of working with Shakespeare and those around them in the realization that the authorship issue is a contentious and important one.

The Shakespeare authorship question is a subject which produces its own genre, has an identifiable history and, as previously stated, interests millions of people the world over. It is also worth saying that it generates much heat and much passion. In these senses, it has an important and ongoing presence in our culture. It exists on the very margins of academia, deemed by most Shakespearean academics as irrelevant, of interest only to fools and fantasists. Yet, many academics, such as those collected here, find the authorship question interesting, important and worthy of analysis in theoretical, sociological and philosophical terms. This collection seeks to provide an analysis of this subject in all its rich diversity and significance. The primary objective is to demonstrate what is possible when academia takes the Shakespeare authorship question seriously. This is the first time it has happened and I wish to thank all of the contributors to this volume for approaching the subject in this serious way. I would hope that everyone interested in Shakespeare can see what they have been missing.

Chapter 1

On not Knowing Shakespeare (and on Shakespeare not Knowing): Romanticism, the Authorship Question and English Literature

Andrew Bennett

Not knowing Shakespeare, not knowing much about his life is crucial to his reinvention within Romanticism. The very high value put on Shakespeare's work in the Romantic period is in fact indissociably bound up with this ignorance of his life: ignorance of Shakespeare accounts for the way his work is valued. Indeed, more generally, bardic ignorance is at work in a new conception of authorship, and therefore even of Literature itself, which has come to characterize the period's literary culture: the Shakespearean author as the centre and the periphery, the author as 'not itself', as, in John Keats's words, 'every thing and nothing' (Rollins 1958, 1: 387). And the emergence of the Shakespeare authorship question in the 1850s may be understood to be a function of this new definition of 'Literature' around a certain conception of Shakespeare. In other words, rather than an arbitrary or contingent dimension of the reception of the body of work most commonly if not uncomplicatedly ascribed to William Shakespeare (and his collaborators), theories that assign authorship of that work to other writers may be seen as intrinsic to both its cultural status and to the new prestige awarded Literature more generally in the early-nineteenth century: it is just because so little is known about Shakespeare that conceptions of literary authorship and of Literature itself come to operate as they do. Shakespeare can only be figured as 'every thing and nothing' to the extent that he is biographically opaque or empty. It is something of a truism to say that English Literature would not be the same without Shakespeare, but one might also suggest that English Literature would not be the same without the many facets of our ignorance of William Shakespeare – and therefore in the end without our, or at least others', doubts about his authorship. There is a certain logic at work here that involves the sense that without the Shakespeare authorship question there would be no such thing as English Literature, at least as it is presently conceived and constituted.[1] There is nothing, we might say, no Literature at least, outside the Shakespeare authorship question.

1

The Romantic construction of the Shakespearean author continues to feature in mainstream contemporary academic discourse. The first paragraph of Stephen Greenblatt's recent high-profile biography of Shakespeare, *Will in the World: How Shakespeare Became Shakespeare*, is exemplary:

> A young man from a small provincial town – a man without independent wealth, without powerful family connections, and without a university education – moves to London in the later 1580s and, in a remarkably short time, becomes the greatest playwright not of his age alone but of all time. His works appeal to the learned and the unlettered, to urban sophisticates and provincial first-time theatergoers. He makes his audiences laugh and cry; he turns politics into poetry; he recklessly mingles vulgar clowning and philosophical subtlety. He grasps with equal penetration the intimate lives of kings and of beggars; he seems at one moment to have studied law, at another theology, at another ancient history, while at the same time he effortlessly mimes the accents of country bumpkins and takes delight in old wives' tales. How is an achievement of this magnitude to be explained? How did Shakespeare become Shakespeare? (2004: 11)

Greenblatt succinctly summarizes many of the key concerns in Romantic and post-Romantic Shakespeare biography and therefore in the construction of literary authorship since the late-eighteenth century. In particular, there is – there must be – a mystery with respect to Shakespeare's *achievement* because of the disjunction between what is known of his upbringing and education and what is thought of as his 'genius': there are, Greenblatt goes on to remark, 'no immediately obvious clues to unravel the great mystery of such immense creative power'; the work 'seems to have come from a god and not a mortal, let alone a mortal of provincial origins and modest education' (12, 13). And as Greenblatt makes clear, Shakespeare's genius includes in particular a sense of his multiplicity, a multiplicity that can be categorized in terms of (a) his apparent familiarity with multiple learned and professional discourses, and (b) his ability to imagine himself into and to perform, through a kind of 'uncanny ventriloquism' (14), an almost unlimited and highly diverse selection of individuals or kinds of individuals: he is 'myriad-minded' (see Coleridge 1983, 2: 19; Schoenbaum 1991: 184), in one cliché; protean in another. Another way of putting these two points is to talk, as Greenblatt goes on to do, about the possibility of making links between Shakespeare's 'timeless work with its universal appeal' on the one hand and a 'particular life', with all its 'humdrum' ordinariness on the other (13) – to talk about Shakespeare's uncanny exemplarity, in other words.

Greenblatt's study also reproduces and reinforces that other feature of Romantic and post-Romantic Shakespeareography: bardolatrous igno-rance. In the first place, the best – most reliable, most scholarly, most authoritative – biographies present a curious combination of a determined and often rather obsessive concentration on empirical and archival research, and at the same time an equally determined use of the imagination to fill in the gaps in historical information. This combination of empirical research and speculative hypothesis has been a feature of such studies at least since the publication of Edmond Malone's multi-volume edition of Shakespeare's works in 1790. As Samuel Schoenbaum comments, although Malone 'uncovered much', the documents that he disinterred 'left untouched the central core of the mystery: the character and spirit and daily life of the greatest of poets' (140). There is, therefore, a predominantly subjunctive voice in such studies: Shakespeare history is largely the history of what the writer *would* have done if he *had* done what he is *imagined* to have done. This is, of course, a direct response to the notable lack of documentation concerning William Shakespeare's life and to the fact that what documenta-tion there is tends to be unilluminatingly legal and financial. Beyond the basic documentary facts, in other words, our knowledge of Shakespeare's life is very limited, and what we know allows us minimal if any engagement with what he thought, felt, believed, said, imagined, desired. The subjunc-tive mood is often, as in Greenblatt's biography, supported by readings from the poems and plays: there is, in Greenblatt and others, an assump-tion that the plays and the poems can be read as keys to the poet's being, as the truth of Shakespeare's subjectivity.[2] And as it is for others writing in this tradition, for Greenblatt it is the sonnets, above all, that allow us insight into the poet. 'There is no mask here', Greenblatt writes of one sonnet: 'One of the startling effects' of the poems, he goes on, is 'an almost painful intimacy' (233). But the plays also allow us a certain perspective on the personality of this mysterious man, serving both as frames for personal revelation and display, and as veils or masks over that personality: what Shakespeare does in his art is to 'transform' everything that he experiences in his life into an 'aesthetic resource' (377). His plays are both reflections on his life and not reflections on his life. In the absence of firm data, in other words, and in order to know the author, we need to look at the compulsions, obsessions, repetitions, allusions and structural patterns, of the plays and poems themselves. And there is an odd circularity here: we investigate Shakespeare's life in order to get a better handle on his writing, but in order to know Shakespeare we resort to interpreting his writings – which can only be fully understood in the context of his life (and so on).

2

Critics have argued that Malone and the Romantics shared the assumption that, as Younglim Han puts it in a recent study of Romantic Bardolatry, Shakespeare 'self-consciously constructed and responded to, his personal identity in his writings', and that a Shakespeare work represents, precisely, an 'internalization of the subject matter' (2001: 79). According to Han, it is this sense of poetic or literary internalization that led to the desire in the late-eighteenth and early-nineteenth centuries to return to, to reconstruct the 'authentic' Shakespeare: 'Malone's accounts of Shakespeare's identity were committed to biographical authorship study by reconstructing Shakespeare's experience and consciousness at the time of writing' (79). But there is another important paradox at work in this, which critics have often overlooked: the ascription of an internalized consciousness to Shakespeare through and in his work (through and in the sonnets, read as personal reflections on personal experience and emotions, in and through the character of Hamlet, with whom the author identifies, and so on), is effected precisely in terms of a certain authorial absence.[3] It is because the Romantics do not know (much) about Shakespeare that he becomes available for a form of authorial–textual identification: his texts can be read as direct transcriptions of an inner self, of a consciousness, to the extent that that hermeneutic is not – cannot be – compromised by our knowledge of the author's personality, his subjectivity.

It is, then, the *lack* of information about Shakespeare that characterizes our *knowledge* of him – and that therefore characterizes the poet himself. This informational vacuum becomes a central issue in Shakespeare appreciation in the mid- to late-eighteenth century. Writing in 1780, for example,

George Steevens comments that all that is known with certainty of Shakespeare's life can be summarized in a single sentence, which he italicizes for emphasis: '*he was born at Stratford upon Avon, – married and had children there, – went to London, where he commenced acting, and wrote poems and plays – returned to Stratford, made his will, died, and was buried*' (in Vickers 1974–1981, 6: 291). Edward Capell had earlier made a similar point, slightly more fully, in the Introduction to his 1768 edition of the works:

> An imperfect and loose account of his father and family; his own marriage, and the issue of it; some traditional stories, many of them trifling in themselves, supported by small authority and seemingly ill-grounded; together with his life's final period as gather'd from his monument, is the full and whole amount of historical matter that is in any of these writings, in which the critick and essayist swallow up the biographer, who yet ought to take the lead in them. The truth is, the occurrences of this most interesting life (we mean, the private ones) are irrecoverably lost to us. (in Vickers, 5: 326)

It is this irrecoverable loss, in other words, that constitutes, for critics and other writers from the mid-eighteenth century, the proper critical relationship with Shakespeare: it is what we do *not* know about him that makes him William Shakespeare.

Edmond Malone is crucial here, of course, as the first scholarly, empirically exacting biographer of Shakespeare, and it is significant that his life of the dramatist is never properly finished, always necessarily fragmentary, even in its final, posthumously edited publication in the 1821 jointly authored and greatly expanded, 21-volume edition of his 10-volume *The Plays and Poems of William Shakespeare* from 1790.[4] The dates are telling, stretching as they do from the beginning to near the end of what we now think of as the era of 'Romanticism', and reflecting the intense desire but final failure during those 30 years to establish the biographical facts, to write a life, of the author William Shakespeare. In fact, however, Malone's documentary biography may itself be understood to be involved in the characterological *absence* on which the Romantic construction of authorship depends. As Margreta de Grazia points out, it is the documentation of Shakespeare's life and the consequent rejection of anecdotes, hearsay, bardolatrous myth and so on, that leads to an 'abstraction' of his life from 'broader social and moral concerns', 'sealing' it, in effect, in an 'historically remote past constructed of authentic papers' (1991: 78).[5] What scholarly biography – biography founded on knowing, empirically and precisely, the

facts of Shakespeare's life – makes explicit is the evacuation of a subjectivity
for which the narrativizing impulse of anecdote had earlier allowed. By
attempting to know more about Shakespeare, we find that we know less, or
know that we know less than we thought we did. The empirical scholarship
of Edmond Malone finally establishes the more general sense of irrecoverable loss experienced in relation to Shakespeare. We know, after Malone,
that we do not know.

And it is this absence of biographical certainty, this large absence of information that allows not only for an over-determination of identification, but
also for a certain structure of identity to be posited for the poet, an identity
that involves both singularity and a certain 'universality', and that comes
indeed to represent the idea and ideal of the poet in general: the author of
Hamlet, Macbeth, and other plays is both an individual who lived and died in
Stratford, a man who has a name, a wife, children, parents, a house and a
pre-theatrical career – a *life* in short – and at the same time an empty shell,
a vacuum, a framework to be repeatedly filled by imagination and projection, not least by means of characterological readings of the plays and
personalized readings of the sonnets. It is this particular kind of identity,
this particular structure of identity, one that combines a certain historical
specificity or individuality with transhistorical generality or 'universality'
that both marks Shakespeare out and at the same time comes to constitute
the literary ideal of authorship in general.

The process by which English Literature is defined in relation to something approaching a vacuum in the available personal or biographical data
regarding the life of its exemplary author, the idea that the author is 'nothing', and the corresponding idea that the author is 'every thing', is in fact
already at work well before the early-nineteenth century, and is an idea that
develops increasing authority as the eighteenth century progresses. It
appears, in particular, as the late-eighteenth-century cliché of Shakespeare
as 'protean'. For Edmund Capell, writing in 1768, Shakespeare is 'this
Proteus, who could put on any shape that either serv'd his interest or suited
his inclination' (in Vickers, 5: 320), while for Elizabeth Montagu, writing in
the following year, he has the 'art of the Dervise' in that he could 'throw his
soul into the body of another man, and be at once possessed of his senti-
ments, adopt his passions, and rise to all the functions and feelings of his
situation' (in Vickers, 5: 330). 'The genius of Shakespeare is unlimited',
remarks William Richardson in 1774: 'Possessing extreme sensibility, and
uncommonly susceptible, he is the Proteus of the drama; he changes himself into every character, and enters easily into every condition of human
nature', Richardson opines (in Vickers, 6: 118–19). 'He could indeed

assume all shapes', comments Edmund Malone in 1780, alluding to but not explicitly mentioning the figure of Proteus that others employ (in Vickers, 6: 291).[6] As Maurice Morgan comments in 1777 on Shakespeare's invention of Falstaff, 'it is really astonishing that a mere human being, a part of humanity only, should so perfectly comprehend the whole' (in Vickers, 6: 171). The astonishment expressed here is part of a response to the question of genius that eighteenth-century critics attempted to address and that Romantic writers developed in their ascription of protean qualities to Shakespeare, their sense both of the exemplary and of the 'magical' or super-human nature of the genius.[7] Astonishment, or at least surprise, is also declared in an anonymous essay from 1792, in which the author ponders a question that still troubles contemporary biographers such as Greenblatt, and which for the anti-Stratfordians was to become a major element in the sceptical case against Shakespeare's authorship – the dramatist's rapid transformation from an 'idle libertine' living in parochial obscurity to a world-class writer at the metropolitan heart of early-modern theatrical production: 'It is in genius, in that divine emanation, which in its nature is inexplicable, that we are to seek the means of resolving this problem', the critic concludes (in Vickers, 6: 574).[8] In a passage that in some ways anticipates Wordsworth's notion of 'spontaneous' poetic composition in his 'Preface', Keats's sense that poetry should 'naturally', like 'Leaves to a tree' in an 1818 letter to John Hamilton Reynolds, and Shelley's conception of the poet in his 'Defence of Poetry' as *unwittingly* producing poetry (see Wordsworth 1992: 744; Shelley in Reiman and Powers 1977: 508; Keats in Rollins 1958, 1: 238–9), but that also foreshadows the anti-establishment position of nineteenth-century Shakespeare-sceptics, this commentator argues that genius involves a crucial element of authorial ignorance:

> [T]he *flatus Dei*, the divinity within, might dictate those comprehensive forms of speech which passed through Shakespeare's mind unnoticed, but as relative to his subject, intirely without that great effect they communicate to others . . . they were not in any sense the result of reflection, labour, and contrivance, like the composition of other writers: from him those wonders fell as the ripe acorn unheeded by the oak. (in Vickers, 6: 574)

It is Shakespeare's comprehensiveness, his universality that needs to be explained because of the way that it transcends the uniqueness, the singularity of an individual, mortal writer. There is a certain impossibility, in other words, in this conception of Shakespearean authorship, because of its definition of Shakespeare as comprehensive and all-encompassing (he had 'the largest and most comprehensive Soul', as Nahum Tate puts it in 1680 (in Vickers, 1: 341); his mind is 'The universal Mirror of Mankind', according to Elijah Fenton, writing in 1711 [2: 265]), and particularly because it seems to be becoming clear that there is a disjunction between the biographical facts and the poet's achievement. The solution to the problem is to reassert the Platonic conception of the poet as fundamentally and uniquely ignorant:[9] the 'speech' that the dramatist produces 'passed through' his mind 'unnoticed'; it lacks the 'great effect' on the author that it has on others; it comes without 'reflection, labour, and contrivance'. As Edward Young comments in his *Conjectures on Original Composition* (1759), 'to neglect of Learning Genius sometimes owes its greater glory': 'Who knows if *Shakespeare* might not have thought less if he had read more?', Young speculates (in Vickers, 4: 405, 407).[10] In other words, despite the importance of originality in eighteenth-century and Romantic conceptions of authorship, the language that Shakespeare produces does not in fact *originate* in him, in his consciousness: it is not Shakespeare that speaks, or writes. It is not in the end his individuality that is being expressed, but something beyond him, outside of him – which also, paradoxically, goes to make up what is understood to *constitute* his individuality. For Hazlitt, writing towards the end of the Romantic era, the very definition of genius involves a certain ignorance or 'unconsciousness': the 'definition of genius is that it acts unconsciously', he declares in an 1826 essay from *The Plain Speaker*, 'Whether Genius is Conscious of its Powers?'. Writers and artists who have 'produced immortal works', Hazlitt goes on, 'have done so without knowing how or why'. His examples of such geniuses are Correggio, Michael Angelo, Rembrandt and of course Shakespeare, who 'appears to have owed almost every thing to chance, scarce any thing to industry or design' (8: 109).[11]

3

Like Coleridge, Hazlitt is particularly insistent on Shakespeare's 'protean' qualities, in fact. This eighteenth-century ideal is firmly embedded in the complex theorizations of genius, authorship and Literature, in successive books, essays and lectures, as well as in the less public discourses of the letters, notebooks and conversations of both writers. And it is, in particular, the Proteus cliché – Shakespeare as 'every thing and nothing' – that the Romantics respond to and develop. Shakespeare, for the Romantics is *uniquely exemplary*. He 'darts himself forth, and passes into all the forms of human character and human passion', according to Coleridge: he is the 'Proteus of the fire and the flood' (1983, 2: 27; 1987, 1: 253; see also Han 154). In the second of Satyrane's Letters, first published in *The Friend* and later as an appendix to chapter 22 of the *Biographia Literaria*, Coleridge tries to summarize the character of Shakespeare by paraphrasing Aristotle on poetry (or, as Coleridge has it, on the poet) in general, as 'an involution of the universal in the individual' (1983, 2: 185).[12] As Coleridge comments in an 1818 lecture, Shakespeare creates through the expression of 'the *universal* which is potentially in each *particular*' (1987, 2: 148). Similarly, in his 1814 essay 'On posthumous fame, – whether Shakespeare was influenced by a love of it' Hazlitt builds on the eighteenth-century tradition of Bardolatry when he argues that Shakespeare 'seemed scarcely to have an individual existence of his own' but rather seemed to 'pass successively' into the identity of his characters (2: 26). Shakespeare's genius, for Hazlitt as for others (especially his acolyte John Keats), involved his ability not to be himself, to 'go out of himself', as Hazlitt puts it in a chapter on the poems and sonnets from *Characters of Shakespeare's Plays* (1817). And this is even why Shakespeare fails as a poet, according to Hazlitt: 'In expressing the thoughts of others, he seems inspired; in expressing his own, he was a mechanic' (1: 266). The 'striking peculiarity of Shakespeare's mind was its generic quality, its power of communication with all other minds', Hazlitt writes in his major statement on this theme from his 1818 lecture at the Surrey Institute on Shakespeare and Milton: as 'the least of an egotist', Hazlitt remarks, Shakespeare was 'nothing in himself' but instead 'all that others were, or that they could become' (2: 208).[13]

In particular, Hazlitt explains the crucial connection between this protean quality and the sense of the insouciant genius, the genius who is not fully aware of what it is that he is doing, in an 1816 review-essay on the English translation of Schlegel's *Lectures on Dramatic Literature* (1815):

> The poet appears, for the time, to identify himself with the character he wishes to represent, and to pass from one to the other, like the same soul successively animating different bodies. By an art like that of the ventriloquist, he throws his imagination out of himself, and makes every word appear to proceed from the mouth of the person in whose name it is spoken. . . . One might suppose that he had stood by at the time, and overheard all that passed. As, in our dreams, we hold conversations with ourselves, make remarks or communicate intelligence, and have no idea

of the answer which we shall receive, and which we ourselves are to make, till we hear it; so, the dialogues in Shakespear are carried on without any consciousness of what is to follow, without any appearance of preparation or premeditation. (1: 300)

Protean, chameleon, ventriloquist, dreamer: Shakespeare is who he is because he is not who he is. For Hazlitt, as for Keats after him, and as for Coleridge, poetry is characterized by authorial exemplarity, by the ability of the author not to be himself and *therefore* to be all others.

This is the law, then, of Romantic authorship. Shakespeare constitutes the model of the Romantic author as transcendent genius. But in order for Shakespeare to figure within Romanticism as the model for the transcendent genius, his identity must be uncertain – our knowledge of his personality and of details of his life must be vague at best: he must be an individual who is not clearly individualized. The genius, after all, must somehow be more than the mortal, fallible, limited, temporally defined human that lives and dies and errs and writes plays and poems. Biographical uncertainty, ignorance with regard to the author's life, must in fact be such that even the very fact of his authorship, of his *being* the author, can be questioned: the known facts must be so limited as to allow for the credible possibility, at least for some, that William Shakespeare is not the author of *Hamlet*, *Macbeth* and other works. In other words, the Romantic condition of (Shakespearean) authorship, and therefore of Literature itself, newly conceived, involves the necessary possibility of the authorship *question*, of the authorship of 'Shakespeare's works being questioned. The Shakespeare authorship question is the logical consequence of the Romantic (re-)invention of authorship itself via the latter's thinking of Shakespeare as the archetypal genius; and this reinvention of authorship is involved in turn in the Romantic (re-) invention of Literature as a function of this strange, uncanny, paradoxical author-figure. Jonathan Bate comments that Shakespeare constitutes the 'authoritative example of Romantic irony', a form of writing in which 'the authority of the author is undermined' (1986: 37). But we might press such an idea further and suggest that Shakespeare offered the very model for the Romantic author, the exemplary Romantic author, precisely on account of his lack of authority, his lack, to use an eighteenth and early nineteenth-century term, of 'authorism'. The essence of Romantic authorship, that central element in the Romantic ideology, is to *lack* authority – that is the author's authority, what constitutes his authorship, and what in the end also comes to define the logic through which the 'authorship question' begins.

Notes

[1] Jonathan Bate briefly makes a similar point in *The Genius of Shakespeare* (1997), when he argues that the Shakespeare authorship question is 'consequent upon a Romantic idea of authorial genius' and that 'in order to have the Genius of Shakespeare, we also have to have the Authorship Controversy' (74, 97); see also Howard Felperin, who argues that the anti-Stratfordians share with the Bardolaters 'an overriding, even obsessive, concern with the "author"' (1991: 135). As Felperin also argues, a pre-condition of the anti-Stratfordian project is the 'paucity of biographical information surrounding Shakespeare' (137). And see Marjorie Garber, who argues that Shakespeare is 'the towering figure he is for us not despite but rather *because* of the authorship controversy' (1987: 11).

[2] For another recent example, see René Weis's comment on Shakespeare's family: 'A strong sense of family runs through Shakespeare's plays', Weis remarks, therefore his parents 'must have run a mostly happy home' (2007: 17). Sometimes this even depends on what Shakespeare failed to write rather than what he put down on paper: it is 'as much what Shakespeare did *not* write as what he did that seems to indicate something seriously wrong with his marriage', Greenblatt comments at one point (2004: 126).

[3] See Gary Taylor's comment that the Romantics (and Hazlitt in particular) 'imagined a Shakespeare who exposed his personality chiefly through an aversion to exposing his personality' (1990: 156). And compare Garber's comment that Shakespeare is 'present as an absence – which is to say, as a ghost': as Garber goes on to comment, were Shakespeare 'more completely known', he would 'not be the Shakespeare we know' (1987: 11). On her chapter on this question, though, Garber is mostly concerned to explore the idea that the plays can themselves be seen as 'thematizing the authorship controversy' (22).

[4] As Younglim Han points out, Malone's attempts to document Shakespeare's life, to establish the authenticity of the canon, and to reconstruct Shakespeare's 'personal experiences through in-depth readings' of his poems and plays in the 1790 edition 'paved the way for Romantic critical practices' (55). But as Han also points out, there is an intrinsic tension between the individualizing impulse of Malone's work on the one hand and the universalizing emphasis of the Romantics on the other (see 70–1). Indeed, Han reminds us that the Romantics tended either to overlook or to castigate Malone's edition (see 73–6, citing Lamb and Coleridge against 'the wretched Malone'), and that they were generally dismissive of textual matters, as if reading Shakespeare through rather than in the particular printed words; see also Taylor (152–3).

[5] But see also page 134, where De Grazia makes the important point that Malone's project as a whole – the life, the chronology of works, the edition of the sonnets – produced a new Shakespearean identity with 'a new focus on previously unprobed interiority' (see also 172–3). On the significance of Malone's edition of the sonnets for a 'Romantic' sense of Shakespearean interiority, together with a sense of his ultimate inaccessibility, see 152–63.

[6] The idea of Shakespeare's capacious or 'protean' imagination is a commonplace in criticism of the mid-eighteenth century onwards: in 1753 Joseph Warton referred to the 'inexhaustible plenty of our poet's invention' (in Vickers, 4: 66),

in 1754 Arthur Murphy remarks on Shakespeare's 'vast imagination' (in Vickers, 4: 98) and in 1765 Edward Watkinson argues that Shakespeare 'seems to have discerned mankind by intuition' and that he is '*master* of every passion' (in Vickers, 4: 541), for example. On Shakespeare as protean, see R. S. White (1996: 10); Jonathan Bate (1986: 14–16); Han (2001: 91–2, 154); Michel Grivelet (1985: 27–46). Romantic allusions to Shakespeare as Proteus include A. W. von Schlegel, *Lectures on Dramatic Art and Literature* (1808–1811), in Bate (1997: 97–9, 109); William Hazlitt, 'On genius and common sense: The same subject continued', in *Table Talk* (1821) in Wu (1998, 6: 36); Coleridge (1983, 2: 27–8; 1957–2002, 2: 2274 – 'that Proteus essence' – and 3: 3247). For John Keats, of course, Shakespeare is the very model of the poet as 'camelion', a poet who 'has as much delight in conceiving an Iago as an Imogen', as he puts it (in Rollins 1958, 1: 387).

[7] On Shakespeare's writing as in effect magic see, for examples, Vickers (3: 299 and 6: 171–2); on astonishment, see also 2: 299, 404, 407–8.

[8] This sense of a disjunction between the work and the man goes back at least to the first anti-Stratfordian, James Wilmot, who decided more than seventy years before Delia Bacon arrived on the scene in the 1850s that Sir Francis Bacon must have written the plays ascribed to Shakespeare: Shakespeare, he opined was 'at best a Country clown at the time he went to seek his fortune in London' and 'co[uld] never have had any school learning', so did not have the erudition to have written the plays (quoted in Schoenbaum 397). For examples of the widespread eighteenth-century concern over this question see, for example, Vickers (2: 404; 3: 431; 4: 173, 305–6; 5: 278, 358, 372, 516, 554; 6: 532).

[9] For Plato's conception of the poet as ignorant, see *Ion* 534 a–b, *Phaedrus* 245a, *Republic* VII 522a, X 602a, *Meno* 99d, *Apology* 22 b–c.

[10] Young's comment perhaps echoes that by Richard Hurd, writing in 1751: it is possible, Hurd suggests, that '*a want of reading*, as well as a vast superiority of genius, hath contributed to lift this astonishing man, to the glory of being esteemed the most original THINKER and SPEAKER, since the times of Homer' (in Vickers, 3: 431); but see Vickers on even earlier versions of this reasoning in the late seventeenth century, in 1: 13–14; for other early examples of this logic, see 2: 191, 193 (but see 217, 219–20 for a counter-argument).

[11] Compare Schlegel (1997: 94–5). See Bate, on 'the traditional English neoclassical view of the Bard as a genius unconscious of his powers' (1986: 13).

[12] See also Coleridge, *The Friend* (1969, 2: 217). Coleridge makes a similar point in *The Friend* when he comments on the way that Shakespeare's plays involve a 'union and interpenetration of the universal and the particular, which must pervade all works of decided genius and true science' (1: 457). For Aristotle on poetry as having both the universality of philosophy and the particularity of history, see Poetics 9: 1–4.

[13] 'He had only to think of any thing in order to become that thing, with all the circumstances belonging to it', Hazlitt comments (2: 209). As Bate remarks (1986: 11), such a conception of Shakespeare in fact echoes that of the mid eighteenth-century critic William Guthrie, who comments in *Essay on the English Tragedy* (1747) that 'The genius, forgetting that he is a poet, wraps himself up in the person he designs; he becomes him' (in Vickers 3: 197).

Chapter 2

Malfolio: Foul Papers on the Shakespeare Authorship Question

Willy Maley

The quest for the truth of the self, our own and others', endlessly fascinating, is precisely endless, since the subject of liberal humanism is a chimera, an effect of language, not its origin. Meanwhile, the social and political are placed as second-ary concerns – naturally, since our democratic institutions are so clearly expressive of what we essentially are. In the subject's hopeless pursuit of self-presence politics can safely be left to take care of itself. And we can be sure that the institutions in question will in consequence stay much as they are.

(*Belsey 1985: 54*)

God is in me, he is the absolute 'me' or 'self', he is that structure of invisible interiority that is called, in Kierkegaard's sense, subjectivity.

(*Derrida 1995a: 109*)

Brink: From Bon Font to Maldon

I have studied literary theory and Renaissance literature for 25 years, but this is my first sortie into the Shakespeare authorship question. I am thus less familiar than others with the terminology, but I do understand some-thing of the politics of faction: anti-Stratfordians, Baconians, Disintegra-tors, Oxfordians, Stratfordians, the Shakespeare Authorship Coalition, Continuity Shakespeare and Provisional Shakespeare, Martexts of various stripes. Generally, I view the recent – post-Theory, post-New Historicist – rise of life-writing in my field with a jaundiced eye, dubbing it 'celebrity studies'. This is partly the result of listening to a distinguished academic babble excitedly about sitting in an office enrapt while listening to a dialogue between their agent and publisher about six figure sums and major book

deals for a Renaissance biography. Not that I think this merely vulgar –
academics need to shore up their incomes somehow, and if you can make a
mint from commercial publishing as a scholar then what's not to like?
Reports of Greenblatt's million-dollar advance for *Will in the World: How
Shakespeare Became Shakespeare* (2004) may have been exaggerated, but they
were used as a way of explaining how a new historicist – who had in fact
always been interested in self-dramatization – came to write a biography
with such a clear populist slant. One newspaper report cited an unattrib-
uted scholarly source saying 'For a million-dollar advance, the author
exists!' (Donadio 2005). That's the million-dollar question. Do you look
that kind of lucre in the eye and say goodbye? But not just money or
sensationalism or the seeking after celebrity of a few scholars drove this
biographical turn. It has deep roots.

Kate Belsey comments, referring to the post-war disillusion with Romantic and Victorian authorship cults; 'For an earlier generation of academics
critical biography was scholarship lite' (2009: 202). In its new ironic, post-
modern guise it is a weightier enterprise. The fact that many of today's
Renaissance biographers were yesterday's new historicists suggests there
was something in the air already – and more than hefty publishing con-
tracts – though the promise of royalties can concentrate the mind. Long
before *Will in the World* (2004), even before *Renaissance Self-Fashioning*
(1980), Stephen Greenblatt authored a study entitled *Sir Walter Raleigh: The
Renaissance Man and His Roles* (1973). In this early work Greenblatt first
advanced the idea of a dramatic sense of life. Most of my own work has been
on one of Raleigh's neighbours on the Munster plantation in Ireland,
Edmund Spenser, a poet whose very existence is something of an elephant
in the room for anti-Stratfordians insofar as he somewhat compromises the
case that someone from a modest background could not be learned and
literate enough to produce lasting literary monuments. Indeed, much of
the authorship debate – barring those whose theories of co-authorship and
collaboration I find compelling – seems to see Shakespeare as a solitary
figure to be replaced by another sole author. In this regard I am as anxious
about the break-up of the Bard as I am about the break-up of Britain – which
is to say not very – and so I cannot share Richard Crinkley's concern: 'One
looks back at the orthodox disintegrationists: here was an almost frenzied
parcelling out of the plays and sections of the plays to a variety of authors
and co-authors' (1985: 521). Scotland is a co-author of Britain, but rarely
credited as such.

I have written elsewhere on the failure of critics to conceive of
co-authorship even when addressing what they know to be collaborative
work (Maley 1999). Other contemporaries are ruled out in a one-man

hunt – and nobody as far as I know is suggesting that the real Shakespeare was a woman, as has been done with Homer (Dalby 2006). Kate Belsey is one of few critics to actually engage with Foucault's opening gambit on individualization and authorship. Belsey has pointed to this reluctance to admit the social milieu of writing, an individualism shared by critics on different sides of the debate: 'the primary source of writing is other writing. Why are we so reluctant to acknowledge this? An empiricist culture longs to find the source of the text in the life of the author, supplanting intertextuality with experience' (2009: 201). Later, Belsey reaffirms this point: 'Critical biographers are obliged to root textuality in experience in order to have a tale to tell: a record of their subject's reading does not make much of a story' (210). But why should this be so? Reading *is* experience. Surely any idea of reading as extra-experiential is pre-critical or at least pre-theoretical. This is exactly Belsey's point: 'Critical biography is not an aid to reading but a substitute for it' (212). As Roger Stritmatter puts it, 'the more a critical work remains tied to the *biographical* mode, the *less* of any significance it tells us about the nature of the Shakespearean *literary* experience' (Stritmatter 2006: 46). Marshall Grossman takes a similar tack in his critique of biographical readings of the Sonnets: 'Strictly speaking, one can't write a life . . . life-writing is best thought of as a defense mechanism, a resistance to poetry and the effects it might have were we to allow it to probe our guilty apprehensions and possibly disclose our malefactions' (2009: 230). For Grossman, 'Only by recognizing the permeability of writing and life can we begin to free Shakespeare's will' (242).

Roland Barthes' 'The death of the author' (1988; 1997) and Michel Foucault's 'What is an author?' (1980) have been key texts in the recent debate. Few critics notice that Barthes bases his essay on Balzac, Foucault on Beckett (with a passing allusion to Balzac). Writing – literature – underpins their arguments. As Belsey notes, 'Foucault's point is that authorship simplifies, dissolves, erases difficulty. Mine is that critical biography reduces the complexity that drew us to the work in the first place' (2009: 211). Belsey archly depicts the reader as suitor with regard to the Sonnets (212). Foucault famously stated that authorship arises not from credibility but from culpability, 'what one might call penal appropriation': 'Texts, books, and discourses really began to have authors . . . to the extent that authors became subject to punishment, that is, to the extent that discourses could be transgressive' (Foucault 1980: 148). In Spenser's *Faerie Queene* the poet Bon Font is punished for transgressing by being renamed Malfont: 'Some one, whose tongue was for his trespasse vyle / Nayld to a post, adiudged so by law' (V.ix.25–6). This classic case of Foucauldian authorial credibility/ culpability set some critics off on a hunt to find the poet in question – and

Elizabethan England was a target-rich environment for subversive versifiers – until Roland Smith pointed out that 'Malfont' or 'Malphant' was a common Irish surname in Cork where Spenser had his Irish estate (Smith 1946: 30–1). More recently in Spenser studies Professor Jean Brink was castigated for daring in a series of essays published in the mid-1990s to question the attribution of *A View of the Present State of Ireland* (Brink 1994; 1997). Spenserians with little expertise in textual scholarship – Maley culpa – were ready to defend the attribution and to close ranks against the raising of a Spenser authorship question, this despite the fact that Spenser had from the beginning in his own work raised the question of authorship (Miller 1979). Spenser published his first major work anonymously, as 'Immerito' (unknown), made 'uncouthe, unkent' his calling card, referred to his literary debut as 'child whose parent is unkent', and adopted the pseudonym of Colin Clout, a name borrowed from another poet, John Skelton. In a characteristically witty but injudicious chapter of my monograph, *Salvaging Spenser* (1997), entitled 'Brinkmanship: a judicial review', I savaged Brink for daring to question the authorship of the *View*, a move I saw as an effort to separate Spenser as poet from Spenser as advocate of colonial violence rather than a careful attempt to examine the evidence. Ten years later, in 2007, asked to write a biographical essay on Spenser for a new guide, I struggled with the task. The list of Elizabethan Edmund Spensers includes one who fathered a son called Hamlet in 1570 (Eccles 1944: 421; Welply 1932: 129). Probably no relation, though given the uncertainty surrounding the sources for his life, anything's possible. For Spenser, two weddings and a funeral can be confirmed. Much else is speculation. Buried in Westminster Abbey, near Chaucer, on 16 January 1599, Camden spoke of Spenser's 'hearse being attended by poets, and mournful elegies and poems, with the pens that wrote them, thrown into the tomb'. Was Hamlet Spenser, then aged 28 or 29, among the mourners? No tomb or verses have been found, and despite the fact that it is a less controversial corpus than Shakespeare's, Spenser's life is as laced with lacunae as other Renaissance writers.

Bourne: Puzzling the Will

> But that the dread of something after death –
> The undiscover'd country, from whose bourn
> No traveller returns – puzzles the will,
> And makes us rather bear those ills we have
> Than fly to others that we know not of? (*Hamlet* 3.1.79–82)

Like *The Bourne Trilogy*, we can divide the Shakespeare authorship question into three distinct phases. Phase 1, 'The bard identity', is the period from Yorick to Garrick when Shakespeare was more than man but less than god. Phase 2, 'The bard supremacy', witnessed the emergence of that spectacular strain of hagiography that sees Shakespeare as the inventor of humanity, as stand-in or understudy for England and the Bible. Just as the cult of the Virgin Queen allowed Mariolatry to persist under a new guise after the Reformation, in the myth of Elizabeth as Gloriana, so the 'Bardonna syndrome', the beginnings of Bardolatry, allowed England to continue to specify its title after Union. Phase 3, 'The bard ultimatum', is the period from Looney to Greenblatt, when acts of bad faith exist alongside an increasing awareness of the precariousness of the Bard Identity. In *The Bourne Ultimatum* (2007), the tagline – 'His identity stolen. His loved ones murdered. His past destroyed' – fits the facts of Shakespeare's story (Marlowe being a murdered friend). But the trilogy is a tetralogy, querying further the status of the corpus. *The Bourne Identity Crisis* (dir: Lara Wood, 2003) features a man who forgets he's gay and thinks he's an assassin (Baxendale 2004: 1481).

In 'What is an author?', an essay wilfully misread by critics on all sides of the Shakespeare authorship question, Michael Foucault remarks:

> If I discover that Shakespeare was not born in the house that we visit today, this is a modification which, obviously, will not alter the functioning of the author's name. But if we proved that Shakespeare did not write those sonnets which pass for his, that would constitute a significant change and affect the manner in which the author's name functions. If we proved that Shakespeare wrote Bacon's *Organon* by showing that the same author wrote both the works of Bacon and those of Shakespeare, that would be a third type of change that would entirely modify the functioning of the author's name. The author's name is not, therefore, just a proper name like the rest. (1980: 146)

Sometimes Foucault is blamed for Beckett or mistaken for Barthes (Foster 2002: 375–6), but his essay on authorship – and more broadly his work on subjectivity – repays close attention. Although Foucault does not include him with Marx and Freud in the category of 'founders of discursivity', it could be argued that Shakespeare fits the bill:

> [W]hen I speak of Marx or Freud as founders of discursivity, I mean that they made possible not only a certain number of analogies, but also (and equally importantly) a certain number of differences. They have created

a possibility for something other than their discourse, yet something belonging to what they founded. To say that Freud founded psychoanalysis does not (simply) mean that we find the concept of the libido or the technique of dream analysis in the works of Karl Abraham or Melanie Klein; it means that Freud made possible a certain number of divergences – with respect to his own texts, concepts, and hypotheses – that all arise from the psychoanalytical discourse itself. (1980: 154–5)

Foucault excludes Galileo and Newton, and the reasons – that 'the initiation of a discursive practice is heterogeneous to its subsequent transformations' (156) – may stand for Shakespeare too, or is the Bard a primary coordinate?

Jacques Derrida defines literature as 'this strange institution which allows one to say everything', and because he believes that literature allows you to say everything, Derrida can say something that wouldn't ruffle any feathers in Stratford-upon-Avon, namely that 'everything is in Shakespeare' (Derrida 1992a: 67). In fact, Derrida goes so far as to say that he'd like to live 200 years in order to become a specialist:

I would very much like to read and write in the space or heritage of Shakespeare, in relation to whom I have infinite admiration and gratitude; I would like to become (alas, it's pretty late) a 'Shakespeare expert'; I know that everything is in Shakespeare: everything and the rest, so everything or nearly. But after all, everything is also in Celan, and in the same way, although differently, and in Plato or in Joyce, in the Bible, in Vico or in Kafka, not to mention those still living, everywhere, well, almost everywhere. (67)

Taking Derrida's essay on *Romeo and Juliet* – 'Aphorism countertime' (1992b), translated into English in 1992 by Nicholas Royle – and his reading of *Hamlet* – *Spectres of Marx* (1993) – as touchstone texts, this essay asks if there is anything outside of Shakespeare, and whether we are his contemporaries or his peers. Derrida's writings on Shakespeare are preoccupied with the politics of the proper name. In this, Derrida comes close to Foucault, for in 'What is an author?', before going on to complicate matters, Foucault wrote: 'The author's name is a proper name, and therefore it raises the problems common to all proper names' (145).

What's in a Name?

Since my own name is, willy-nilly, the source of some amusement on occasion, I am interested in the sound of names, their resonance. When

J. T. Looney published his *'Shakespeare' Identified in Edward de Vere, 17th Earl of Oxford* (1920), he would have been wise to have assumed a pseudonym, as Warren Hope and Kim Holston pointed out:

> The best trained and most highly respected professional students of Shakespeare in the colleges and universities of England and the United States contemplated the seemingly seamless argument represented in *'Shakespeare' Identified,* and quickly discovered a flaw in it. The book was written by a man with a funny name. They found their argument against Looney where they had found their arguments in favor of William Shakespeare: on a title page. (Hope and Holston 1992: 116, cited Stritmatter 2006: 41)

Looney's is not the only proper name to elicit improper amusement or anxiety. The quest for origins is a fraught one, as Jacques Derrida has taught us, he who gave up his own name – 'Jackie' – as well as his Algerian accent – or 'Franco-Maghrebian', to use his preferred term – in order to pass in Paris (Derrida 1998). Sometimes names have to be changed to fit the nomenclature. Derrida's name change was his personal passport to the public sphere:

> I changed my first name when I began to publish, at the moment I entered what is, in sum, the space of literary or philosophical legitimation, whose 'good manners' I was practicing in my own way. In finding that Jackie was not possible as the first name of an author, by choosing what was in some way, to be sure, a semi-pseudonym but also very French, Christian, simple, I must have erased more things than I could say in a few words (one would have to analyze the conditions in which a certain community – the Jewish community in Algeria – in the '30s sometimes chose American names, occasionally those of film stars or heroes, William, Jackie, and so forth). (Derrida 1995b: 343–44)

William is a fair name, but some surnames – or their speakers – hiss like snakes in the grass or serpents in gardens. Names can injure as well as entertain. In an interview, Stephen Greenblatt, who as a student at Cambridge was close to the Monty Python team, recalled how his name was taken in vain by the satirists:

> In one show, in a long list of names of people who've been killed by a deranged dwarf, the name 'Stephen J. Greenblatt' is read out, and it's a

laugh line! It took me a while to *get* it, to understand that for the English
the actual *name* 'Stephen J. Greenblatt' is itself funny, just like they think
it's funny on the BBC to say 'Solly Zuckerman'. It took me *years* of living
in England to be able to hear that little note of risibility that they intro-
duce into their voice at the name of the *other*, as it were. I don't really *mind*
all that much, but at first I found it puzzling that the audience laughed.
I don't think of my name as being so hilarious! But then, it's not, say,
'John Major'. (Greenblatt 1994: 122)

The same parochialism and prejudice that wants an ordinary Joe or Will for
its national Bard can discriminate against names that appear to come from
outside. And as I've shown elsewhere, 'John Major' is not 'John Major'
either, or at least we must distinguish between the sixteenth-century Scottish
historian who invented Britain and the twentieth-century Prime Minister
who contributed to its demise (Maley 1995).

Being Maladjusted: Time out of Joint

Derrida sees hauntology, absence and disjuncture as key to addressing the
ghost – the 'Thing' – that is Shakespeare, and fixes on Marcellus asking
Horatio to speak to the ghost of Hamlet's father 'as a scholar':

There has never been a scholar who really, and as a scholar, deals with
ghosts. A traditional scholar does not believe in ghosts – nor in all that
could be called the virtual space of spectrality. There has never been a
scholar who, as such, does not believe in the sharp distinction between
the real and the unreal, the actual and the inactual, the living and the
non-living, being and non-being ('to be or not to be', in the conventional
reading), in the opposition between what is present and what is not, for
example in the form of objectivity. Beyond this opposition, there is, for
the scholar, only the hypothesis of a school of thought, theatrical fiction,
literature, and speculation. (1993: 11)

In his readings of *Hamlet* and *Romeo and Juliet*, Derrida sees plays preoccupied by times and names, forms of address:

'The time is out of joint': time is *disarticulated*, dislocated, dislodged, time
is run down, on the run and run down . . . *deranged*, both out of order and
mad. Time is off its hinges, time is off course, beside itself, disadjusted.
Says Hamlet. Who thereby opened one of those breaches, often they are

poetic and thinking peepholes . . . through which Shakespeare will have kept watch over the English language, at the same time he signed its body, with the same unprecedented stroke of some arrow. (1993: 18)

Shakespeare watches over the English language, and over England, as a kind of shorthand or synonym for both, guards against change as a source or core that cannot be compromised, and will only be shared provided tribute is returned to the fount. For Derrida, 'Shakespeare' is a name attached to an opening and a breach of being, a tear in time, an interrogation of the name: 'This is the stroke of genius, the insignia trait of spirit, the signature of the Thing "Shakespeare": to authorize each one of the translations, to make them possible and intelligible without ever being reducible to them' (1993: 22).

In an interview with Derek Attridge, speaking of his essay on *Romeo and Juliet*, Derrida admits he 'did not have the necessary competence to read this play "in its period"', before going on to say:

This brings us back to the question of the structure of a text in relation to history. Here the example of Shakespeare is magnificent. Who demonstrates better that texts fully conditioned by their history, loaded with history, and on historical themes, offer themselves so well for reading in historical contexts very different from their time and place of origin, not only in the European twentieth century, but also in lending themselves to Japanese or Chinese productions and transpositions? (1992a: 63)

Derrida is attentive to the authorship question – hence his allusion to 'the *Romeo and Juliet* which bears Shakespeare's signature' (Derrida 1992a: 69) – and alive both to the singularity of the play and to its survival beyond its immediate contexts, its openness to multiple readings:

Disjunction, dislocation, separation of places, deployment or spacing of a story because of aphorism – would there be any theatre without that? The survival of a theatrical work implies that, theatrically, it is saying something about theater itself, about its essential possibility. And that it does so, theatrically, then, through the play of uniqueness and repetition, by giving rise every time to the chance of an absolutely singular event as it does to the untranslatable idiom of a proper name, to its fatality . . . to the fatality of a date and of a rendezvous. Dates, timetables, property registers, place-names, all the codes that we cast like nets over time and space – in order to reduce or master differences, to arrest them, determine then – these are also contretemps-traps. (1992b: 419)

Here, Derrida comes close to Greenblatt, whose essay 'Shakespeare and the exorcists' makes this very point about the larger culture within which the plays – in this case *King Lear* – are set (Greenblatt 1985). Exorcism is an apt way of describing the marvellous possessions of the Shakespeare authorship question. The name of the author, like the name of the rose, has an echo that runs through writing as well as law and nature. Derrida cites Juliet's argument to Romeo, but only in order to deconstruct it: 'A rose remains what it is without its name . . . (Supposing that the rose, all the roses of thought, of literature, of mysticism, this "formidable anthology", absent from every bouquet . . .)' (1992b: 427). Our names survive us, and language carries – bears witness to – accents and scents. Derrida speaks of 'the aphorism of *Romeo and Juliet* . . . Shakespeare's play of that title', a play with proper names that depends on a proper name:

> It belongs to a series, to the still-living palimpsest, to the open theater of narratives which bear his name. It survives them, but they also survive thanks to it. Would such a double survival have been possible 'without that title', as Juliet put it? And would the names of Matteo Bandello or Luiga da Porto survive without that of Shakespeare, who survived them? And without the innumerable repetitions, each staked in its particular way, under the same name? Without the grafting of names? And of other plays? 'O be some other name . . .' (1992b: 433)

Derrida then puts his finger on author and title alike: 'The absolute aphorism: A proper name' (1992b: 433). Shakespeare is shorthand, the ultimate aphorism.

Bard Times

Speaking as a spectator rather than a participant, the Shakespeare authorship question appears to be a maelstrom. As one bridge-building critic, Richmond Crinkley, Director of Programs at the Folger Shakespeare Library from 1969 to 1973, observed, 'the question of the authorship of Shakespeare's work rouses wild passions in people otherwise placid and uncontentious' (1985: 515). According to Crinkley,

> What drives the arguments for the authorship of Oxford, Derby, and Bacon is that the biography of William Shakespeare of Stratford is such a mass of lacunae. It is not just the want of sufficient relevant biographical

facts that breeds doubt. It is the absence in William Shakespeare of a life with anybody living in it. (517)

Crinkley has characterized the debate in a way that partly explains its marginal status within Shakespeare studies:

> As one who found himself a contented agnostic Stratfordian at the Folger, I was enormously surprised at what can only be described as the viciousness towards anti-Stratfordian sentiments expressed by so many otherwise rational and courteous scholars. In its extreme forms the hatred of unorthodoxy was like some bizarre mutant racism. (518)

Crinkley sees Shakespeare as 'For democratically inclined scholars . . . an archetype of the self-made man' (520), but surely most writers throughout history are not aristocrats, they are common people? Even an agnostic like Crinkley falls foul of snobbery and the privileging of so-called experience over reading, so that 'there is a pervasive ease with which the playwright inhabits an aristocratic world', as though a familiarity of what is all too readily alluded to as 'court life' cannot come from books (521). Would historians of the courts of Elizabeth and James view Shakespeare's depictions of royal circles with such credulity?

For Mark Twain, Shakespeare was 'a Brontosaur: nine bones and six hundred barrels of plaster of Paris' (Stritmatter 2006: 39, citing Twain 1909: 49). But was Shakespeare a playwright? Freud had his doubts: 'I am almost convinced that behind the figure of Shakespeare lies a great unknown: Edward de Vere, 17th Earl of Oxford' (cited in Stritmatter 2006: 44). Perhaps there was a dramatic unconscious, a pool into which Will dipped his quill, more as an auditor or editor than an author in the modern sense. According to Roger Stritmatter,

> In private correspondence with Looney, Freud was even more candid about his belief: 'I have known you as the author of a remarkable book, to which I owe my conviction about Shakespeare's identity as far as my judgment in this matter goes'. (2006: 44)

But Stritmatter like so many others falls for the idea that the Stratford man could not have become the literary giant who penned *Hamlet* and the rest:

> In place of the world-weary and cynical dogma that the bard was a sort of literary idiot savant, the Oxford story reveals a literary oeuvre connected

in many intimate particulars to the actual lived experience of a real, flesh-and-blood author, whose life's work was to transcend his own suffering through the therapeutic power of art. (Stritmatter 2006: 46)

Was Joyce a literary idiot savant? The starving artist is more than a cliché, it's an historical reality.

Robert Hume speaks of Dryden's dilemma in his *Essay of Dramatick Poesy:*

Dryden's critical dilemma in the *Essay* is both political and cultural. England was a small, marginal, rather backward country that had disgraced and enfeebled itself in a Civil War and had just embarrassed itself in a signally unsuccessful war against the Dutch. Dryden is massively intimidated, not only by the classics but by the French, and one of the best measures of the degree of his intimidation is his noisy and jingoistic insistence on rejecting their influence. (1997: 62)

Thus Hume can conclude: 'If Shakespeare had not existed he would have had to be invented – as, in a sense, he was' (62). Shakespeare was enlisted in the interests of sabre-rattling, and in this his name was too good to be true: 'Shakespeare constituted a line of defense against French encroachment' (Hume 63). Thus 'Shakespeare's works were . . . successfully appropriated to fit what became the dominant, nationalist ideology of mid-Eighteenth century England' (Hume 67, citing Dobson 1992: 12).

You Complete Me

How many co-authors had Shakespeare? Brian Vickers, a leading disintegrator, subscribes to the heresy of the 'collaborative mode' (2007: 312). According to Vickers: 'We must recognize that every dramatist of whom we have record took part in collaborative authorship' (317). Vickers points out that the Oxford *Complete Works* do lend ear to the idea of co-authorship: 'The only modern edition open to these scholarly developments has been the Oxford *Complete Works*, where Middleton (*Timon of Athens*), George Wilkins (*Pericles*) and John Fletcher (*Henry VIII* and *The Two Noble Kinsmen*) are acknowledged as co-authors' (346). According to Vickers:

The notion of a 'Complete' Shakespeare, as I understand it, means a collection of all the plays and poems that he wrote. But if we turn our attention from his works to the way that we look at Shakespeare in his time, a complete view would recognize that, as a commercial dramatist in the hugely competitive London Theater world, he undoubtedly shared the writing of some plays in his canon. In the judgment of those scholars who have kept up with authorship studies in the last twenty years, a title such as *The Complete Works of William Shakespeare* should now be followed by the words '*Assisted by Thomas Nashe, George Peele, Thomas Middleton, George Wilkins, John Fletcher, John Davies of Hereford, and Others*'. (311)

Curiously, Vickers speaks of another scholar yielding to the French disease of post-structuralism: 'Gordon McMullan succumbed to the spell of Foucault's antirational and antihistorical pronouncements. Like Foucault, McMullan was unaware that authorship existed as a clearly articulated concept, with many of the attributes it has today, from the Greeks to the Elizabethans' (348). Vickers gets his knickers in a twist over Foucault, whom he should really regard as an ally, not a foe. Foucault's insistence on an ethical principle 'not designating writing as something completed, but dominating it as a practice' (1980: 142) is not that far removed from Vickers' own efforts to secure justice for Shakespeare's co-authors: 'To wish to identify the playwrights who worked together with Shakespeare on some projects, making their own special talents available, is a simple instance of justice' (352). Foucault's genealogical reasoning would chime with Vickers' efforts at recovery, though the two might part company where Foucault sees such acts of recovery as stages on a road to anonymity and indifference to authorship: 'The purpose of history, guided by genealogy, is not to discover the roots of our identity but to commit itself to its dissipation' (Foucault 1977: 162). Jeffrey Knapp's question, 'What is a Co-author?', is arguably answered in Foucault's original essay (Knapp 2005).

Courtney Lehmann takes us back to first principles in her essay on Baz Luhrmann's *Romeo + Juliet*:

According to the *Oxford English Dictionary*, the word *author* appears typographically in 1550. However, the semantic status of the word *author* as a harbinger of 'originality' is considerably restricted by its use at this time as a variant of *auctor*, a term derived from scribal culture designating a quintessentially medieval conception of authorship-as-transcription rather than origination. This ideology reduces authorship to a pastiche ensemble of 'speech in a dead language' – quite literally, the words of ghostly fathers, or *auctors*, whose authority is preserved through scribal and cultural regimes of repetition. (2001: 194)

Whatever the Renaissance idea of authorship, modern critics insist on the idea of a literary life, a life in literature, and the capacity to see the author's face, faith, family and fantasies in a work of art. Shakespeare is claimed as a writer with a special interest in life-writing. According to René Weis,

> As a dramatic biographer rather than an historical dramatist, Shakespeare is the most Plutarchan of English writers. That the creator of two royal Richards and several kingly Henrys should himself prove so elusive a life-writing subject is of course partly due to the tenuousness of a certain kind of trace history in the records. (2009: 217)

Since Joyce's deadly parody of it in *Ulysses*, such readings of Shakespeare's life through his work are rare. Yet Weis persists:

> Suggesting that Shakespeare wrote his own experience of life into his plays and poems has become anathema, but why this should be so is not at all self-evident. That names from real life and indeed historical events find their way into Shakespeare's plays has worried this generation of literary critics arguably more than any before it. In the wake of *The Verbal Icon* by W. K. Wimsatt (1954) and its excoriating of the author's presence and intentions in his or her own writings, it has become intellectually suspect to believe that literature and life can be intimately related when almost every previous generation took it for granted that they were. (224)

The sonnets, on which so many recent critics have written so ably and eloquently, remain a site of contestation. For Weis, Shakespeare's heart as well as his art is at stake: 'That his life and works demonstrably merged at the margins suggests that he did not see them as separate at all, and to this the *Sonnets*, arguably the most wilfully (as it were) misread set of poems historically, bear eloquent witness' (227). Personally, I prefer Marshall Grossman's approach of asking why critics wax biographical and hence autobiographical in their commentaries on Shakespeare:

> How is it that so many apparently rational individuals, over so long a time, have been undone, not merely by the assumption that the sonnets tell of events in a life, but by an obsessive desire to move through their episodic narration to the ground of lived experience from which they are assumed to have sprung – to identify an actually existing young man, rival poet and dark lady by whom the sonnets' shabby and sad story was acted out? The story of this story, the long history of literate men and women possessed

by the idea that the sonnets record something crucial of Shakespeare's maddeningly undocumented life and that 'the key' to the sonnets and the life is the identities of the participants in the events on which they are based, poses questions of its own. (2009: 229)

Looking for signs of life in a literary text is a fraught enterprise, if on occasion a profitable one. For Foucault, 'A private letter may well have a signer – it does not have an author' (1980: 148), yet he recognizes that authors' letters, literary letters, can assume an importance beyond their immediate content or context, becoming part of a writer's corpus. According to Alan Stewart, however, 'The bad news for literary biographers is that early modern writers almost never discuss their writing in letters: reading Philip Sidney's voluminous surviving correspondence, one would never know that he had written the *Arcadia, Astrophil and Stella* and *The Defence of Poesie*, in a thousand letters, Francis Bacon almost never talks natural philosophy' (2009: 300). Spenser's 1580 correspondence with Harvey is an exception, since these letters were intended for publication and thus constitute a staged exchange.

Who You Gonna Call?

Shakespeare is a sort of understudy for nation and religion, monarchy and empire. When those categories and concepts and allegiances are under siege or in crisis, 'who you gonna call?' If for Foucault (and for Belsey after him) the Shakespeare authorship question in its original framing has its origins in what Foucault calls 'the privileged moment of *individualization* in the history of ideas' (1980: 141); for Michael Dobson Shakespeare is an eighteenth-century invention of English nationalism; for Robert Hume a matter of editing; for Andrew Murphy a question of publishing; for Jonathan Bate the product of Romanticism – but isn't the author cult itself exactly a product of Romanticism, in which case to question it is actually to critique the Romantic construction of Shakespeare? (Stritmatter 2006: 44); for Jacques Derrida Shakespeare stands sentry over the English language; and then for Charles LaPorte we must look to the religious crises and controversies of the Victorian era, including the impact of Strauss's *Life of Jesus Christ*, for evidence of the origins of bardolatry.

For LaPorte, 'the Shakespeare Question arose at an important moment in the history of hermeneutics, when the confluence of romantic literary enthusiasm and historical Biblical scholarship had established the right cultural atmosphere for widespread speculation about how such inspired texts as Shakespeare's come into being' (2007: 609). Laporte speaks of 'the Biblolatry of Bardolatry', the way in which – and there are echoes here of Terry Eagleton's account of the rise of English and the transfer of power from pulpit to lectern – the Victorians earthed some of their ecclesiastical energies in Shakespeare at a time when faith was in doubt and fiction had to fill the breach. The 'Shakespeare redemption' was the answer to the prayers of those experiencing a crisis of faith, and his canonization is directly linked to questions of faith and doubt of a theological nature. LaPorte dates this crisis to the English translation by George Eliot of the ultimate biography, David Friedrich Strauss's *Das Leben Jesu* (1835) as *The Life of Jesus* (1846):

> For English readers, the higher criticism made its first big splash with George Eliot's translation of Strauss's *Life of Jesus*. In many ways, the higher criticism and *Sturm und Drang* bardolatry came from the same scholarly nexus of early romantic historicism. Yet when these two strains of thought reunited – or, rather, collided – in the mid-Victorian period, questions about the authorship of Shakespeare would echo through the world. (613)

After pointing out the ways in which Ralph Waldo Emerson, Walt Whitman, Henry James and Mark Twain joined the debate, LaPorte remarks:

> It has sometimes been argued that a disproportionate number of the early anti-Stratfordians were American and that this number suggests an American need to reconfigure the cultural legacy of their former colonizer. Given the number of Scottish critics, it would be truer to say that these early scholars tended not to be English. The post-colonial argument applies equally to Scotland, however, and here the Shakespeare Question also coincides with the mid-century controversy on Spasmodic poetry, in which working-class Scots poets were ferociously denounced for their pretensions to a religiously nuanced form of poetic inspiration. The claim that working-class poets must not aspire to Shakespearean inspiration fits perfectly with the idea that Shakespeare's works must have been secretly written by a more respectable author. (617–18)

Coincidentally, Robert Crawford has argued that Robert Burns was the original of the Bard and that not only were Scottish publishers behind the invention of Shakespeare and Scottish educationalists behind the teaching of English literature, but Scottish critics and readers in their appreciation of Burns gave rise to Shakespeare as counterweight national bard (2005). There is a lot of classism as well as classicism in the invention of Shakespeare. In *A Room of One's Own*, musing on Shakespeare's sister, Virginia Woolf attacked the elitist idea that literary talent is the exclusive province of makers of means: 'Yet genius of a sort must have existed among women as it must have existed among the working classes. Now and again an Emily Brontë or a Robert Burns blazes out and proves its presence' (Woolf 1929; 1992: 63). If a Burns can blaze out, why not a Shakespeare?

Charles LaPorte is surely right when he says that 'Victorian religious controversy established many of the terms in which the Shakespeare Question was debated, including its existence in the first place' (624). And right too to point to the present as a place where such motives persist:

> This is perhaps the final way in which it mirrors Victorian Biblical controversies. Mainstream nineteenth-century Shakespeare scholars generally presumed that Bacon's doubts about Shakespeare's identity would be quickly put to rest, just as conservative Christians hoped that the higher criticism would be exploded. On the other hand, Victorian Baconians felt confident that Shakespeare's long-held disguise was crumbling, just as liberal adherents to the higher criticism assumed that the literal interpretation of the Bible would soon disappear altogether. None of these disappearances have taken place, and the Victorian drama continues to shape both Biblical and Shakespearean interpretation for enormous numbers of people. (624)

If indeed 'anti-Stratfordians still regularly depict university English faculty as a sort of morally bankrupted clergy determined to defend their Stratford bard against extensive evidence of his inauthenticity', then, says LaPorte:

> Such mistrust of an academic clerisy derives from a religious history that predates English departments. The Victorian religious atmosphere, in other words, brought to life problems of historical and literary hermeneutics that are not easily dispelled. And the translation of Strauss's *Life of Jesus* stands as an important monument in this religious history. It became the model for the type of romantic hermeneutics that made speculation about authorship a necessary part of understanding sacred texts. It deeply unnerved the Victorians, and the Shakespeare Question arose quickly in its wake. (625)

The evangelical appropriation of Shakespeare arguably has its roots in the Reformation as much as the nineteenth century. If religious fervour lies behind bardolatry then we must remember pagan passions too. English literature's other origin is of course as the poor person's classics. Those Victorians who were classicists would have had before them many examples of authorship questions, including Hippocrates, whom Foucault mentions, and of course Homer, a founding figure in authorship studies (Graziosi 2002). There are many parallels between the fourth and sixth centuries BC and the eighteenth and nineteenth centuries AD.

From Touchstone (http://www.touchstone.bham.ac.uk/) to Treadstone, from Lear to Looney, from the Folio to the Folger, Shakespeare is an elusive figure – 'good Master What-ye-call't' . . . 'Is thy name William?' – whose mystery is part of his glamour. In *The Bourne Identity* (2002), Jason Bourne, an amnesiac agent working for Treadstone, a secret arm of the CIA, comes up against an agent called 'The Professor', who, when Bourne has close to killed him, says with his dying breath: 'Look at us. Look at what they make you give.' Let that stand as my epitaph, or at least my exit line.

Chapter 3

The Authorship Question: An Historian's Perspective

William D. Rubinstein

So far as I am aware, no academic historian has ever written on the Shakespeare authorship question. This in itself is curious, since the question of who wrote Shakespeare's works is an historical one, to which the normal concepts of historical evidence surely apply. Additionally (as far as I am aware), no academic historian, one employed as a university professor or lecturer in History, has ever written a biography of Shakespeare. Indeed, rather curiously, it would be considered eccentric if a university lecturer in History were known to be working on a new biography of Shakespeare. This strange reality goes far in explaining why Shakespeare studies have taken the direction they have during the post-war period, and why the Shakespeare authorship question has been the grand taboo of academic Shakespeare scholars. During the past fifty or sixty years, the great bulk of serious studies and biographies of Shakespeare has indeed been written by university academics, but these have almost invariably been professors and lecturers in English Literature departments. To non-academics, this distinction may seem trivial, but in my opinion it is of some considerable importance in understanding why the authorship question is taboo to so many academics.

Before turning to this point, it is worth making an equally important one: until well into the twentieth century, most Shakespearean scholars were not academics at all, but well-educated (or self-educated) amateurs of a type almost totally crowded out today by the growth of university research and learning. Until the Second World War, virtually all eminent and important Shakespearean scholars were educated amateurs. For instance, Edmond Malone (1741–1812), Shakespeare's first real biographer and the first man to produce a chronology of Shakespeare's works, was a barrister; James Halliwell-Phillipps (1820–1889), one of the most important of nineteenth-century Shakespeare scholars, was a librarian (at Jesus College, Cambridge);

Howard Staunton (1810–1874), author of *Memorials of Shakespeare* (1864) and the first to publish a photographic reprint of the *First Folio* (1864), was a journalist (and the world's strongest chess player of his time) and so on. This tradition of the gifted non-academic lived on well into the twentieth century, producing arguably its greatest example in Sir E. K. Chambers (Edmund Kerchever, 1866–1954), who was a senior civil servant in the Department of Education. Until his retirement in 1926, Chambers conducted his research into all aspects of the Elizabethan theatre in his spare time. Down to the First World War and beyond, intellectual journals such as *The Fortnightly Review* published innumerable articles about Shakespeare by intelligent amateur writers who seemed to have something important or interesting to say, notwithstanding the fact that they held no academic position and in some cases had not even attended a university. It seems apparent that this intellectual reality made for freer, more open and less bounded discussion than is the case today. This intellectual reality should also be kept in mind when today's orthodox Stratfordian academics dismiss anti-Stratfordian theorists as 'mere amateurs': until the First World War or even later, virtually all Shakespeare scholars and researchers were 'mere amateurs', and most of what we know and accept about Shakespeare's life emerged from 'amateur' scholarship.

To my knowledge, the earliest eminent writer on Shakespeare who was employed as a university academic in the modern sense was Edward Dowden (1843–1913), who was professor of English Literature at Trinity College, Dublin from 1867 until his death. The career of Sir Sidney Lee (1859–1926), arguably marked the transition: from 1883 until 1913 he was, first, assistant editor, and then editor of the *Dictionary of National Biography*, and wrote its entry on William Shakespeare. From 1913 to 1924 he was professor of English at London University, the point at which academics began to crowd out the amateurs. Charles William Wallace (1865–1932), who with his wife Alfreda discovered the Belott-Mountjoy lawsuit, containing a previously unknown Shakespeare signature, was professor of English Dramatic Literature at the University of Nebraska from 1910.

Since the Second World War, this period of transition has given way to university hegemony. A number of well-known recent Shakespeare scholars and biographers – such as the late Eric Sams and Ian Wilson – have not been employed as academics. Nevertheless, it is safe to say that 95% of the men and women who have produced books or articles on Shakespeare during the past 40 years have been university academics, generally publishing in scholarly journals or in academic presses. Nearly all of the best-known recent orthodox biographies of Shakespeare – by Park Honan (1998),

Stephen Greenblatt (2004), James Shapiro (2005), René Weis (2007) and Jonathan Bate (2007), among many others – have been by university academics in Britain or America.

In many respects, this profound change represents a gain for accurate research methodology and scholarly acumen. In other respects, however, this evolution has carried with it its own set of dangers for our understanding of the life of Shakespeare, or the author of Shakespeare's works. First, as noted, all or virtually all of these scholars have been located in English Literature departments, and none or virtually none is an academic historian. However, academics in the two disciplines are trained to do quite different things. Historians work from a variety of primary and secondary sources, treated objectively, critically, and in a wider context, to build up a picture of the most plausible sequence of events via the best evidence. Clashes of opinion about the past, even the most fundamental facts of past life, comprise the very heart of historical debate. Historians' reputations are made in significant part by the novelty of their interpretations of the past, provided, of course, that the actual evidence leads to a novel interpretation. Historical journals largely consist of novel interpretations. In a university History department, it would not be considered *outré* to suggest that someone else wrote Shakespeare's works, provided that evidence for this viewpoint could be cogently presented. Although I have written highly unorthodox works on the Shakespeare authorship question, none of my academic colleagues in History has ever expressed any hostility to my views on this matter, and most, I am quite sure, would concede that I was making telling points. Academic historians of Elizabethan and Jacobean England, too, realize that the mainstream of public debate in that time and place was over politics and religion, leading to the Civil War, with economics and foreign affairs also highly important. They are perfectly aware that Shakespeare and his works were utterly marginal and insignificant to the mainstream of public life and debate, and would find no difficulty in accepting the fact that Shakespeare was not 'Shakespeare' – the English national poet – until the mid-eighteenth century. If the evidence showed it to be likely that William Shakespeare the actor was the 'front man' for the real author, few academic historians would, I think, dismiss this as *ipso facto* nonsense.

This tolerant attitude should be contrasted with the probable attitude of academics in English Literature departments towards those who would raise the authorship question as a serious issue. This attitude was set out bluntly by Professor Alan H. Nelson, formerly Professor of English at the University of California, Berkeley. He is, ironically, a leading pro-Stratfordian who has written a comprehensive biography of Edward de Vere, seventeenth Earl of Oxford, which dismisses claims that he wrote Shakespeare's plays as mythical. Nelson notes that 'I do not myself know of a single Professor of English in the 1300-member Shakespeare Association of America who questions the identity of Shakespeare', and concedes that 'there exist indeed professors of law, mathematics, medicine, psychology, sociology, and even theatre studies among the ranks of the unbelievers' (Nelson 2004). He then frankly discusses the reasons for this variation between disciplines:

> Anti-Stratfordians attribute this lop-sided alignment to internal professional discipline: anyone who expresses a reservation [about Shakespeare as author] will be denied tenure, drummed from the ranks, returned to civilian life. I agree that antagonism to the authorship debate from within the profession is so great that it would be as difficult for a professed Oxfordian to be hired in the first place, or to gain tenure, as for a professed creationist to be hired or to gain tenure in a graduate-level Department of Biology. (2004)

This iron wall of hostility apparently permeates – and prevents – any possible discussion of the authorship question among most English Literature academics. It prevents even the admission that such a question might actually exist. On the leading academic internet discussion group about William Shakespeare, 'Shaksper' (*sic*), any issue related to the life and works of Shakespeare, his milieu, or subsequent commentary or performances may be discussed – with one exception. The authorship question is strictly taboo, and no messages relating to it may be posted. It seems inconceivable that a frankly anti-Stratfordian paper could be presented, or accepted for presentation, at an academic conference organized by university English Literature departments.

There are perhaps two main reasons for this state of affairs, one plausible and the other far less so. It is unquestionably true that most anti-Stratfordian theories were and are egregious, and (at the very least) border on the crackpot, frequently entailing secret codes embedded in Shakespeare's texts; secret, illegitimate children of Queen Elizabeth; alleged autobiographical references throughout the plays, and the like, put by obviously untrained amateur theorists. One can readily understand why the organizers of Shakespearean journals, conferences and websites would wish to have nothing to do with most such amateur theorists, who also tend to be unusually persistent and single-minded. However, this does not explain why they would also dismiss out of hand academically trained, obviously sophisticated and intelligent anti-Stratfordians, some of whom are university academics. A glance at recent sophisticated anti-Stratfordian books and articles will show that their quality has risen enormously in recent years, and, at their best, differ little from orthodox academic writings on Shakespeare. The fact that most anti-Stratfordians are 'amateur historians' without a university position even when university educated and intelligent also suggests a second, powerful reason why this universal disdain exists; that giving any legitimacy whatever to a body of amateurs *ipso facto* delegitimizes academic scholars of Shakespeare. Not only would this be to admit amateurs as equal participants in an important discussion with university academics, it would also be to undermine the very professional status of English Literature academics, a threat increased by the growing marginalisation of English Literature and other arts disciplines within the university structure, elbowed aside in the battle for student numbers and resources by practical and pre-professional disciplines. Fear of the loss of professional status is surely one important reason for the iron wall which exists around the academic discussion of the authorship question, where the field is dominated by amateurs. This situation appears to be wholly the product of the post-1918, and especially post-1945, hegemony of university English Literature departments in the serious study of Shakespeare and his works. The current state of affairs would have been virtually unrecognizable during the nineteenth century, when gifted amateurs outside of university life were the most significant voices among Shakespearean scholars. They were far more flexible and untroubled by any need to erect iron walls to protect their status.

But is the authorship question a viable one to be addressed, or is it merely the creation of crackpots? In my view, there are at least three reasons for historians (and others) to question whether William Shakespeare, the actor who was born in 1564 and died in 1616, wrote the works attributed to him. First, there are no sources from Shakespeare's lifetime which unequivocally make it plain that the Stratford actor was the author of his supposed works. There are, of course, many contemporary sources about Shakespeare, for instance his baptismal record and his will, but none, from his lifetime, which record someone saying 'I saw Master Will Shakespeare at the theatre with his newe playe *Hamlet*, which he showed me to read and explained ye plot' – none. There are, in fact, no contemporary sources which unequivocally state that he was a writer. If these existed, there would be no authorship question. But there are two further points here which make this fact even more curious than it seems at first glance. First, there is ample evidence of the authorship for virtually *every* other significant author of the Elizabethan and Jacobean period which unequivocally shows that they – these particular human beings – were indeed authors. Diana Price's important work, *Shakespeare's Unorthodox Biography: New Evidence of an Authorship Problem* (2001), sets this out in detail. For instance, the royal pension awarded to Ben Jonson was increased in 1630 in consideration of 'Those services of his wit and his pen' (cited in Price 306). The Merchant Taylors Company in London recorded that it was 'to conferr with Mr. Benjamin Johnson the Poet, aboute a speeche' (306). In 1597 Jonson was imprisoned for writing *The Isle of Dogs*. In 1614 John Felder wrote a Preface to his *Titles of Honour* in which he referred to a book 'in the well-furnisht Librarie of my beloved friend that singular Poet M. Ben: Jonson' (306). Numerous elegies were written to Jonson when he died in 1637. For virtually every other well-known literary contemporary of Shakespeare similarly clear and unambiguous statements can readily be found which show, beyond any doubt, that each of these men was indeed an author. *Nothing* of a similar nature exists for Shakespeare. This takes us to the second consideration about this point: when we compare Shakespeare with his literary contemporaries, we must never forget that he is probably the most intensively studied and researched human being in history. Quite literally every scrap of paper surviving from Shakespeare's lifetime has been examined and poured over precisely to find some reference, however indirect, to Shakespeare's life, and, in partic-ular, his supposed life as an author. It is safe to say that for every literary critic, historian or archivist who has closely studied or researched the life of Ben Jonson – let alone a lesser-known Elizabethan or Jacobean literary figure – five hundred have conducted research on the life of Shakespeare. Any original discovery in a primary source which unequivocally linked Shakespeare the Stratford actor with the works he supposedly wrote would make its discoverer world-famous, and presumably lead to academic pro-motion and financial success in publishing and on the lecture circuit. Yet, to reiterate, nothing has ever been found about Shakespeare's sup-posed literary career, in striking contrast to the ease with which so many lesser figures can unequivocally be regarded as authors from contemporary evidence. Although Stratfordian orthodoxy holds that this state of affairs is not unusual, in fact it is so implausible as to *ipso facto* imply that there is something very much amiss. In contrast to Shakespeare, although Christopher Marlowe died in a tavern brawl at the age of only 29, we have, for instance, a letter from the playwright Thomas Kyd, probably written in mid-1593, to Lord Keeper Puckering noting his 'first acquaintance with this Marlowe', who had been 'writing for his [Lordship's] plaiers' (cited in Price 313). Also in existence is George Peele's tribute to Marlowe, written three weeks after his death, 'unhappy in thine end, / Marley [*sic*], the Muses darling, for thy verse' (cited in Price 312). There is, in other words, not the slightest doubt that those who knew him regarded Christopher Marlowe, the man who was born in 1564 and died in 1593, as the author of the plays which are attributed to him. Strikingly, there is absolutely nothing similar in Shakespeare's lifetime; that is, unequivocally noting that the Stratford actor was also a playwright, and no funeral elegies upon his death, although vastly more scholarship has attempted to find anything relating to Shakespeare as a supposed writer. Indeed, in the whole of the twentieth century only two new pieces of information of any significance have been discovered about Shakespeare's life that were not known about in Victoria's reign. The first is the Belott–Mountjoy lawsuit of May 1612, discovered by the Wallaces around 1910, in which Shakespeare gave evidence in a lawsuit in which one Stephen Belott, a women's headdress maker, sued Christopher Mountjoy for failure to provide his daughter, whom Belott had married, with a promised dowry and legacy (Nicoll 2007; Schoenbaum 1991: 467). Shakespeare appeared in this lawsuit because he had lodged in the Mountjoy household in Cripplegate eight years earlier. Essentially, Shakespeare stated that he could remember nothing about Belott's claim. He was identified in the court transcript as 'of Stratford upon Avon . . . gentleman' (not as resident in London). The lawsuit contains not one word which would suggest that he was a writer; he was presumably lodging in Cripplegate as an actor and theatre-sharer with the King's Men. Secondly, in the 1920s the will was found of the Catholic Alexander Houghton, a wealthy landowner of Lea, Lancashire, who died in 1581, in which he left a legacy to Sir Thomas Hesketh of '. . . all my instruments belonging to musics, & all manner of play clothes, if he be minded to keep & do keep players', and asked Hesketh 'to be friendly unto Fulk Gillom and William Shakeshafte now dwelling with me' (Honigmann 1998: 136). From this dubious evidence there has grown an elaborate theory, now the subject of many works, which states that 'Shakeshafte' was Shakespeare, that the playwright was a secret Catholic, and that he spent two years in a Catholic household in Lancashire before joining Lord Strange's acting company and moving to London and immortality. One might assume that a wealthy testator would know the correct name of someone in his household whom he has mentioned in his will, and Shakeshafte is evidently not Shakespeare, but that has not deterred the many proponents of this theory, most famously expounded in E. A. J. Honigmann's *Shakespeare: The 'Lost Years'* (1985; 1998). Apart from Houghton's will, Shakespeare has no known associations of any kind with Lancashire and, moreover, must have been in Stratford for his wedding with Anne Hathaway in November 1582, and presumably for his intimacy with her before that. No accounts of Shakespeare's youth, even the earliest from the late seventeenth century, mention Lancashire, but merely that he left Stratford for London. Shakespeare might have been a secret Catholic, but he was certainly baptised, married and buried as a conforming Anglican, and his daughters married Anglicans, one (John Hall) a noted Puritan. Yet in the absence of any other evidence about Shakespeare's early life, this far-fetched tale has taken flight as the basis for biographies which roll off the press at least on an annual basis. Rather astonishingly to anyone unfamiliar with the actual biographical record of the life of William Shakespeare produced by so many hundreds of researchers, *that's it*: literally nothing else has been discovered of any significance about Shakespeare's life since 1900 – absolutely nothing.

As is well-known, the surviving material in Shakespeare's handwriting consists of six signatures, all dating from 1612–1616, towards the end of Shakespeare's life. Three are on legal documents and three on his will. One of these latter signatures reads 'By me, William Shakespeare', the only words – apart from his name – by Shakespeare which survive. Again, this is certainly remarkable. Shakespeare maintained two households, in Stratford and London, presumably writing from one place to the other, and must have carried out a considerable number of business transactions, none of which survive. There are, of course, no universally accepted literary manu-scripts in Shakespeare's handwriting. The closest approach to one is the so-called 'Hand D' of the manuscript of a play – *Sir Thomas More* – rediscov-ered in 1844, and consisting of thirty-two handwritten pages by six different authors. The 147 lines which have become known as 'Hand D' have been attributed to Shakespeare since around 1871 on the basis of the similarity of handwriting and style. There are, however, many problems with this attribution. Most obviously, of course, we do not know what Shakespeare's handwriting looked like apart from the signatures noted above. *Sir Thomas More* is generally dated by scholars to either around 1592–1593, at the start of Shakespeare's career, or to around 1603, the generally accepted view today. There are problems with both dates. In 1592–1593, the basis of the handwriting comparison is purely with Shakespeare's signatures twenty or more years later. Gary Taylor, a leading Shakespearean scholar, has dated 'Hand D' to 1603 on the basis of stylistic similarities with Shakespeare's known work around this time (Taylor 1989: 120–3). The problem here is that the other contributors to the *More* manuscript – Anthony Munday, Henry Chettle, Thomas Dekker and perhaps Thomas Heywood – all wrote for the Lord Admiral's Men, the rival company to the Lord Chamberlain's/ King's Men to which Shakespeare belonged and was a 'sharer', that is, a part owner. Shakespeare had no known connection with the Admiral's Men, and nor did the other authors ever work for Shakespeare's company. It seems improbable that 'Hand D' could have been Shakespeare, despite the complicated arguments offered by Taylor that this was likely (102–03). Moreover, the play dealt with a controversial subject in English history in the fairly recent past, and was censored by Edmund Tilney, Master of the Revels. Shakespeare's company was in serious trouble in 1601 over its apparent alliance with the Earl of Essex in the period just before the 'Essex rebellion', including its performance of *Richard II,* and it seems implausible, to say the least, that Shakespeare would wish to become involved with another incendiary political text at, it would seem, almost precisely the same time. The theory put forward by Carol A. Chillington that 'Hand D' is John Webster's (1980), seems at least as plausible. As noted, there are no other manuscripts by Shakespeare, either literary or of any other description.

The second reason to question whether Shakespeare was the actual author of the works attributed to him is that he almost certainly could not have done what he must have done to have written his works, a point made again and again by anti-Stratfordians. For instance, many Italian scholars who are familiar with Shakespeare's works believe that he must have visited Milan, Verona, Venice, Padua and Mantua, since he is conversant with details of their local geography which could only have been known to a visitor (Grillo 1949; Magri in Malim 2004: 45–106). William Shakespeare was never known to have visited Italy: he might have done, but there is no record of his having tried to obtain a passport from the records of English travellers overseas at the National Archives, and nor has anyone ever claimed that he did. Shakespeare apparently used as sources for his plays a range of works in French, Italian and Spanish which had not been translated into English. Even orthodox Stratfordians such as Samuel Schoenbaum, who conceded that 'Shakespeare didn't have access to translations' of these works, offer no suggestions as to how – or why – he would have read them or used them in his plays (Schoenbaum 1991: 103). Diana Price has noted that where *Romeo and Juliet* deviates from Arthur Brooke's poem, on which it is largely based and which it does in four important instances, it agrees with the original Italian version by Luigi da Porto of which no known English or even French translation existed at the time (Price 248). How did Shakespeare read the Italian version, and why use it rather than Brooke's *Tragicall Historye of Romeus and Juliet,* which had appeared in 1562? As is well-known, Shakespeare had no formal education past the age of thirteen in a village school. He certainly did not attend Oxford or Cambridge, the only two universities in England at the time – although even this has been disputed, strangely enough. According to Claire Asquith, a leading contemporary proponent of the secret Catholic Shakespeare thesis, *Love's Labour's Lost* demonstrates a detailed knowledge of Oxford University and its academics, and she suggests that he might have attended the university around 1580 under an assumed name and then studied in the English College in Rome, where English Catholics went to study (2003: 27–8). There is, of course, no evidence of any kind that Shakespeare was at Oxford (or in Rome), but the apparent familiarity of the author of his works with that University requires explaining, as do many other aspects of his astonishing erudition. For instance, Shakespeare apparently had a keen interest in astronomy and his works show a familiarity with Galileo's findings, which did not become public knowledge until 1610, after they were written (Usher 2002). Michael Wood has tried to explain Shakespeare's knowledge of 'the new astronomy' in his BBC television series *In Search of Shakespeare* by claiming that he learned about it by talking to casual drinkers at local taverns. This preposterous claim is equivalent to asserting that a writer today, one without a higher degree, made erudite comments about quantum physics in his writings by discussing the subject with customers in a local pub. From such facts as these about Shakespeare and his learning one may reasonably infer that he was a highly educated man, multi-lingual and at the cutting-edge of Europe's 'new learning', who was arguably educated at Oxford. This is not – and the point cannot be stressed enough – a product of 'snobbery', of discounting William Shakespeare as author because he was not a nobleman, but simply a series of reasonable inferences from Shakespeare's texts.

There is, moreover, the apparent sheer physical impossibility of Shakespeare of Stratford doing what he was supposed to have done; pursue a joint career as an actor and a prolific playwright. The orthodox view of Shakespeare's career was put by Professor James Shapiro in his *1599: A Year in the Life of Shakespeare:*

> Shakespeare and his fellow [theatre] sharers spent their mornings rehearsing and their afternoons performing alongside hired men and boys who were needed to fill out the cast of approximately fifteen. Except for a break during Lent and the occasional closing of the theatre due to a scandal or plague, performances went on all year round. As Elizabethan audiences expected a different play every day, actors had to master a score of new roles every year – as well as recall old favourites needed to flesh out the repertory. (Shapiro 2006: 23)

Shapiro neglects to add that the Chamberlain's/King's Men went on lengthy exhausting tours of provincial cities, or that it frequently performed at Court. Besides this, Shakespeare was maintaining two households three days' travelling time apart, and must have travelled between them at least several times each year. Shapiro does note that 'new plays were acquired from a score of freelance dramatists who were paid on average £6 a play (at a time when a schoolmaster might earn £20 a year)' (23). Despite this, Shapiro sees nothing unusual in espousing the orthodox claim that 'what little free time Shakespeare had at the start of his working day must have been devoted to reading and writing . . . [and] providing his company with, on average, two new plays a year' (23).

That Shakespeare actually lived like this – needless to say – beggars belief and appears to have been virtually impossible. Shakespeare would, unquestionably, have been physically and mentally exhausted by this regimen before he penned one word of a new play. In modern times, it is difficult if not impossible to point to a single famous playwright who was both an actor and a playwright at the same time; if there were any, their output was only a tiny fraction of Shakespeare's. No one who could earn a liveable income as a successful playwright would conceivably continue as a performing actor on a daily basis. Nor did anyone actually live like this in Shakespeare's time. Only six persons with entries in the *Oxford Dictionary of National Biography* deceased between 1590 and 1640 are described as 'playwrights and actors'. None wrote more than two or three plays when they were actually employed as actors. Some playwrights, such as Ben Jonson, started as actors, but had certainly left the stage when they wrote the bulk of their work.

The third, and perhaps most important single reason why it is difficult to accept that the Stratford man wrote the works attributed to him is that, to a remarkable extent, there is no real mesh between his life and the evolutionary trajectory of his works, accepting the orthodox chronology of when they were written. What little is known about Shakespeare's biography has virtually no explanatory power in understanding why he wrote a particular work when he did, or why he changed the direction and thrust of his works, as he occasionally did. Orthodox biographers of Shakespeare have long been puzzled by this complete failure for the facts of Shakespeare's life to account for or explain the surprisingly clear evolutionary pattern of his works, and have, basically, long since given up trying to do so. The obvious conclusion, that Shakespeare's biography and his works cannot be satisfactorily meshed because we are dealing with two different men, the actor and the author, with quite different life trajectories, is, of course, never drawn by orthodox biographers. The author killed off Falstaff, his most popular character, for no apparent reason in 1598–1599, rather than milk him in five more plays, to the financial advantage of the Chamberlain's Company. Centrally, the author appears to have suffered a traumatic experience of some kind in 1601, leading to a comprehensive alteration in the nature of his works: out went the Italianate Comedies and triumphalist Histories, in came the great Tragedies and the 'Problem Plays'. The author was apparently pleased when Queen Elizabeth died in 1603 ('The mortal moon hath her eclipse endured . . . Incertainties now crown themselves assured, / And peace proclaims olives of endless age'– these lines from Sonnet 107 are taken by most commentators to refer to the death of the Queen), and Shakespeare produced no memorial poem or tribute to her memory. The author's plays from 1603 are, it is often argued, part of the oppositionist politics of the post-Essex rebellion. The author was apparently keenly interested in the London Virginia Company and had access to the Strachey Letter, a confidential document about the Bermuda shipwreck circulated only to directors of the Company. The author evidently was a friend of Lord Southampton's, since he dedicated two poems to him, while Southampton is widely believed to have been the 'onlie begetter' of Shakespeare's Sonnets.

In contrast, the actor was none of these things. He had no reason to kill off Falstaff in 1598–1599, which was directly detrimental to the financial interests of him and the Chamberlain's Men. He suffered no known traumas in 1601. Most orthodox scholars attribute the great break of 1601 either to the death of Shakespeare's son Hamnet (although this took place five years earlier and in the interim Shakespeare wrote the Falstaff plays), or to the death of Shakespeare's father in this year (although he was 37 at the time and there is no evidence that he was close to his father. Shakespeare did not follow his father's trade and spent most of his career in London, not Stratford). The actor had absolutely no reason to be pleased when the Queen died and no reason not to have written a memorial tribute. The actor had no known political profile and engaged in no political activities of any kind, presumably because of the extreme dangers which Elizabethan politics threatened to a nobody in a marginal occupation who unwisely engaged in them. The actor had no conceivable connection with the London Virginia Company. He was not among the 570 men (whose names are known) who each paid £12 to buy a share in the Company, and plainly had no access to its confidential documents. Shakespeare appears at the time to have been living almost full-time in Stratford, not in London. There is no reason to suppose that Southampton ever set eyes on Shakespeare, unless he saw the Stratford actor in a play, and no sense in which he could have been the 'onlie begetter' of Shakespeare's Sonnets. It is obviously inconceivable that Shakespeare, an unknown provincial actor, would have addressed Sonnet 10, which urges its addressee to marry and beget children 'for love of me' to a powerful earl, unless he wanted to be made shorter by the head. There is another extremely telling point, as curious as it is disconcerting to orthodox biographers of Shakespeare. Shakespeare had two surviving children, both daughters, Susannah and Judith. Judith was certainly illiterate, and was unable to sign her name. In 1611 'she twice made her mark as witness to a deed for the sale of a house' (Schoenbaum 13). In other words, the daughter of the greatest writer in history, an author renowned for creating strong female characters such as Portia and Cordelia, one of his two surviving children, was illiterate, and unable, among other things, to read his plays.

It should surely seem clear from this that we are dealing with two separate and distinctive men, the author and the actor, whose life trajectories were plainly quite different and cannot be meshed or conflated into each other. In the case of Shakespeare the actor, we actually know, or can readily infer, a considerable amount about his life trajectory and its aims. The central aim of his life was, clearly, to use the money he made in London to become a recognized gentleman and man of property in Stratford, and to found a dynasty. He seems to have pursued these aims quite single-mindedly. He had no known literary or cultural interests or aims of any kind and, despite his status as the greatest writer in history, remarkably little interest in the London intellectual world once he retired, aged 47 or so, to Stratford.

***

In the absence of a firm biographical underpinning of facts and sources, such as is the case with virtually any other historical figure, all orthodox biographies of Shakespeare take liberties with, or actually invent, facts about the supposed playwright, such as no historian would allow for a moment in an academically credible biography of an important man or woman in the past. With the possible exception of accounts of religious figures such as Jesus, who lived thousands of years ago, Shakespeare appears to be absolutely unique in the extent to which academic and other serious biographers routinely take liberties with the meagre historical records of Shakespeare's life. The ease and ambiguity with which this is invariably done contrasts, and rather ironically, with the contempt orthodox Shakespearean scholars demonstrate towards 'amateur historians' who offer biographies of their favourite alternative candidate. One might here consider, for example, a recent, very typical biography of the Bard, *Shakespeare Revealed: A Biography* by René Weis, Professor of English at University College, London, which was published by the distinguished London publisher John Murray in 2007. As an orthodox biography, it is no worse, and probably better than, most of the other recent biographies which pour forth with such extraordinary regularity. Weis writes well, with a distinct lack of pretentiousness, and knows his sources.

So far, so good. However, Weis like so many others, has to create a 444-page biography by speculation, near-inventions and a long series of implausibilities as facts, in a manner which would not be tolerated for one moment in the published biography of any other historical figure, especially by an academic. Shakespeare is probably the only person in history of whom reputable publishers will regularly bring out long biographies whose claims are unsupported by any real evidence whatsoever. This strange reality may best be illustrated by considering four different claims about Shakespeare made by Weis in his book.

Weis accepts without question the hoary tale first propagated by Nicholas Rowe, Shakespeare's earliest biographer (writing in 1709), that Lord Southampton, to whom *Venus and Adonis* and *Rape of Lucrece* were dedicated, gave Shakespeare £1000 'to enable him to go through with a purchase which he had in mind' (115). According to Weis, 'This gift . . . perhaps helped to redeem both Shakespeare's father's debts and his own fines, as well as funding the acquisition of his property' (115). This claim, which is unsupported by any evidence whatever, is plainly nonsensical, as level-headed scholars have repeatedly pointed out. £1000 then was the equivalent of at least £1 million today. It was, roughly, 200 times as large as the annual income of a workingman in 1600, which would more accurately make it equivalent to at least £4 million today. For someone, even a nobleman, to give this sum to a little-known writer and actor for no apparent reason is absurd, and, in any case, Southampton was in no position to part with it. According to the entry on Southampton by Park Honan in the *Oxford Dictionary of National Biography*:

The myth that Southampton gave him £1000 is unfounded . . . Southampton had little but enthusiasm to offer any poet. He hardly had funds to spare; he lived on a fixed allowance and faced paying a gigantic fine to [Lord] Burghley, plus another vast sum to get his estates out of wardship. After he turned twenty-one in 1594, his need for money became desperate. In November of that year, he leased out part of Southampton House [his London mansion], and a few years later had to sell off five of his manors. (www.oxforddnb.com/wriothesley)

Needless to say, although Southampton left extensive papers, no evidence for any such gift to Shakespeare has been found. Indeed, Shakespeare is not mentioned in any surviving document that Southampton wrote.

Weis states flatly, as if it were a matter of accepted fact, that 'Shakespeare built up the library in New Place [his house in Stratford], and it was he who created the "study" which existed in the house many years after his death' (251). As everyone who has read about Shakespeare's life will surely know, however, there is no direct evidence that Shakespeare owned a single book, let alone a library. As has been repeatedly pointed out, Shakespeare did not mention any books in his will, and one known to have been owned by him has never been found. The 'study' Weis introduces by sleight-of-hand was the 'study of books' mentioned in the will of Shakespeare's son-in-law, Dr. John Hall, drawn up just before he died in 1635, nineteen years after Shakespeare's death (Dobson and Wells 2007: 177). There is no reference to this 'study of books' anywhere else, and none from Shakespeare's lifetime. Hall and his wife, Shakespeare's daughter Susannah, inherited New Place and lived there after 1616. Hall was a learned and well-regarded physician who had graduated from Cambridge and is believed to have studied medicine in France; his own father had also been a physician of note, and was known to have owned many books. In an oral will dictated to his son-in-law Thomas Nash, Hall left his 'study of books' to Nash (177). In other words, and in pointed contrast to Shakespeare, Hall made special mention of his own books. There is no evidence of any kind that they had been owned by Shakespeare, or concerned anything besides medicine. More tellingly, there is no evidence that the room Hall used as a 'study of books' had been employed for that purpose by his father-in-law. There is no evidence – none – that this 'study' had been 'created' by Shakespeare; New Place had been built around 1490. There is some indirect evidence that Shakespeare carried out repairs on the house when he bought it in 1597, but none whatever that he created a 'study'. Similarly, there is no evidence that, prior to 1616, it was used as a 'study' or housed a single book. Furthermore, surely any valuable books in Shakespeare's 'library' would have been specifically mentioned in his will, with particular recipients noted from among his London writing and acting friends. Weis's statement here seems to sail very close to the wind in its disingenuousness.

Somewhat strangely, Weis (163–76) believes that Shakespeare was lame as, in several of his Sonnets, Shakespeare mentions this lameness. In Sonnet 37, he states; 'So, I, made lame by Fortune's dearest spite. / Take all my comfort of thy worth and truth.' Virtually without exception, all commentators believe that Shakespeare was here writing metaphorically, and that his 'lameness' referred to his inability to carry out his practical aims. Weis, however, believes that Shakespeare meant this literally, although he also notes that no one among his contemporaries who commented personally on Shakespeare, ever mentioned his lameness. Shakespeare, I suppose, might have been lame, although this sits rather uneasily – to put it mildly – with Weis's further mention that 'probably on foot' Shakespeare often walked 'the hundred-odd miles from Stratford to London. People as a rule walked far more then', he adds, and 'there was as yet no regular coach service between London and the Midlands' (85). Shakespeare's acting company, moreover, frequently toured the country, giving performances in many provincial towns. Presumably a lame man would have lagged far behind, cursing his faster colleagues and being cursed or laughed at by them. Was this really likely?

Weis also believes that the 'Dark Lady' of the Sonnets was Emilia Lanier (*nee* Bassano), whose Italian, probably but not definitely Jewish father, was a leading musician in London. This woman was a talented poet in her own right. According to Schoenbaum, Bassano was first proposed as the 'Dark Lady' by A. L. Rowse (558), and Weis has accepted his identification with little in the way of acknowledgement. Rowse's claim was apparently based on the misreading of an Elizabethan text, as has been widely noted (Schoenbaum 559). But there are many other difficulties, as usual, in accepting Lanier as the 'Dark Lady'. While she was the daughter of an Italian-born musician, Baptista Bassano, her mother was an Anglo-Saxon Englishwoman, Margaret Johnson. There is no direct evidence that she was 'dark'. Although Weis confidently states that 'Her skin colour would probably have been olive rather than English "white"', because she came from 'a Venetian Jewish musical dynasty' (148), Sephardic Jews, such as Spinoza or Disraeli – as someone named Weis ought surely to know – have exactly the same skin colouration as any other Europeans. There are, moreover, no pictures of Lanier, so Weis is simply making an assumption. He also suggests that the character 'Baptista' in *Taming of the Shrew* was named for Lanier's father. Apart from the implausibility of this suggestion *per se*, Baptista Bassano died in 1576, when Shakespeare was 12. Shakespeare plainly never met him and there is no reason to suppose that he ever heard of him.

Emilia Lanier was, moreover the mistress of Henry Carey, Lord Hunsdon, who was at once Queen Elizabeth's cousin; the Lord Chamberlain, responsible for licensing all plays; and the Patron of Shakespeare's acting company, the Lord Chamberlain's Men. It is thus difficult to think of anyone less likely to have been the object of Shakespeare's attempts at seduction, when his efforts were guaranteed to result in the loss of both his career and his life. As evidence for his claim about Lanier, Weis cites an anecdote in a

1759 work by one Thomas Wilkes, who stated that Shakespeare tried to seduce a 'young lady . . . the favourite of an old rich merchant' (151–2). However, Hunsdon was not a 'merchant', but a noble landowner and courtier, and no one at the time, if this anecdote is factual, would have confused the two ranks. Finally, there is not one iota of evidence that Shakespeare has Lanier in mind as his 'Dark Lady': the claim is pure surmise.

To reiterate, I have made these points about Weis's biography not because it is strikingly egregious but because it is absolutely typical of the near-fiction which orthodox biographers of Shakespeare must produce in the absence of facts, moreover facts which have failed to surface despite 400 years of searching. It is surely time for orthodox Stratfordians, especially academics, to take courage in both hands and think about the life of the author of Shakespeare's works with the possibility of an entirely different paradigm not automatically and *a priori* dismissed.

Chapter 4

The Distraction of 'Freud': Literature, Psychoanalysis and the Bacon– Shakespeare controversy

Nicholas Royle

It is the ear of the other that signs.

(*Jacques Derrida 1985*)

1

In his three-volume biography, Ernest Jones refers to a letter of 1922 in which Freud confessed 'that there were two themes that always perplexed him to distraction (*bringen mich immer aus der Fassung*)'. One was 'occultism' or 'the question of telepathy'; the other was 'the Bacon–Shakespeare controversy' (Jones 1957: 419, 462).[1] What is the Bacon–Shakespeare controversy? Why did Freud (to borrow Jacques Derrida's words) lose his head on this subject? Who wrote Shakespeare? Or, what might the criteria be for determining the authorship of a particular text or number of texts? And how out of touch is all this with the question of telepathy?

The 'Bacon–Shakespeare controversy' is a misnomer. The question concerns whether or not William Shakespeare really wrote the plays, poems and sonnets attributed to him: Francis Bacon is only one of the candidates put forward as the 'real' author. There have been plenty of others, as Samuel Schoenbaum makes clear in the 100 page section of his *Shakespeare's Lives* entitled 'Deviations' (1970: 529–629).[2] Among them are Chapman, Raleigh, Jonson, the 6th Earl of Derby, the 5th Earl of Rutland, the Earl of Southampton, Edward Dyer, William Seymour, Patrick O'Toole of Ennis, Michel Agnolo Florio, his son John Florio, Anne Whateley, Edward de Vere, Christopher Marlowe, James I, Fulke Greville, Sir Thomas North, Queen Elizabeth and even 'occult forces' (Schoenbaum 573). Some anti-Shakespeareana or 'anti-Stratfordian' discourse argues for collaborative authorship: such theories are designated 'groupist' and would include Harold Johnson's *Did the Jesuits Write Shakespeare?* (1910), H. T. S. Forrest's *The Five Authors of 'Shakespeare's Sonnets'* (1923) and Gilbert Slater's *Seven Shakespeares* (1931) (Schoenbaum 591 ff.).

The identity of the author as Shakespeare was not questioned until nearly a hundred and fifty years after his death. Only in the second half of the nineteenth century did the 'controversy' emerge as such. Delia Bacon's 'William Shakespeare and his plays; an inquiry concerning them' was published in *Putnam's Monthly Magazine* in 1856; William Henry Smith's privately circulated letter to Lord Ellesmere, entitled 'Was Lord Bacon the author of Shakespeare's plays?', came a few months later. Expansion was rapid. Schoenbaum writes: 'By 1884 the authorship controversy had stirred France, Germany, and India, as well as England and the United States, and it had produced over 250 books, pamphlets, and articles' (554). At this stage Bacon was the principal competitor and his position was bolstered in the 1880s when Baconians, stimulated by the fact that their master knew and wrote about ciphers, started producing 'cryptographic', 'cryptanalytical' theories. As Schoenbaum observes, 'The endeavour to strengthen the Baconian case took ever more extravagant forms' (583); but increasingly, too, other competitors were being put forward. The quantity and quality of published material in fact becomes quite overwhelming. Finally even the scholarly Schoenbaum may seem in danger of losing his head.[3]

And what of Freud? A letter to Martha Bemays in 1883 suggests an early inclination towards a groupist (rather than specifically Baconian) position: 'it seems to me that there is more need to share Shakespeare's achievement among several rivals than to burden another important man with it' (cited by Jones 459). Any later leanings towards Baconianism were finally to be wiped out by a book called *Shakespeare Identified in Edward de Vere, Seventeenth Earl of Oxford* (1920), written (as Ernest Jones pleasurably informs us) by 'an author with the unfortunate name of Looney' (460). Freud read this book twice (in 1926 and 1927) and became, says Jones, 'practically convinced of his conclusions' (460). Is it coincidental that it was in this decade also that Freud started to publish and proclaim openly his views on telepathy and the occult? Is it coincidental that what offered perhaps the most acute contemporary account of the 'Bacon–Shakespeare controversy', James Joyce's *Ulysses*, should have appeared between the time of publication of Looney's book and the time of Freud's first reading it, mediating between lunacy and psychoanalysis, shuttling between them? Perhaps. These questions will return.

Why did the so-called Bacon–Shakespeare controversy arise? Why were
Freud and so many others obsessed, distracted by it? Samuel Schoenbaum
suggests that 'it is perhaps a mistake to pursue a rational explanation' (554).
But in his very next sentence declares: 'Yet one can understand the
emergence of an anti-Stratfordian movement out of midcentury unease
over the Shakespeare of the popular understanding'. This at least gestures
towards the broadly but clearly political issue: Shakespeare the poacher, or
ex-butcher, whose parents were illiterate, etc., couldn't possibly have been
the bard; only an aristocrat could. And later Schoenbaum will offer
a further explanation, one that is in keeping with his prevailing emphasis
on the lack of 'academic credentials' (615) among most anti-Stratfordians.
Books like Looney's are appealing because, in them, 'Sober literary history
is metamorphosed into a game of detection . . . . To such a game the culti-
vated amateur can give his leisure hours in hopes of toppling the supreme
literary idol and confounding the professionals' (602–03).

But most of all, and most provocatively perhaps, Schoenbaum makes use
of psychoanalytic concepts in order to explain the controversy: the concepts of identification and ambivalence, family romance and rescue fantasy,
for example. In dealing with the case of Freud, in particular, the use of
psychoanalytic theory becomes decisive, and Schoenbaum here relies quite
heavily on an article by Harry Trosman, 'Freud and the controversy over
Shakespearean authorship', published in 1965. Trosman glosses that familiar but strange affiliation between psychoanalytic discourse and detective
fiction: 'Looney's book must have made an immediate appeal to Freud
because to a large extent Looney's method resembled his own' (Trosman
1965: 493). He also employs the concepts of family romance and rescue
fantasy. Schoenbaum follows, and picks up as well Ernest Jones's noting
a similarity between Freud's attitude to the author 'Shakespeare' and
the argument in 'Moses and Monotheism' that Moses was an Egyptian.
Schoenbaum writes:

> Such obsessions reflect the operation of the Family Romance fantasy. The
> child, reacting against disappointment with the imperfections of his par-
> ents, compensates by replacing them with others of higher birth; he must
> be a stepchild or adopted. In later life such fantasies of parental idealiza-
> tion are transposed to a Moses – or [Earl of] Oxford. (612)

And what of Looney? Schoenbaum reiterates Trosman's account of the
bizarre scene in which Looney attempts to deposit with the Librarian of
the British Museum a sealed envelope containing written testimony to his

'priority of discovery' (Trosman 481) vis-à-vis the Earl of Oxford's authorship. In doing this, Trosman argues,

> Looney could well imagine that eventually his identity would be revealed as the original instigator of the Oxfordian position. In the same way that [Looney] states credit must be given 'to the great Englishman' who actually authored the plays, credit would then be given to him who had actually made the Oxfordian discovery first. (465)

And Schoenbaum adds: 'Looney's deliverance of his idol from depreciation and obscurity exemplifies the rescue fantasy, interpreted by Freud as the son's defiant wish to settle his account with his father for the gift of life' (613).

Finally, there is the concept of ambivalence. Here Schoenbaum refers to the manifestations of 'filial ambivalence throughout the dreary pages of anti-Stratfordian discourse: on the one hand, denigration of the drunken, illiterate, usurious poacher from the provinces; on the other, ecstatic veneration of the substitute claimant, aristocrat and deity' (612). This kind of manifestation of ambivalence is obvious enough in Looney's *Shakespeare Identified* – the book Freud reread, says Schoenbaum, 'with no accessions of doubt' (609). What goes for Looney, goes for Freud.

Ambivalence is clearly in play in Freud's own remarks, in his 'Address Delivered in the Goethe House at Frankfort' in 1930, on the value of biographies of great writers such as Goethe and Shakespeare:

> But what can these biographies achieve for us? Even the best and fullest of them could not answer the two questions which alone seem worth knowing about. It would not throw any light on the riddle of the miraculous gift that makes an artist, and it could not help us to comprehend any better the value and effect of his works. And yet there is no doubt that such a biography does satisfy a powerful need in us. We feel this very distinctly if the legacy of history unkindly refuses the satisfaction of this need – for example in the case of Shakespeare. It is undeniably painful to all of us that even now we do not know who was the author of the comedies, tragedies and sonnets of Shakespeare; whether it was in fact the untutored son of the provincial citizen of Stratford, who attained a modest position as an actor in London, or whether it was, rather, the nobly-born and highly cultivated, passionately wayward, to some extent *déclassé* aristocrat, Edward de Vere, seventeenth Earl of Oxford, hereditary Lord Great Chamberlain of England. (Strachey et al. 1973–86: 14, 470–1)

Freud goes on to argue that the 'powerful need' which biography can satisfy consists in bringing us closer to the artist 'as a human being'. This in turn involves the concept of ambivalence. A movement, then, towards 'degradation', since 'our reverence . . . regularly conceals a component of hostile rebellion' (471–2). Freud's own ambivalence towards the author of the comedies, tragedies and sonnets is thus explicit: ambivalence is 'a psychological fatality', he says; 'it cannot be altered without forcible suppression of the truth and is bound to extend to our relations with the great men whose life histories we wish to investigate' (472). But in the case of Shakespeare – in the absence of the greatly desired 'biography' or 'life history' – Freud's ambivalence is forced to operate at the level of the proper name of the author: what more magnificent degradation one might ask, than to deny Shakespeare authorship of 'his' oeuvre?

But at this point we must pause. Briefly we have seen how Schoenbaum, following Trosman, seeks to use psychoanalytic theory to 'explain the unconscious origins of anti-Stratfordian polemics' (Schoenbaum 613). This entails a troubling paradox: namely, that both writers employ psychoanalytic theory in order to explain what Schoenbaum calls a 'surprising and sad' (608) aberration on the part of the founder of psychoanalytic theory. In *The Post Card* (1987), Jacques Derrida has demonstrated, through a reading of *Beyond the Pleasure Principle* (1920), how the institution of psychoanalysis is inextricably tied up with the name of its founder. There are threads here leading into the 'Bacon–Shakespeare controversy': we propose to analyse them.

Freud's own suspicions about the name of the first Baconian in print – Delia Bacon – clarify the stakes. Any inclination towards a strictly Baconian position was much diminished when (as Jones puts it) Freud 'heard that one of the founders of the Baconian idea was a Miss Bacon, of Boston, which suggested a personal reason for the cult' (459–60). It is a question of the proper name. Freud's losing his head, being driven to the point of distraction over the 'Bacon–Shakespeare controversy', cannot be reduced simply to notions of family romance or rescue fantasy, whatever their exemplary status or value. Freud's engagement is, besides anything else, an engagement with the power of the proper name, his own and Shakespeare's. It is a question of the interrelations of proper name, institution and monumentalization.[4] Of 'psychoanalysis' and 'literature'.

Schoenbaum's 'Deviations' confirms the conclusions reached by the Friedmans some years earlier (Friedman and Friedman 1957).[5] Anti-Stratfordian writings are exposed for all their 'intrinsic worthlessness' and 'ignorance of fact and method' (Schoenbaum 627–8); there are no grounds

for believing a Baconian or indeed any other-author theory; Freud was
wrong; in the absence of firm 'evidence' to the contrary, we should continue to suppose that the author of the plays and sonnets was William
Shakespeare.

And yet, despite a systematic rubbishing of anti-Stratfordian positions,
doubts may recur. As the Friedmans conclude their study of 1957: 'As to the
main issue – we are left where we were: unable to state positively who wrote
the plays' (280). Samuel Schoenbaum's own interest in the complexities of
this topic is reflected in an earlier study, *Internal Evidence and Elizabethan
Dramatic Authorship*, in 1966. He includes, among his final remarks, the
following:

> We want to know; something there is that doesn't love an anonymous
> play. And so scholars use internal evidence as a basis for attribution. Some
> of the hypotheses are much better supported than others; some are
> almost certainly correct. But all of them remain hypotheses. Despite the
> safeguards devised, a subjective element resides in all attribution work,
> and even the utilization of electronic computers will not eliminate the
> need for the exercise of scholarly judgment. (1966: 218)

What's in a name? Who wrote Shakespeare? How useful are the established
notions of internal and external evidence in formulating a solution to this
question?

Let us then turn to a more recent theorization of these problems – to a
text which pursues this questioning, works over the limits of 'scholarly judgment', disrupts distinctions between 'internal' and 'external evidence' and,
finally, opens up new ways of thinking about authorship in general.

2

Derrida's *Signsponge* has been described as 'the most irruptive essay
on literature' to have appeared in English this century (Rand in Derrida
1984a: xi). It is also one of Derrida's most difficult texts, as well as one of his
most daring. Explicitly and provocatively 'taking chances', the essay necessarily articulates itself in the uncanny and perhaps finally undecidable space
between science and belief.[6] As regards the question of literary criticism, it
would appear to represent a particularly strange and intense challenge.
For nothing in the thought of *Signsponge* would permit a critical return to
the realms of so-called rationality or commonsense. *Signsponge* is simply

irreducible to them. The essay effectively summarizes the unprecedented range of its concerns:

> The critic and the philologist (and various others) . . . may wonder whether a certain piece of writing is indeed assignable to a certain author, but as regards the event of the signature, the abyssal machinery of this operation, the commerce between the said author and his proper name, in other words, whether he signs when he signs, whether his proper name is truly his name and truly proper, before or after the signature, and how all this is affected by the logic of the unconscious, the structure of the language, the paradoxes of name and reference, of nomination and description, the links between common and proper names, names of things and personal names, the proper and the non-proper, no question is ever posed by any of the regional disciplines which are, as such, concerned with texts known as literary. (Derrida 1984a: 24, 26)

Derrida's *Signsponge* works on the work of Francis Ponge, works on his name. It is concerned with notions of proper name and signature.

Why write? What can writing do? A writer 'expresses his name, and that is all. Across the entire corpus' (Derrida 70). Richard Rand has elaborated:

> The drive is to take the proper name, one's own name, and convert it into the signature, a mark that will never perish. One can go so far as to say that the artist doesn't give a damn about his work; he cares only about the survival of his signature. (Rand 1982: 55)

There is always some signature, there are always signature-effects; but the signature does not just happen in a self-identical way. As Derrida makes clear in 'Signature event context':

> In order to function, that is, in order to be legible, a signature must have a repeatable, iterable, imitable form; it must be able to detach itself from the present and singular intention of its production. It is its sameness which, in altering its identity and singularity, divides the seal. (1982: 328–9)

This strange logic of sameness and singularity, of repetition and alterity, operates as the condition of possibility of the signature. 'The necessarily invisible quotation marks surrounding the proper name' (Derrida 1984a: 8) must be acknowledged. The signature can never be purely and simply present, proper, self-identical, singular; it always involves, as well, (non-simple) absence, the improper or non-proper, and otherness. The notion of otherness is introduced, for example, as soon as one raises questions about 'the line between the autography of one's proper name and a signature' (54). As Derrida does in *Spurs*: 'What, after all, is handwriting? Is one obliged, merely because something is written in one's hand, to assume, or thus to sign it? Does one assume even one's own signature?' (1979: 127).

Otherness is linked to the notion of 'the thing'. The drive is to leave one's mark in the text itself; but

> [B]y not letting the signature fall outside the text anymore, as an under-signed subscription, and by inserting it into the body of the text, you monumentalize, institute, and erect it into a thing or a stony object. But in doing so, you also lose the identity, the title of ownership over the text: you let it become a moment or a part of the text, as a thing or a common noun. (Derrida 1984a: 56)

Always the strange and paradoxical logic – that 'the stony monumentaliza-tion of the name (is) a way of losing the name' (26); that 'The signature is the placement in abyss (of the proper) itself: exappropriation' (132). There is always this 'double band' of the signature

> stretched between the need to become a thing, the common name of a thing, or the name of a generality losing the *idion* in order to inscribe the colossal, and, on the other hand, the contrary demand for a pure idioma-ticity, a capital letter unsoiled by the common, the condition of the signa-ture in the proper sense. (64)

There may be 'the momentary singularity of a certain coitus of signatures' (50) and this may consist in a certain union of signature ('pure idiomatic-ity') and countersignature (that of 'a thing' or 'a generality'). It may consist in 'the *rebus* signature, the metonymic or anagrammatic signature'; but 'these are the condition of possibility and impossibility. The *double bind* of a signature event' (64).

The only desire is to leave one's mark, to monumentalize one's name. The entire problematic comes forcefully in a single sentence in *Glas*: 'The signature is a wound, and there is no other origin for the work of art' (Derrida 1986c: 184). So what in the name of 'Shakespeare'? How would *Signsponge* work in relation to the texts of 'Shakespeare'?

3

Freud's reading of *Hamlet*, in *The Interpretation of Dreams* (1900) (Strachey et al. 4), illustrates with an almost embarrassing clarity the dangers of literary psychobiography. To take Hamlet as a real person, who has a 'mind' or 'unconscious' which can be probed and analysed; to declare that Hamlet's 'distaste for sexuality' would be shared 'more and more' by Shakespeare himself. Freud also writes that,

> *Hamlet* was written immediately after the death of Shakespeare's father (in 1601), that is, under the immediate impact of his bereavement and, as we may well assume, while his childhood feelings about his father had been freshly revived. It is known, too, that Shakespeare's own son who died at an early age bore the name of 'Hamnet', which is identical with 'Hamlet'. (Strachey et al. 4: 367–8)

It is now generally supposed that John Shakespeare's death did not antedate the composition of *Hamlet*; but it is known that Shakespeare's only son, Hamnet – 'of which name Hamlet is a variant form' (see Blakemore Evans 1974: 1828) – was buried at Stratford on 11 August 1596, aged 11. Again, what interests us here is the name; and the fact that Freud, if only in passing, draws attention to it.

Freud's observations on the psychogenesis of Hamlet are rendered absurd by his own simple but amazing footnote, added in 1930: 'Incidentally, I have in the meantime ceased to believe that the author of Shakespeare's works was the man from Stratford' (Strachey et al. 4: 368, n.1). But then *Ulysses* returns, interloping and interlooping, between 1900 and the 1930 footnote, carrying on the analysis. As Stephen Dedalus says of the Ghost: 'To a son he speaks, the son of his soul, the prince, young Hamlet and to the son of his body, Hamnet Shakespeare, who has died in Stratford that his namesake may live for ever' (Joyce 1974: 188–9). In humour and in rigour *Ulysses* goes beyond Freud's account and, like the *Portrait* before it, explores the entire domain of the signature and proper name. Stephen says:

> He has hidden his own name, a fair name, William, in the plays, a super here, a clown there, as a painter of old Italy set his face in a dark comer of his canvas. He has revealed it in the sonnets where there is Will in overplus. Like John O'Gaunt his name is dear to him, as dear as the coat of arms he toadied for, on a bendsable, a spear or steeled argent, honorificabilitudinitatibus, dearer than his glory of greatest shakescene in the country. What's in a name? (1974: 209)

Allusions to the 'fair name' in *As You Like It* (5.1.22) and the Sonnets (e.g. 57, 135, 136, 143), to the coat of arms granted to John Shakespeare in 1596, to one of the Baconians' favourite cryptonyms ('honorificabilitudinitatibus'), in *Love's Labour's Lost*, (5.1.41) and to Robert Greene's 1592 attack on the playwright as 'the onely Shake-scene in a countrey' (see Blakemore Evans, 1835) – all of these culminate in the quotation from *Romeo and Juliet*: 'What's in a name?' (2.2.43).

The idea of Shakespeare's authorship of Psalm 46, on the basis of the 46th word in, and the word 46 off the end; punning references to the name 'Will' in the sonnets; the sonnets' preoccupation with the name (for instance, 71, 72, 76, 95, 111) and, more specifically, with poetry as monumentalization (for instance, 18, 19, 55, 63, 65, 74, 81, 107) – these are perhaps well-known. There are also contemporary descriptions of Shakespeare which link the ideas of name and monument – early meldings in the formation of the Shakespeare–England–Monument–Institution (S.E.M.I.) chain, even if it is only half the story. One could unearth Leonard Digges's 'To the Memorie of the deceased Authour Maister W. Shakespeare' (Blakemore Evans 71), which appeared in the *First Folio*:

> SHake-speare, *at length thy pious fellowes giue*
> *The world thy Workes: thy Workes, by which, out-liue*
> *Thy Tombe, thy name must when that stone is rent,*
> *And Time dissolues thy Stratford Moniment,*
> *Here we aliue shall view thee still* . . .

Blurred syntax brings 'name' and 'Tombe' together. In Milton's 'Epitaph on the admirable Dramaticke Poet' (1630) (in Blakemore Evans, 1845), the name requires no physical monument:

> What neede my Shakespeare for his honour'd bones,
> The labour of an Age, in piled stones
> Or that his hallow'd Reliques should be hid
> Vnder a starre-ypointing Pyramid?
> Deare Sonne of Memory, great Heire of Fame,
> What needst thou such dull witnesse of thy Name?
> Thou in our wonder and astonishment
> Hast built thy selfe a lasting Monument.

The name is itself a monument. It has been monumentalized into some other 'stony thing'. And there is an athanasy of the name – so long as appropriation, quasi-hypnotic identification, a singular kind of transfer-ence, translation no doubt, maintain 'William Shakespeare' as the thing ('my *Shakespeare*', a monument of 'wonder and astonishment', enough to 'make us Marble' as line 14 of Milton's poem has it).

4

What's in a name? In Denmark. This will have been my hypothesis, in four parts: (i) that *Signsponge* (and Derrida's other work on the signature and proper name) appears to offer a way of identifying Shakespeare as author, a way which at the same time tampers with traditional scholarly distinctions between 'internal' and 'external evidence', questioning the very idea of signing and appropriation (by the author, by the reader, in the name of the author, and so on); (ii) that *Hamlet* can be read not only as a text signed, on the 'inside', by Shakespeare, but also as a text which is specifically *about* the idea and act of signing; (iii) that the logic of this reading can be extended to other 'Shakespeare' texts; and (iv) that, finally, all of this can be linked up with the question of psychoanalysis, and above all with the proper name of 'Freud'.

Engaging disruptions between internal and external, Derrida argues that 'In the form of the whole name, the inscription of the signature plays strangely with the frame, with the border of the text, sometimes inside, sometimes outside' (1984a: 120). And again, 'a small part of the text, (the) *signature*, takes hold of the text, which it covers to the point that it also makes the text into a small part of itself, and therefore overflows it' (122). William Shakespeare expresses his name, and that is all, across the entire corpus – for example, the strange body of *Hamlet*. 'That every word doth almost tell my name' (sonnet 76): this proposition would no longer involve simply that second modality of signature which Derrida characterizes as 'the set of idiomatic marks' which have 'no essential link with the form of the proper name' (54).[7]

Derrida notes that,

> The proper name, in its aleatoriness, should have no meaning and should spend itself in immediate reference. But the chance or the misery of its arbitrary character (always other in each case), is that its inscription in language always affects it with a potential for meaning, and for no longer being proper once it has a meaning. (118)

He shows how this functions in and around the name 'Francis Ponge' – most elaborately in terms of the notion of 'sponge' (*éponge*, hence *signe-éponge, signé-ponge*). A similar situation clearly presents itself with Shakespeare. Again, it is crucial to stress that this is not a matter of 'authorial intention', nor even of 'consciousness' or 'unconsciousness'. As Derrida points out in a discussion in *The Ear of the Other*: 'obviously this is not something one can decide: one doesn't disseminate or play with one's name. The very structure of the proper name sets this process in motion (1985: 76).

At the most obvious, commonsensical level then – before the others or not – the name has the at least doubly categorematical signification hinted at by Leonard Digges's hyphenation 'SHake-speare': a verb and a noun which, separately ('spear' as verb) or together, suggest action and force. As with the name of Fortinbras, literally 'strong-in-arm' (Jenkins 1982: 163). Etymologically the spear marks many names, among them Roger ('fame-spear'), Oscar ('god-spear'), Edgar ('happy-spear'), Gerald ('spear-wielding'), Gerard ('spear-hard'), Gervase ('spear-servant') and – since *Hamlet* beckons – Gertrude ('spear-might'). This, then, would be the immediately remarkable thing: that the idea of what Derrida refers to as the third modality of the signature, 'the fold of the placement in abyss where . . . the work of writing designates, describes, and inscribes itself as act (action and archive)' (1984a: 54), this idea is (banally) named in the name itself. Both as action (shaking, spearing, shaking a spear) and as archive (spear-shaking as flourish and as paraph).

'Shake hands'– as in sonnet 28, to seal a compact – this is Shakespeare: no need, always other, impossible, it won't have been his thing.

Dispersal and decomposition – the task of turning the name, as Derrida puts it, 'into a blazon or legendary *rebus*' (1984a: 60) will nevertheless be manifest in 'so many sigils, or abbreviated, interrupted, and condensed signatures' (96). So many signature-effects. Richard Rand has said of Wordsworth's poetry:

[T]here are many, many places, in 'Tintern Abbey' and in 'Michael' for instance, where the language develops a certain thickness and all the graphemes and phonemes of the name William Wordsworth suddenly begin to fulminate. It's not accidental. The letters are scattered, dispersed like the body of Orpheus. (1982: 55)

Transfer these remarks to Shakespeare and Hamlet, and let's start again with Hamlet's first encounter with the Ghost. This 'event' might be read as precisely a dramatization of sealing/signing – from the opening 'Mark me' – 'I will' (1.5.2) – to the reportedly 'wild and whirling words' used by Hamlet afterwards:

> And so, without more circumstance at all,
> I hold it fit that we shake hands and part:
> You, as your business and desire shall point you –
> For every man hath business and desire,
> Such as it is – and for my own poor part. (1.5.127–31)

These lines supposedly reveal nothing, like the Ghost's:

> But that I am forbid
> To tell the secrets of my prison-house,
> I could a tale unfold whose lightest word
> Would harrow up thy soul, freeze thy young blood,
> Make thy two eyes like stars start from their spheres,
> Thy knotted and combined locks to part,
> And each particular hair to stand an end
> Like quills upon the fretful porpentine.
> But this eternal blazon must not be
> To ears of flesh and blood. List, list, O list!
> If thou didst ever thy dear father love – (1.5.13–22)

Strange *occupatio* – saying without saying, saying by not saying, remaining by disappearing, the strangest folding-unfolding of all: signature or blazon in abyss. There is a certain thickening in these lines, most clearly in 'Make . . . stars start . . . spheres'; but an anticipation of the secret has perhaps been blurred together in Hamlet's prelude, his pledge of attention in the Ghost's presence: 'Speak; I am bound to hear' (1.5.6). And only to fall apart. For it is a question of the ear. Here, in the Ghost's speeches, one could trace all the sounds of 'e(a)r(e)' – right through to the critical injunction to 'Remember' and to the final repetitions of 'Swear'.

Leave the demonstration there, at least a moment, it will have already disappeared, as if into thin air. 'But soft, methinks I scent the morning air . . .' (1.5.58). A similar showing can be made for all the rhyming, miming and quasi-hallucinatory variants of 'shake/s'. A few instances, then, along with a few versions of '(sp)ear(e)', from a few lines of the remain-or-disappear, 'To be, or not to be' overheard soliloquy: 'heart-ache', 'shocks', 'heir', 'sleep', 'perchance', 'there's', 'shuffled', 'pause', 'there's', 'makes', 'bear', 'scorns', 'spurns', 'takes', 'make', 'bare', 'bear' (3.1.62–76) and so forth.

Who's there?

For it is a question of the ear – and of proper name and signature – from the first two words of *Hamlet* onwards. The significance of the ear in the play can no longer be confined merely to considerations of theme (poisoning, eavesdropping, etc.) or imagery ('the whisper', i.e. rumour, 'the whole ear of Denmark', etc.). Hamlet's response to hearing the Ghost lights the way: hearing must be supplemented by writing. In order to remember what he hears, Hamlet must 'set it down' (1.5.107) in writing. A notion of writing becomes decisive for the memorization of what is heard; it thereby suggests itself as a necessary condition for acts of memory, hearing, speaking and even the so-called experience of self-presence.[8] Writing commemoration. The 'ear', with all its more or less audible variants, is violently, uncontrollably caught up in signature and signature-effects.

Hence, from before the beginning, the (ex)appropriateness of the manner of King Hamlet's death. This, together with a recurrent association of ear and specifically verbal poison (e.g. 3.2.227–30; 4.5.88–91; 4.7.101–4), might be used to initiate a demonstration of how the structure of the signature obeys a logic analogous to that of the *pharmakon* ('poison' as well as 'remedy', etc.) in Derrida's *Dissemination*, not to mention that of the sponge (1981: 61–171).[9] Ear, wound, mark and name are repeatedly linked. They gather as folds and forms of signature. It may be a matter of listening for the impossible – and of glimpsing constellations of certain phonemes and graphemes, as in 'assail your ears' (1.1.34), 'with a hideous crash / Takes prisoner Pyrrus' ear' (2.2.472–3), 'He would drown the stage with tears, / And cleave the general ear with horrid speech' (2.2.556–7), 'A knavish speech sleeps in a foolish ear' (4.2.22–3), 'Will nothing stick our person to arraign / In ear and ear' (4.5.93–4).

Or of hearing 'nothing but ourselves' (3.4.135).

5

Signing: this is the 'essential' subject of *Hamlet*. What can hearing do? What kind of mark can sound leave?

KING: How fares our cousin Hamlet?

HAMLET: Excellent, i'faith, of the chameleon's dish. I eat the air, promise-cramm'd. You cannot feed capons so.

KING: I have nothing with this answer, Hamlet. These words are not mine.

HAMLET: No, nor mine now, –

(3.2.92–7)

On Hamlet's final retort, Harold Jenkins quotes Johnson: 'A man's words, says the proverb, are his own no longer than he keeps them unspoken' (1982: 293). But writing, it should be clear, is scarcely different. Again and again *Hamlet* will focus on notions of proper sealing, proper signing – from the 'seal'd compact' (1.1.89) between Fortinbras and King Hamlet, which precedes the play, to the pharmaco-pharmaceutical compact between Laertes and Claudius ('Now must your conscience my acquittance seal . . .' (4.7.1)). The identification between Hamlet and Horatio moves at the level of names and seals – and what must not be forgotten:

> HAMLET: I am glad to see you well.
>   Horatio, or I do forget myself.
> HORATIO: The same, my lord, and your poor servant ever.
> HAMLET: Sir, my good friend, I'll change that name with
>   you.
>
>   (1.2.160–2)

Later, Hamlet will say, as near the ear as possible,

> Dost thou hear?
> Since my dear soul was mistress of her choice,
> And could of men distinguish her election,
> Sh'ath sealed thee for herself. (3.2.62–5)

And this sealing ('Shath-spearing') seals the text – or rather opens the possibility of its being narrated. In the final transfer, in the midst of so much aphony, such polyphony, hearing is (impossibly) encrypted:

> If thou didst ever hold me in thy heart,
> Absent thee from felicity awhile,
> And in this harsh world draw thy breath in pain
> To tell my story . . . (5.2.351–4)

Hamlet comes right up to Horatio's ear, even in writing: 'I have words to speak in thine ear will make thee dumb; yet are they much too light for the bore of the matter. . . . He that thou knowest thine, Hamlet' (4.6.22–8). But who wrote this? According to the first Sailor it was 'th'ambassador' (4.6.9). The question of the authenticity, propriety and properties of Hamlet's handwriting is raised more than once. 'Came this from Hamlet to her?' (2.2.113), Gertrude asks, when Polonius is providing 'proof' of the nature of his 'madness'. And later, in response to the letter announcing Hamlet's 'sudden and more strange return', Laertes asks, 'Know you the hand?' – and the King avers: ''Tis Hamlet's character' (4.7.45–9). Criticism may variously inscribe the significance of Hamlet as a playwright – inside or outside the play? what play? neither in nor out, and both together as well? – and may variously assess which (if any) of Hamlet's 'dozen or sixteen lines' (2.2.535) are inserted in *The Mousetrap*; but these ruminations stop short of the question of handwriting, the authenticity of 'character', seal or signature. How many plays does Hamlet write, or how many write Hamlet?

> Being thus benetted round with villainies –
> Or I could make a prologue to my brains,
> They had begun the play – I sat me down,
> Devis'd a new commission, wrote it fair –
> I once did hold it, as our statists do,
> A baseness to write fair, and labour'd much
> How to forget that learning, but, sir, now
> It did me yeoman's service. Wilt thou know
> Th'effect of what I wrote? (5.2.29–37)

Like Derrida's shopping list, handwriting is linked with forgetting (1977: 185).[10] Difficult to imagine a theory of autography without absence, forgetting, otherness, death – perhaps to precisely the degree that it is difficult to imagine the labour of *forgetting* how to write clearly and legibly ('fair'). And the nature of the handwriting here is crucial, like the nature of the seal: a matter of life and death.

A letter may not reach its destination; equally, it can kill. The letter which should have brought Hamlet's death brings the deaths of Rosencrantz and Guildenstern – thanks not only to Hamlet's unforgotten ability 'to write fair' but also to the seal or signature:

HORATIO:　How was this sealed?
HAMLET:　Why, even in that was heaven ordinant.
　　　　　I had my father's signet in my purse,
　　　　　Which was the model of that Danish seal,
　　　　　Folded the writ up in the form of th'other,
　　　　　Subscrib'd it, gave't th'impression, plac'd it safely,
　　　　　The changeling never known. (5.2.47–54)

Who signs and seals? And where? Monstrous impropriety and multiple divisions of the seal. Hamlet's signature, or subscription, is both proper and improper – and neither. 'That Danish seal' is, madly, both King Hamlet's and his murderer's; and Hamlet's 'model' (small copy or exact likeness) signs, undecidably, the internal ruptures and divisions of this seal.

How to distinguish between Claudius and old Hamlet? Again, Hamlet invokes the idea of seals, characterizing his father as,

> A combination and a form indeed
> Where every god did seem to set his seal
> To give the world assurance of a man.
> This was your husband. Look you now what follows.
> Here is your husband, like a mildew'd ear
> Blasting his wholesome brother . . . (3.4.60–5)

Hamlet's father was a wholesome form covered with seals, and Claudius is 'a mildew'd ear'. Contrast or comparison? What is the status of 'assurance'? It is this last word which occurs again, in the graveyard scene:

HAMLET: . . . Will his vouchers vouch him no more of his
          purchases, and double ones too, than the length
          and breadth of a pair of indentures? The very
          conveyances of his lands will scarcely lie in this
          box, and must th'inheritor himself have no more,
          ha?
HORATIO: Not a jot, my lord.
HAMLET: Is not parchment made of sheepskins?
HORATIO: Ay, my lord, and of calveskins too.
HAMLET: They are sheep and calves which seek out
          assurance in that . . . (5.1.106–15)

If 'assurance' (glossed by Jenkins as 'certainty of possession' and 'legal deed securing this' [1982: 383]) is part of a play of signature, along with 'seek', 'parchment' and 'sheepskins', it is signature in abyss. What is the legitimacy or propriety of 'a pair of indentures'? Surely there is no point in writing. Writing is absurd. There is no permanence in it, no certainty of possession, either in or beyond itself, no possibility of proper monumentalization. What can writing do? What kind of mark can writing leave?

Ear, wound, mark and name: we come back to this chain. In doing so, we should underscore the suggestion that 'writing' be understood in a less narrow sense: just as it has an essential, as well as supplementary relation to the ear, to hearing and the voice, so it extends into the body and a suppos-edly extra-linguistic world of action. Remember: wounding the ear – which is happening all the time – is inextricably linked up with the marking of the name. Words, 'spoken' as well as 'written', produce violent, 'physical' effects. But we cannot any longer separate these fields – even if Hamlet seems to, for example, in reference to Gertrude:

> I will speak daggers to her, but use none.
> My tongue and soul in this be hypocrites:
> How in my words somever she be shent,
> To give them seals never my soul consent. (3.2.387–90)

Any 'assurance' must deliquesce – at least once Hamlet '*Thrusts his rapier through the arras*' (3.4.23), into 'the ear / Of all their conference' (to adopt Polonius's earlier description, in 3.1.186–7), and once Gertrude 'repeats' (by what uncanny machinery or kind of dramaturgic telepathy?):

> O speak to me no more.
> These words like daggers enter in my ears.
> No more, sweet Hamlet. (3.4.94–6)

We will have to say that everything in *Hamlet* follows, in a circular or 'counter' (4.5.110) fashion, from the idea of the 'wounded name' (5.2.349), of telling it, telling its story, inscribing and monumentalizing the name, producing 'wonder-wounded hearers' (5.1.250) and 'a living monument' (5.1.292). It is not only Hamlet, or Horatio, who is thus situated. All the doubling in the play feeds into this loop. Another 'double', Laertes, brings together 'voice' and wounded name, when he rejects Hamlet's request for pardon:

> . . . but in my terms of honour
> I stand aloof, and will no reconcilement
> Till by some elder masters of known honour
> I have a voice and precedent of peace
> To keep my name ungor'd. (5.2.242–6)

'But stay, what noise?' (4.7.161). The duel must come, even if – like the battle between Norway and Poland – it 'hath in it no profit but the name' (4.4.19).

Another 'double', Claudius, is also articulated on to the loop, inscribed in the ear, wound, mark, name chain. As when he calculates, for example,

> [So envious slander],
> Whose whisper o'er the world's diameter,

As level as the cannon to his blank,
Transports his poison'd shot, may miss our name
And hit the woundless air. (4.1.40–4)

A remark by Derrida may advance our reading and allow us to move it beyond *Hamlet*: 'In the question of style there is always the weight or *examen* of some pointed object. At times this object might be only a quill or a stylus. But it could just as easily be a stiletto, or even a rapier' (1979: 37). The question of style will also entail the notion, and deposition, of a signature. Especially in the case (and chance) of a name like Shakespeare. It can be traced across the entire ever-'changeling' body of *Hamlet*, from the 'quills upon the fretful porpentine' to the 'treacherous instrument' (5.2.322) which kills Hamlet, Laertes and Claudius. One must look for so many pointed objects – pins, partisans, swords, arrows, daggers, points, quills, bodkins. And above all, no doubt, as most provocative linking of the question of style and signature, the rapier. Signature-effects proliferate in those lines about the 'eyrie of children', for example, lines crucial to the dating of the play: 'These are now the fashion, and so berattle the common stages – so they call them – that many wearing rapiers are afraid of goosequills and dare scarce come thither' (2.2.339–42).[11] Almost as provocative, in their way, as the 'shak[ing] . . . parsnip' in the *Sir Thomas More* additions (see Blakemore Evans 1687).

But what is a signature? Who signs? How to sign, where and when? How to seal, how to monumentalize, how to leave a mark in or as writing? The validity of these questions is interdependent with that of the play's relentless exploration and questioning of death and mourning, memory and remembering, of the present and presence. Validity as legitimacy (questions of law and institutions) and as durability (questions also of monuments and monumentalization). Everything in *Hamlet* which questions memory and self-presence is finally a question of (the impossibility of a proper) signing.

All remembering is in the name of something.[12] In the Derrida-Ponge description, signing is associated with the notion of the wager and the duel.[13] *Hamlet* offers an elaboration of this association. It embraces yet exceeds all the forms of wager and compact in the play – for instance, between King Hamlet and King Fortinbras, Claudius and Gertrude, Polonius and Laertes and Ophelia, Hamlet and Horatio, Polonius and Reynaldo, Polonius and Claudius, Claudius and Fortinbras, Claudius and Gertrude and Rosencrantz and Guildenstern, Hamlet and the Players . . . . It exceeds also the singular compact between Hamlet and the Ghost Hamlet – ostensibly sealed by the written 'word', 'Remember me' and the swearing to silence by Hamlet's sword. It is, as such, neither the duel between Hamlet and Laertes, nor the longer one which has gone on between Hamlet and Claudius and to which Hamlet refers when dismissing any guilt over Rosencrantz and Guildenstern:

> 'Tis dangerous when the baser nature comes
> Between the pass and fell incensed points
> Of mighty opposites. (5.2.60–2)

It is neither characterological, nor thematic, nor even an event. Rather *Hamlet* is, from start to finish, and spreading before and after them, the impossible dramatization, deferral and enactment, presentation, analysis and abyssing of the signature.

Impossible because always other – and the other thing. What will Shakespeare's thing have been? One might say the ear, or Hamlet, or, with Hamlet, that 'The play's the thing' (2.2.600) or again 'The King is a thing' (4.3.27); one might say woman, the Ghost, Oedipus complex, objective correlative, memory, mourning and so on. Any and all of these would only be a way of seeming to bring close the impossible, the inaudible-unspeakable, the unnamably other.

6

What's in a name?

The preceding remarks and suggestions would furnish a basis for the discussion and analysis of other putatively 'Shakespeare' texts. Circling in a gradual but determined fashion back to the question of the proper name of 'Freud', let us sketch very rapidly some possible approaches to three other plays: *Romeo and Juliet, Antony and Cleopatra* and *The Tempest*.

> What's in a name? That which we call a rose
> By any other word would smell as sweet;
> So Romeo would, were he not Romeo call'd,
> Retain that dear perfection, which he owes
> Without that title. (2.2.43–7)

Name, word, title: Romeo and Juliet. Familiarity pleads unsettling here, and not only in the manner of Virginia Woolf's supplement to Gertrude Stein's 'A rose is a rose is a rose': '– Is it?'

Left to reverberate, 'What's in a name?' becomes more than simply a rhetorical question. Gulielmus. It would take a central role in a reading of *Romeo and Juliet* at the level of the uneasy tones and effects of its language: a 'most excellent and lamentable tragedy' of the *alea* and power of proper names; of love, identification, transference figured as figures of rhetoric, through a metaphorics of light, writing and reading – by the visible materiality of the signifier; of letters, communications and telecommunications at least one of which fatally fails to reach its destination; of an uneasy final confusion of monumentalization and encrypting, rounding on names – an unease which is also, perhaps, an uneasiness of signing.[14] Like Juliet's 'O happy dagger. / This is thy sheath. There rust, and let me die' (5.3.168–9), Romeo goes out with a paraph, and with a sign of the impossible contract:

> O here
> Will I set up my everlasting rest
> And shake the yoke of inauspicious stars
> From this world-wearied flesh. Eyes, look your last.
> Arms, take your last embrace! And lips, O you
> The doors of breath, seal with a righteous kiss
> A dateless bargain to engrossing Death. (5.3.109–15)

This bargain can be compared with Hamlet's 'quietus' (1.3.75). 'Engrossing' means not only 'purchasing in gross, in large qualities' or 'illegally monopolizing or amassing', but also 'writing a legal document' (Gibbons 1980: 227): Death (capitalized and capitalizing as proper name) writes, and must (impossibly) sign or 'seal' as well. Datelessness and monumentalization. Unease through a multiplication of monuments – the monument where Romeo and Juliet die, the monument proposed to commemorate them, and the monument entitled *Romeo and Juliet*. A question, finally, of names and sealing a compact at any rate, in which the proper name of Verona itself must participate:

> CAPULET: O brother Montague, give me thy hand.
>   This is my daughter's jointure, for no more
>   Can I demand.
> MONTAGUE: But I can give thee more,
>   For I will raise her statue in pure gold,
>   That whiles Verona by that name is known,
>   There shall no figure at such rate be set
>   As that of true and faithful Juliet.

CAPULET: As rich shall Romeo's by his lady's lie,
             Poor sacrifices of our enmity. (5.3.295–303)

Proper name and signature, monument and monumentalization in *Antony and Cleopatra* require a reading of such concentration and subtlety that I can only give the most hesitant of outlines. Space seems to close in.

Will you walk out of the air?

I have suggested that the ear, and a labyrinthine kind of phone-book gathering around the sounds of 'e(a)r(e)', is a signature-effect, and site of sealing, in *Hamlet*. The operation can be transferred to the air in *Antony and Cleopatra*. One would have to listen to the ear as well, and to those other kinds of signature-effect touched on in the discussion of *Hamlet*; but read also for a thread perhaps, for knots of 'rare', 'yare', 'mare', 'chare' and so many more familiar others, leading to 'air'. Or not. Cleopatra is, says Antony, 'Like a right gipsy, that at fast and loose / Beguil'd me, to the very heart of loss' (4.12.28–9). John Ingledew glosses 'fast and loose' as follows: 'a game of deception formerly played at fairs by gipsies. Having tied a knot in a belt or string, the gipsy would get people to bet that it was real (*fast*), and would then pull the two ends, removing the knot and showing that it was only an apparent one (*loose*)' (1983: 158). Whether there is nothing, just air, or a knot, or not: the incipient hallucinosis of this alternative – if it is one – is tied to dissolution, air, signature, seal and death. In the power of its serenity and affirmation, Cleopatra's death may be breathtaking – like the resumption of an after-life, or living on – a trick or snare, or not a knot. This mad suspension, between 'knot' and 'not', 'Shakespeare' and 'air', death and living on, and so on, is also caught by Caesar as he remarks on Cleopatra's corpse:

> she looks like sleep,
> As she would catch another Antony
> In her strong toil of grace. (5.2.344–6)

'Toil' as 'net' or 'snare' (but not 'labour'?) goes back at least to Antony's entangling and sealing:

> Now all labour
> Mars what it does: yea, very force entangles
> Itself with strength: seal then, and all is done.
> Eros! – I come, my queen: – Eros! – Stay for me,
> Where souls do couch on flowers, we'll hand in hand,
> And with our sprightly port make the ghosts gaze. (4.14.47–52)

Antony's 'Stay' anticipates Cleopatra's final words, an aposiopesis like a suspension in air, of mark and step: 'What should I stay –' (5.2.312). It lives on, undecidable, like an effect of fast and loose, or of the serpentine syntax of her preceding address to the asp: 'With thy sharp teeth this knot intrinsicate / Of life at once untie.' (5.2.303–04).

Signsponge draws attention to ways in which the notions of signature and resolution are linked. There is irresolution in *Hamlet* – for rapid convenience call it structural, if you wish, rather than characterological – and this would clearly complement the reading of *Hamlet* as a scene of signature. With *Antony and Cleopatra* resolution tends to be dissolution: dissolving, melting, discandying, vanishing. Not nothing; rather, transformation in and as 'air'. Hence the scattering of signature-effects, perhaps, in the clouds of Antony's lines:

> ANTONY: Eros, thou yet behold'st me?
> EROS: Ay, noble lord
> ANTONY: Sometime we see a cloud that's dragonish,
>   A vapour sometime, like a bear, or lion,
>   A tower'd citadel, a pendent rock,
>   A forked mountain, or blue promontory
>   With trees upon't, that nod unto the world,
>   And mock our eyes with air. Thou hast seen these signs
>   They are black vesper's pageants.
> EROS: Ay, my lord.
> ANTONY: That which is now a horse, even with a thought
>   The rack dislimns, and makes it indistinct
>   As water is in water.
> EROS: It does, my lord.
> ANTONY: My good knave Eros, now thy captain is
>   Even such a body. (4.14.1–13)

And, with Cleopatra, the idea of some kind of appropriation of 'air' goes back to Enobarbus's early description:

>   From the barge
>   A strange invisible perfume hits the sense
>   Of the adjacent wharfs. The city cast
>   Her people out upon her; and Antony,
>   Enthron'd i' the market-place, did sit alone,
>   Whistling to the air; which, but for vacancy,

>Had gone to gaze on Cleopatra too,
>And made a gap in nature. (2.2.211–18)

At which impossible rarefaction, Agrippa exclaims 'Rare Egyptian!' And in the final scene Cleopatra will affirm: 'Husband, I come: / Now to that name, my courage prove my title! / I am fire, and air' (5.2.286–8). And again, 20 lines later:

>CHARMIAN: O, break! O, break!
>CLEOPATRA: As sweet as balm, as soft as air, as gentle.

What will 'air' be? What kind of thing? Perhaps both the 'vapour' of 'mechanic slaves / With greasy aprons, rules, and hammers' (5.2.208–12) and 'power': signature and countersignature of air and Shakes-paraph which is by the same gesture disappearance, vanishing; signature as a common thing and as a monument of power. Shake. It is a question of a structure analogous to the logic of what Derrida terms *pas* (both 'not' and 'step'), which we might render *knot-a-step*, or of an aposiopesis which is at the same time in some sense paraphonic:

>I saw her once
>Hop forty paces through the public street,
>And having lost her breath, she spoke, and panted,
>That she did make defect perfection,
>And, breathless, power breathe forth. (2.2.228–32)

As with the mournful, airy power of the colossal imaging of Antony, in Act 5, scene 2 (75ff.), it seems to be a question of an impossible and absolutely singular sounding or voice, one that could 'shake the orb' while being identified with 'all the tuned spheres' (5.2.84–5).

A pair? – appear and disappear. How to round off, embrace, clasp or name? 'No grave upon the earth shall clip in it / A pair so famous' (5.2.357–8).

>Who's there?
>Indeed, that is out o' th' air.

Can you hear lightning?

The Tempest begins with 'a tempestuous noise of thunder and lightning heard' and in the midst of it, of so many waves, in the first seventeen lines, the ghostly shapes of a signature might be heard, like lightning, for instance in 'here', 'cheer', 'speak', 'yarely', 'bestir, bestir', 'cheerly, cheerly', 'yare, yare!', 'take', 'care', 'where', 'hear', 'mar our labour', a stressed thread leading through to the Boatswain's 'Hence! What cares these roarers for the name of King?' (1.1.16–17). Or knot. The name is here, in *The Tempest*, as both 'roar' and (musical) 'air'. Are you awake?

'Shake it off. Come on.' (1.2.309)

The Tempest's concern with the power of language is a concern with the hyp-notic power of sound. It is a matter of the relations between hypnosis and literature, in short that of a hypnopoetics (Derrida 1988: 31–41).

No need to repeat the numerous arguments for seeing Prospero as a figure of the playwright or the text as an allegory of 'the story' of Shakespeare's life. Our only interest is in the name, the signature, the William-Shakespeare-text. Everything in the text is to be heard – right 'To th'syllable' (1.2.504) – and everything will come down to the name. Between the impropriety and violence of the 'roar' and the clear, formal beauty of the (musical) 'air'; or rather, passing through them. Or knot.

The *OED* defines 'paronomasia' as 'a playing on words which sound alike; a word-play; a pun'. It specifies its derivation from the Greek verb παρονομαζιειν, 'to alter slightly in naming'; but warns against confusing it with another word, 'prosonomasia' which is, 'properly, a calling by a name, a nicknaming', and derives from the Greek προσονομαζειν, 'to call by a name'. We shan't confuse them, or make a paronymous botch of them, properly speaking. Nevertheless it is clear that the names of Miranda (see 1.2.428–31, and 3.1.36–8) and Caliban (as cannibal or oth-erwise deformed, to the syllable, as "Ban, 'Ban, Cacaliban', at 2.2.184) traverse both terms – let alone that of Prospero (there is play, perhaps, on 'prosper' at 2.1.69, 2.2.2, and 4.1.104). For the name 'Prospero' is also a paronomasia of the proper name of Shakespeare, and even of the 'proper' itself. Prosperonomasia: 'Prospero' as (impossibly proper) signature-effect.

Shake off slumber, and beware:
Awake, Awake! (2.1.299–300)

Ariel too – that spirit 'which art but air' (5.1.21) and which, by the most lightening paronomasia, carries the air in its name.

What is fascinating, or spell-binding, is the (impossible) chance of saying the name, not only of letting the name be signed or inscribed in the text, in accordance with the kinds of signature-effects so far indicated, but also of letting *The Tempest* finally say nothing at all except the name. Between 'Prospero' and 'Ariel', 'roar' and 'air', the dramatization of the signature as sound – as something holy, majestic, monumental.

But can it be heard? Are you awake? For instance, in these exchanges:

ALONSO: Wherefore this ghastly looking?
GONZALO: What's the matter?
SEBASTIAN: Whiles we stood here securing your repose,
                   Even now, we heard a hollow burst of bellowing
                   Like bulls, or rather lions: did't not wake you?
                   It struck mine ear most terribly.
ALONSO: I heard nothing.
ANTONIO: O, 'twas a din to fright a monster's ear,
                   To make an earthquake! sure, it was the roar
                   Of a whole herd of lions.
ALONSO: Heard you this, Gonzalo?
GONZALO: Upon mine honour, sir, I heard a humming,
                   And that a strange one too, which did awake me:
                   I shak'd you, sir, and cried . . . (2.2.304–14)

One might hear Shakespeare, nothing, a roar, or 'humming' air. Or knot. Frank Kermode glosses the lines about the bellowing, earthquaking sound as 'Possibly an allusion to the many accounts of terrifying noises on unexplored islands, from Hanno up to date' (1979: 60). Perhaps; but more obvious is the way in which the hearing of this sound anticipates Alonso's experience in Act 3:

GONZALO: I' th' name of something holy, sir, why stand you
                   In this strange stare?
ALONSO: O, it is monstrous, monstrous!
                   Methought the billows spoke, and told me of it;
                   The winds did sing it to me; and the thunder,
                   That deep and dreadful organ-pipe, pronounc'd
                   The name of Prospe . . . (3.3.95–9)

Difficult to hear in all the noise. Wake up still in sleep. Where should this music be? The trees are toppling.

The power of sound, the musical forces of language: these constitute the spell within and of the play, crossing and recrossing the borders to form a singular, multiple knot. Knotty oak and arms.

> [I have] 'twixt the green sea and the azur'd vault
> Set roaring war: to the dread rattling thunder
> Have I given fire, and rifted Jove's stout oak
> With his own bolt; the strong-bas'd promontory
> Have I made shake, and by the spurs pluck'd up
> The pine and cedar: graves at my command
> Have wak'd their sleepers. (5.1.43–9)

This extraordinary paraph coincides with the abjuration of rough magic: a kind of disappearing in order to remain. Being 'bound up' (1.2.489), 'knit up' (3.3.89), in 'bondage' (3.1.41) – this is all undone ('Untie the spell', says Prospero at 5.1.253), only in order that the other begins, already will have begun. A knot. Or not.

> It is a sleepy language, and thou speak'st
> Out of thy sleep . . . (2.1.206–7)

What happens? Will all have 'melted into air, into thin air' (4.1.150) – fast and loose. By me, William Shakespeare.

7

Appalled by his disregard, by the fact that he didn't seem to give a damn about his plays, about having them properly written down, edited or printed, Delia Bacon supposed that Shakespeare must have 'cared for them precisely as a tradesman would – cared for them as he would have cared for tin kettles, or earthen pans and pots, if they had been in his line, instead' (cited in Schoenbaum 1970: 535). That will do, in part: a line in stony objects.

While greasy Joan doth keel the pot.[15] Greasy aprons, rules and hammers. The thin air of things. Dissolves into insignificance. After all, to adopt Derrida's words, the question of the name is never more 'than a little, insignificant piece of the whole corpus. And his work is so little the product of his name that it springs rather from an aptitude for doing without it' (1984a: 116).

One or two final threads of insignificance to pick out here, which may turn out to be one or more, to close, or not.

First thread. Derrida writes: 'To signify oneself in the insignificant (outside meaning or concept), isn't this the same thing as signing?' (1984a: 40). One might pursue this question through an analysis of what is classically recognized as a mark of Shakespeare's 'greatness': his facility for engaging with, representing the ordinary, the banal and insignificant, the everyday. And, suggestively in accordance with Derrida's formulation of 'style', a facility for this facility itself: 'easie numbers' (as Milton's poem has it) – a style which appears to advance in advance, weaving (itself) away, throwing off (everything in) its path, like just so much insignificance, not worth a jot, and yet, by precisely this self-effacing movement, letting a mark or signature be left (Derrida 1979: 39 and passim).

Second thread. The notion of marking the insignificant can be thought in terms of being resolute. Lacan emphasizes the idea of the duel in *Hamlet* and how the objects offered in the wager ('six Barbary horses' against 'six French rapiers and poniards, with their assigns, as girdle, hanger, and so' [5.2.144–7]) take on 'the character of what is called a *vanitas* in the religious tradition'. The notion of signature might then affect the context and sense of Lacan's observation that Hamlet 'stakes his resolution against the things that interest him least in the world, and he does so to win for someone else' (Lacan 1977a: 30). Marking both the insignificant and the *objet a*.[16] This can be generalized: doesn't work on signature and signature-effects open up the possibility of a redescription, a transformation of the very grounds, of psychoanalysis, of the concepts of 'ego' and 'narcissism', 'identification' and 'transference' and of the entire (insignificant) psycho-pathology of everyday life?

Not forgetting the forgetting of proper names, not least that of Freud, the Freudian slip, the slip or slip-knot of 'Freud'.

One has to try the argument out on various people, but Arnold Zweig proves stubborn. Enthusing about Edward de Vere, Freud writes to Zweig in 1937: 'I do not know what still attracts you to the man of Stratford . . .. It almost irritates me that you should support the notion' (Freud 1970: 140). Nearly a year earlier, anticipating a visit from Zweig, Freud had written: 'You must bring Looney back with you. I must try him on others, for obviously with you I have had no success' (132). Does this remind us of anything?

A month earlier, in May 1936, this time to Stefan Zweig: 'For with the biographer as with the psychoanalyst we find phenomena which come under the heading of "transference"' (Freud 1961: 426).

Analysts have been embarrassed about Freud's involvement in the Bacon–Shakespeare controversy; it is seen as a curious aberration, perhaps best forgotten, comparable to his involvement with the question of telepathy. Yes, let's try to forget about it.

Or knot. In which case wouldn't this curious aberration operate according to the logic of what Derrida has called an 'unanalysed remainder'? (1987: 519). Then far from being an eccentric or whimsical concern out on the margins of Freud's thought, the Bacon–Shakespeare controversy and all that it entails would be alive and stirring at the heart of the inside. Like 'telepathy', and like 'hypnosis' too. Here we might attend to the emphasis given, in the remarkable work of Mikkel Borch-Jacobsen (1989b), to the ineffaceably constitutive role of hypnosis in the institution of psychoanalysis; and in particular to the way in which hypnosis comes back, in ghostly fashion, to the centre-stage of Freud's later work.[17] In various and interconnected ways, all three – hypnosis, telepathy, the Bacon–Shakespeare controversy – would lead us to focus on notions of a radical alterity, fictionality and literarity.[18] All three might thus also be seen to figure the concealed and unacknowledgeable distractions of 'distraction' itself, within the conceptuality and the historical emergence of psychoanalysis.

The Bacon–Shakespeare controversy as the distraction of 'Freud': as with 'telepathy', the issues involved would be of the order of a foreign body or an encrypting. Set up, supervised by 'Shakespeare'. What could this mean? *Hamlet*-signed. Freud's suspicions were aroused by the name of Delia Bacon; perhaps it is less strange that he appeared not to see, in the letters of the name 'de Vere' (and even the alternative, 'Oxford'), a scattered projection of his own name. In any case, psychoanalysis is situated as a discourse disturbed, haunted, disrupted by signature and proper name – by an inability to sign well, among other things to sign, countersign or be signed by, literature.

But what if Looney and his disciple Freud were correct after all, and the author really was de Vere? Wouldn't that name function just as satisfactorily in producing supposed signature-effects of 'ear' and 'air'?

Or perhaps Leonardo, the existence of whose 'Academia Vinciana' Freud doubted – an institution, as Freud pointed out, 'postulated from the existence of five or six emblems' (Strachey et al. 14: 222). In a footnote he quotes Giorgio Vasari:

> [Leonardo] lost some time by even making a drawing of knots of cords, in which it was possible to trace the thread from one end to the other until it fanned a completely circular figure. A very complex and beautiful design of this sort is engraved on copper; in the middle can be read the words 'Leonardus Vinci Academia'. (Strachey et al. 14: 222, n. 1)

Notes

1 Following the French version of 'distraction' as '*perdre la tête*', Jacques Derrida has treated the first of these themes in his 'Telepathy' (1988). The present essay is in certain respects a complement to that work.

2 For another account of the Bacon–Shakespeare controversy, especially from a more literary theoretical perspective, see Garber (1987), esp. 1–27.

3 Thus at the end of a hundred pages of scrupulous documentation, Schoenbaum cannot refrain from interposing: 'Perhaps at this pause in the narrative the writer may be permitted to drop for a moment the historian's mask of impersonality and give vent to private emotion. This section ["Deviations"] has been the cruellest assignment I have ever confronted. The sheer volume . . . appals . . .' (627).

4 In this way we might then reconsider: what, essentially, is anti-Stratfordian discourse? It is an engagement with the question and power of the proper name. Schoenbaum's 'Deviations' seems repeatedly to verge on a recognition of this, on the decisiveness and essentiality of naming – but without naming it as such. Shakespeare's name as the one to conjure, to juggle with, all the time, but also the proper names of the anti-Stratfordians themselves: J. Thomas Looney, Sherwood E. Silliman and George M. Battey, for instance. 'How innocently appropriate are some anti-Stratfordian names!' exclaims Schoenbaum (625). The question of what is 'innocent' or 'appropriate', we would note, is necessarily bound up with notions of the illegitimate, the proper and improper. Throughout anti-Stratfordian writings, it is a matter of the appropriations, the property and propriety of proper names. And always also expropriation, the non-proper, the improper. The title, the name of the author and the thesis of one anti-Stratfordian study dramatizes this with a certain hilarity: *Our Elusive Willy: A Slice of Concealed Elizabethan History*, by Ira Sedgwick Proper, which argues that William Seymour, illegitimate son of the Earl of Hertford and Lady Catherine Grey, was christened as 'William Shakespeare'. If Schoenbaum recounts this (613) in a perfectly 'proper' and 'sober' fashion, he treats *Wie was Shakespeare*, by F. Louise W. M. Buisman-de Savornin Lohman, a little more directly: 'the most remarkable feature of this effort, if one may judge from the English summary graciously appended, is the name of the authoress' (616). But Schoenbaum's stress on names is largely inadvertent, clearly subordinate to more 'fundamental' considerations of scholarly exposition, commentary and judgment. A slight drawing apart, displacement or deviation, however, and 'Deviations' might be readily articulated onto a critical analysis of proper names, a meditation on the institutional and monumental significance of the proper name of Shakespeare. What Celeston Demblon called '*l'ex-boucher stratfordien*' (cited by Schoenbaum, 619) might become a kind of *lex-bouchon*, a reading-stopper, the distraction of a traffic-jam or catastrophic pile-up around the reading of a name.

5 The Friedmans' concern is to show how 'claims based on cryptography can be scientifically examined, and proved or disproved' (1957: xv). Thus before coming to reject the arguments for the use of a bi-literal cipher, for example, they carefully establish what we might call a necessary undecidability: 'For even if a claim to authorship were found in the *First Folio*, using Bacon's bi-literal cipher,

this in itself would not be conclusive. The message could have been inserted by the printer himself, playing an elaborate hoax on posterity.' (92).

6 The phrase 'taking chances' alludes to the collection of essays, *Taking Chances: Derrida, Psychoanalysis, and Literature*, eds Joseph H. Smith and William Kerrigan (1984c), especially Derrida's own contribution, 'My Chances / *Mes Chances*: A Rendezvous with Some Epicurean Stereophonies', 1–32. For another essay specifically concerned with 'science' and 'belief', see Derrida's 'No Apocalypse, Not Now (full speed ahead, seven missiles, seven missives)' (1984b).

7 Derrida distinguishes what he calls 'three modalities of signature' (1984a: 52). The first is,

> The one that we call the signature in the proper sense . . . the act of someone . . . engaged in authenticating (if possible) the fact that it is indeed he who writes: here is my name, I refer to myself, named as I am, and I do so, there-fore, in my name. I, the undersigned, I affirm (yes, on my honour). (52, 54)

The second is 'the set of idiomatic marks that a signer might leave by accident or intention in his product' and which have 'no essential link with the form of the proper name as articulated or read "in" a language': this is what is often called 'the style, the inimitable idiom of a writer, sculptor, painter, or orator' (54). The third and most enigmatic is designated 'as general signature, or signature of the signature' (54): it might be described as a kind of writerliness or self-referentiality which is able to efface itself, thus ensuring that 'it is the other, the thing as other, that signs' (54). Derrida's *Signsponge* is concerned to explore the singularity with which the Francis-Ponge-text combines all three modalities.

8 For more extended treatment of these questions, see my 'Nuclear *Pieqe: Mémoires of Hamlet* and the time to come' (1990b).

9 The sponge, in Derrida's account of Ponge, figures the very (im)possibility of the signature. The weird character of the sponge as both proper (clean, dry) and improper (soiled, wet), both itself (empty) and other (full of what is not itself), is evoked by Hamlet's 'knavish speech' to the sponges called Rosencrantz and Guildenstern: 'When [the King] needs what you have gleaned, it is but squeezing you and, sponge, you shall be dry again' (4.2.18–20). Ned Lukacher has also noted the relation between the poisoning of Hamlet's father and Shakespeare's signature: 'The manner of the crime is in effect Shakespeare's own signature in the play, the inimitable mark of his originality. With the ear-poisoning, Shakespeare signs his text twice, once as the author on the title page and again, in a kind of antonomasia, by dismantling his proper name into the common nouns that compose it: ShakespEARE' (1986: 227). Lukacher does not, however, elaborate on the strange logic of this signature-effect.

10 The apparent need for Hamlet to write down the Ghost's 'word', in Act 1, scene v, may correspondingly be illuminated by Derrida's example of the shopping list:

> *At the very moment* 'I' make a shopping list, I know (I use 'knowing' here as a convenient term to designate the relations that I necessarily entertain with the object being constructed) that it will only be a list if it implies my absence, if it already detaches itself from me in order to function beyond my 'present' act and if it is utilizable at another time, in the absence of my-being present-now,

even if this absence is the simple absence of memory that the list is meant to make up for, shortly, in a moment, but one which is already the following moment, the absence of the now of writing, of the writer maintaining [*du maintenant-écrivant*], grasping with one hand his ballpoint pen. Yet no matter how fine this point may be, it is like the *stigmé* of every mark, already split. The sender of the shopping list is not the same as the receiver, even if they bear the same name and are endowed with the identity of a single ego. Indeed, were this self-identity or self-presence as certain as all that, the very idea of a shopping list would be rather superfluous or at least the product of a curious compulsion. Why would I bother about a shopping list if the presence of sender to receiver were so certain? (1977: 185).

11 See Jenkins's notes on 255–6 and 470–2 (1982); and for the notion of dating as itself a form of signing, see Derrida's fascinating 'Shibboleth' (1986b).

12 For extended analysis of the ways in which 'We cannot separate the name of "memory" and "memory" of the name; we cannot separate the name and memory', see Derrida's *Mémoires: for Paul de Man* (1986a: 49 and passim).

13 In *Signsponge* (1984a) too, we should note, this strange 'duel' must 'carry on to the death' (14). It is a question of the impossible (mute) challenge of what Derrida calls 'the thing' – that is to say, the 'entirely other' (12) – and of a law of debt and forfeit which is indeed 'more than life-long' (70).

14 For a somewhat different and much more detailed account of the character and effects of the proper name in *Romeo and Juliet*, see Derrida's 'Aphorism Counter-time' (1992).

15 This is the refrain with which *Love's Labour's Lost* closes: see 5.2.920, 929 (Blakemore Evans 1974: 212).

16 In this way we might be drawn to reconsider, for example, Lacan's analysis of the appearance of the skull in Holbein's 'The Ambassadors' (1977b). Lacan notes that 'This picture is simply what any picture is, a trap for the gaze. In any picture, it is precisely in seeking the gaze in each of its points that you will see it disappear' (89). The anamorphic skull in this painting offers us, according to Lacan, 'the imaged embodiment of the *minus-phil* (-φ)] of castration' (89): we might additionally, or rather, wish to trace its figuring of hollow bone (*hohl bein*).

17 In his 'Hypnosis in Psychoanalysis' (1989b), Borch-Jacobsen observes:

> Psychoanalysis no doubt did found itself on the abandonment of hypnosis – but only, it must be recognized, to see hypnosis reappear, sometimes under other names or in other forms, at the crossroads of all questions; hence, the importance of reconsidering this so-called abandonment, not so much to initiate a 'return to hypnosis' as to examine, in light of the questions Freud was asking himself in his last phase, the reasons why in his first phase he had believed, rather too quickly, that these issues were settled. In other words, what is important is to reconsider what Freud called the 'prehistory' of psychoanalysis, to return to it with the suspicion that this 'prehistory' belongs to a certain future of psychoanalysis rather than to a long-dead past. (95–6)

See also his 'Talking cure' (1990).

18 Hence Borch-Jacobsen's elaboration, for instance in *The Freudian Subject* (1989a), of the notion that 'under hypnosis, *I* no longer distinguish myself from the

other – I *am* the other' (140) and of the logic whereby 'The so-called subject of desire has no identity of its own prior to the identification that brings it, blindly, to occupy the point of otherness, the place of the other (who is thus not an other): an original alienation (which is thus not an alienation); and an original lure (which is thus not a lure, either)' (48). Thus the subject, for Borch-Jacobsen, is 'born in myth, in fantasy, in art' (238). Hence also our attention, in the present essay, to ways in which proper name and signature are inextricably bound up with a logic of the nonproper, exappropriation and the entirely and unnamably other. For a preliminary exploration of the interrelations of telepathy and literarity, see my 'Telepathy: From Jane Austen and Henry James' (1988). As regards what puts the Bacon–Shakespeare controversy in touch with the question of telepathy, let us merely add here the hypothesis that it would be difficult to imagine a theory of telepathy which would not involve, as a quasi-essential condition, the identification of a (so-called) proper name. In this context we might recall the suggestive anecdote recounted by Ernest Jones, in the chapter on 'Occultism':

> . . . Ferenczi was now getting venturesome. Seeing a soldier in a tramcar he made a guess at his name and as they got out asked him, 'Are you Herr Kohn?' The astonished man answered in the affirmative. Freud found the story 'uncannily beautiful', but could not attribute it to telepathy because the man could hardly be expected to carry a visual picture of his name about with him. He said afterwards, however, that he was impressed by Ferenczi's argument that a man's name was a sensitive area and thus could more easily be communicated to a stranger. (415)

Chapter 5

No Biography: Shakespeare, Author

Sean Gaston

Shakespeare gave us a Shakespeare.

Edward Young (1759: 78)

Shakespeare is like God: unparalleled creation, and no biography. Or, perhaps more accurately, he is like Jesus Christ, whose scraps and traces of an unprovable and unproved life sustain the belief in a more than human life, in an exception without example. Like Christ, Shakespeare can never be reduced to biography. No matter how deft, how light, how ingenious the attempts of the Stephen Greenblatts, Jonathan Bates or Michael Woods, not only can 'William Shakespeare' never be reduced to a biography, but nor can 'Mr. William Shakespeares Comedies, Histories, & Tragedies' be reduced to a biographical narrative (Bate 1998; Greenblatt 2004; Wood 2003). Accident, chance or purpose have marked a historical impasse, an irrecoverable and irreducible trace of the past that resists the writing of the life: from the start, *historia* (which can never begin with the assurance of what was *first*, but only with the indefinite displacement of what was *before*) has precluded *bios* (Gaston 2007b). From the start, even before Aubrey's anecdotes in the 1680s of the butcher's son who would make speeches while he slaughtered animals, this historical impasse had wounded the biographical (Aubrey 1958: 275).

But like Christ, this absence of biography has created a perpetual future *of* the past: the life and the works are always ahead of us, always full of an elusive promise. If there were a biography there would be no 'Shakespeare'. No biography: that's Shakespeare. For Christianity, the historical wounding of the biography of Jesus Christ gave rise to, or was a product of, those spectacular concepts that broke with both nature and history, and founded a religion: the virgin birth, the trinity, the resurrection. In his not particularly good book, *Foucault's Pendulum*, Umberto Eco made one very good point: from its many inceptions, Christianity has always relied on and been reinvigorated by conspiracies and secret societies, by the passion of the passionate search for the key to all mythologies, and even those secrets and secret societies that appear to challenge and resist Christianity are already part of the ceaseless restitution of Christianity (Eco 1989). It is the endless hunt for the hidden details of the life of Jesus Christ the man that has kept Christianity alive and well.

Christianity has overcome the impasse of history by turning the absence of biography into an exceptional onto-theology. Both the absence of biography (beyond the hagiography of the Gospels) *and* the never ending hunt for biography have perpetuated the exemplary divinity of Jesus and ensured that any temporality or finitude will always be preceded by a timelessness that gathers and presents itself to itself: the body and spirit of Christianity is always *there*, from the start. This timeless origin of the life and works of William Shakespeare is perhaps all the more egregious when one recalls that remarkable temporal event in the lifetime of Shakespeare: the changing of calendars from the Julian to the Gregorian system in 1582 in the Catholic countries of Europe. While it would be another 170 years until Britain and its colonies adopted the Gregorian reforms, from 1582 the 11-day discrepancy in the new calendar meant that all correspondents and travellers to and from England would experience a remarkable time lag: travelling from France, you could arrive ten days *before* you had left. Time was unavoidable (Gaston 2007a).

It is hardly surprising that both the absence and the hunt for the biography of William Shakespeare, author of plays and poems, remains *par excellence* within the body and spirit of Christianity. Whether in a quasi-negative theology, which finds an exalting hyper presence in the unique absence of the biography of 'Shakespeare author', or in the interminable labour of searching for the blinding epiphanies of life and light in the great 'ocean of words' that so haunted Plato's Parmenides, 'Shakespeare, author' has become an onto-theological concept (Plato 1892b: 137a). These theological imperatives mark the cul-de-sacs of Shakespeare scholarship. For Shakespeare to be unlike anyone else, he must be *no one*. All biographical narratives of 'Shakespeare' become a Nietzschean challenge: Shakespeare has a life, therefore Shakespeare is dead. At the same time, while there is a need for this absence, this hollow space to be untouchable, there is also a need to touch everything, to be invited or charged with the task of filling this sublime gap, of reconstituting and resuscitating the works and life of William Shakespeare, author. This need and this contradictory demand – don't touch, touch everything, celebrate the absence, reconfigure the presence – is irresistible. Discover the secrets of the resonating absence and the still untapped presence of Shakespeare!

'Shakespeare' must *either* uniquely be no one *or* he must be someone unique. It is perhaps the quasi-theological force of this either-or injunction that haunts all writing on 'Shakespeare, author'. Long before the rather dubiously named Delia Bacon questioned the authorship of the plays and poems of William Shakespeare, Shakespeare was singled out for his unique capacity to be everyone *and* no one. There is no Shakespeare and that is his true genius. In this sense, Peter Sellers was a true Shakespearean of the twentieth century. In 1802, Samuel Taylor Coleridge evoked this Shakespeare as no one as the secret of his authorial genius:

> It is easy to cloathe Imaginary Beings with our own Thoughts & feelings; but to send ourselves out of ourselves, to *think* ourselves in to the Thoughts and Feelings of Beings in circumstances wholly & strangely different from our own: *hoc labor, hoc opus*: and who has achieved it? Perhaps only Shakespeare. (Coleridge 1956–1973: II 810)

In the 1817–1818 letters of that ardent critic of romanticism Keats, 'Shakespeare, author' is imbued with all the negative capabilities that William Wordsworth lacked. 'The poetical character', Keats insisted, 'is not itself – it has no self – it is everything and nothing' (Keats 1958: 1 193, 387).

We poets, the romantics suggested, we can only aspire to being Shakespeare, we can only dream of being *absolutely* no one, of not being. As old Parmenides had warned, and after him Hegel, such aspirations to the *absolute* difference of not-being can only reinforce the great project of being. The assured alternative of *either* absence *or* presence remains within the ontological tradition (Derrida 1990a: 154, 244). As Andrew Bennett has suggested, Keats does not perhaps simply evoke an idealizing and quasi-theological vision of the unique and absolute not-being of 'Shakespeare, author', but rather a *relative* relation to the 'either-or' of being and not being which, more recently, Lévinas and Derrida have discerned in their readings of Plato (Gaston 2007c; Bennett 2005; 1995: 56–9).

As Proust suggests in *The Search for Lost Time* through the character of the writer Bergotte, inventing the biographies of so many others debilitates and undermines one's own capacity for autobiography: 'Perhaps the more the great writer developed at the expense of the little man with the beard, the more his own personal life was drowned in the flood of all the lives that he imagined, until he no longer felt himself obliged to perform certain

practical duties, for which he had substituted the duty of imagining those
other lives' (Proust 1989: 602). Borges seems, as ever, at once close to and
distant from the romantic tradition when he argued for the pathos of a
Shakespeare that suffered from having 'no one in him' and who, as actor
and playwright, discovered the terrible capacity to be anyone and everyone:
'no one has ever been so many as this man'. For Borges, Shakespeare, the
'many and no one' leaves us would-be biographers only with 'a bit of
coldness', an 'emptiness' (Borges 1985: 284–5).

There is something beguiling about the genius of being no one. Like the
virgin birth, it creates a perfect concept for resisting the mundane and the
merely human. In this sense, the resistance of biography becomes an index
of creative genius. 'Painters must begin by cutting out their tongues',
Matisse said (DeLillo 1999: 78). And I want to say, yes – real art must get
away from the tawdriness and narcissism of the confessional, of the cliché
of the artist who just says 'I I I' over and over again. Yes, there must be the
silence of Rilke and Hölderlin, a pure break and assured absence of the
gods, and the necessary violence of cutting out the tongue. But would
'Shakespeare, author', simply embrace this implicit acceptance of a godlike noble silence founded on a classical brutality, of an idealizing denigration of speaking and the corporeal body? 'Nay then, I'll stop your mouth',
Chiron says to Lavina before she reappears on the stage with her tongue cut
out and her hands cut off (Shakespeare 1997a: 2.3.184). Can one ever avoid
such *violence* in the absolute denial of biography? 'She hath no tongue to
call nor hands to wash, / And so let's leave her to silent walks': the violent
birth of the artist that transcends the life, and then finds they have no hands
(2.4.7–9).

If the urge for no biography is irresistible, and with 'Shakespeare, author'
most of all, the urge for the restitution of biography is equally inescapable.
It is perhaps also one of the legacies of romanticism that we can no longer
draw a clear distinction between the life and the work. A few years before
Coleridge and Keats began to celebrate Shakespeare as no one, Disraeli's
father, Isaac D'Israeli, was beginning to gather his curiosities of literature,
charting the chaotic and entertaining lives of authors, arguing that it is the
work that makes the life. Writing invents the literary character, invents
character as a kind of literary affect. It is hardly fortuitous that the word
autobiography was first coined by the translator William Taylor of Norwich
in a review of one of D'Israeli's books (Good 1981). Despite I. A. Richards,
Wimsatt and Beardsley, and a host of worthy structuralists, since at least the
1880s when Nietzsche insisted that 'every great philosophy' was 'a kind of
involuntary and unconscious memoir', and certainly since Strachey, Freud,

television and the 1960s, the J. D. Salingers of this world are the exception. Dennis Potter's anguished cry in his last plays *Karaoke* and *Cold Lazarus* of 'No biography!' is a dream, a return to an age of discretion and anonymity that probably never existed (Nietzsche 1968: 203).

'When we read the poetry of *King Lear*', Stephen Dedalus says in *Ulysses*, 'what is it to us how the poet lived?' (Joyce 1992: 242). In his 1944 review of Salvador Dali's autobiography, George Orwell touched on a silent fear in the persistent hunt for the Shakespearean biography, namely that the newly discovered biography would make all the difference:

> If Shakespeare returned to earth to-morrow, and if it were found that his favourite recreation was raping little girls in railway carriages, we should tell him not to go ahead with it on the ground that he might write another *King Lear*. (Orwell 1946: 125)

And this is part of the problem for Shakespeare scholars. Whether in the hagiographies of the early saints, in Saint Augustine, in Suetonius's gossip about the Roman emperors or in the first fragments of Greek biography or the extraordinary lives of the Patriarchs in *Genesis*, biography has always been here (Momigliano 1971). The writer's dying cry of 'No biography!' at the end of Potter's *Karaoke* is followed in *Cold Lazarus* by a Rupert Murdoch figure in the not too distant future exploiting the innermost memories of the writer's head and broadcasting them on television, until, influenced by the extremist group Reality Or Nothing (*RON*), a technician unplugs the writer and liberates him, letting him die at last (Potter 1996). Potter's works suggest that there is a certain freedom from biography for the writer in death, but also that the death of the author is just the beginning of biography.

If the romantic period can be said to mark a heightened interest in the incompatible injunctions that Shakespeare should at once be uniquely no one and be someone unique, it is perhaps telling that the Shakespeare authorship question was revived from the 1850s to the 1920s, a period marked, as Hillis Miller had suggested, by the disappearance of God (Derrida 2005; Miller 1963). Though predating *The Origin of Species* by three years, Delia Bacon's case for Francis Bacon raises the question of how the true author of the plays and poems of Shakespeare might be naturally selected. To no more than gesture to this late nineteenth century reinvention of 'Shakespeare, author', one would, as Darwin suggests, have to come to the conclusion that the works of Shakespeare 'had not been independently created, but had descended, like varieties, from other species' (Darwin 1998: 4). Nor is it fortuitous, as Nicholas Royle has suggested, that

Looney makes his case for the Earl of Oxford in the age of Freud or that Freud himself is persuaded by 1930 'that the author of Shakespeare's works' was not 'the man from Stratford' (Freud 1982: 266 n. 1).

One would perhaps have to analyse the Darwinian and Freudian legacy of attribution to begin to approach the more recent pathology of questioning Shakespeare authorship. For example, how does one respond to a work that connects the case for the Earl of Oxford as the author of Shakespeare's plays and poems to a discovery of the true author of the anonymous Martin Marprelate tracts, the satirical attacks on bishops and the Anglican Church in 1588–1589 that marked the rise of the Calvinist and Puritan church militants and led to the death of two of the suspected authors, John Udall (c.1560–1592) and John Penry (1559–1593)? (Cross 2004; Lake and Questier 2002: 505–20; Pierce 1911).[1] This is the argument made by Elizabeth Appleton in *Anatomy of the Marprelate Controversy 1588–1596: Retracing Shakespeare's Identity and that of Martin Marprelate.* Appleton finds not one, but two names (Appleton 2001).

While the hunt for the true author or authors of the Martin Marprelate tracts goes on, Patrick Collinson, Regis Professor of History Emeritus at Cambridge, has suggested that Job Throckmorton (1545–1601) was the most likely candidate (Collinson 2004). In the asymmetry that characterizes much of the Shakespeare authorship debates, one can contrast the authority of Collinson to the rather anxious supplementary supports for Elizabeth Appleton's book. The back cover of the *Anatomy of the Marprelate Controversy* both confirms and weakens Appleton's academic standing by presenting her academic qualifications: 'Elizabeth Appleton graduated from London University with B. A. Honours in Modern History and studied at *Hautes Études Internationales* in Geneva, Switzerland'. Does she have an M. A.? Does she have a doctorate? Is she one of *us*? And what exactly is this *Hautes Études Internationales* in 'Geneva, Switzerland', as we might mistake it for that other Geneva in Idaho? But this anxiety about *place*, about getting the place right, is itself not entirely removed from the Shakespeare authorship controversy, since the one constant, the one anchor, in the fleeting and shifting and possibly dubious identity of 'Shakespeare, author', is Stratford-upon-Avon in Warwickshire. Stratford is the Bethlehem or even Jerusalem of Shakespeare studies.

The pathos of the back cover of Appleton's book is reinforced by the two prefaces, which rather oddly come after her own introduction, both disconnecting her introduction from the main thesis and giving an unusual prominence to these other introductory voices. The prefaces are written by two men whose names are presented in a sea of acronyms: the 'Rev. Francis

Edwards, SJ, F. S. A., F. R. Hist. S.' and 'Dr. Daniel Wright, B. A., M. A., M. Div., Ph. D'. On the one hand, this overcompensation of institutional affiliations can only recall Appleton's lack of academic credentials. On the other hand, it stands as a strange act of defiance. After all, hardly any of the great writers in English literature went to university, or distinguished themselves at university. Why is it that *we*, we with all the acronyms, we of the university, are the only ones who can speak with authority about those who didn't have or didn't care about acronyms?

To draw a rather frail analogy to illustrate the importance of the history of an unavoidable relationship between those who are 'inside' and 'outside' of the university, in an influential article from 1950, 'Ancient history and the antiquarian', the great and formidable classical historian Arnaldo Momigliano argued that the gentlemen amateur antiquarians of the eighteenth century played a critical role in the development of the modern academic study of antiquity. While in this period the professional university-based historians tended to rely on ancient literary sources to write sweeping universal histories, because of their interest in collecting non-literary sources, such as coins, inscriptions, statues, vases and archaeological evidence, the antiquarians made a crucial contribution to the emergence of a historical method that had to take into account both the difference between 'original' and 'derivative' sources and the difference between 'collecting' and 'interpreting' facts. In other words, Momigliano suggests, while the 'outsiders' ultimately changed and improved the methods of the 'insiders', the 'insiders' also raised important questions that the 'outsiders' could never have formulated on their own (Miller 2007; Momigliano 1966).

In the first of the two prefaces to *Anatomy of the Marprelate Controversy*, Appleton is described as 'a brilliant "outsider", but not without friends and supporters in the discerning academic world' (Edwards 2001: lv). This sentence could detain us for a long time. What is 'the *discerning* academic world', and how would one distinguish it from the undiscerning world? What does it mean to have friends in the academic world? Can one be an academic and have friends? Is a friend, and even more a 'supporter', still an academic? Does our own need for anonymous peer review, for an assessment without names, do anything else than reinforce the power of friends and supporters in 'the discerning academic world'? And what does it mean to be an academic and a friend to a 'brilliant "outsider"'? The author of the first preface had perhaps already put a subtle strain on this endorsement when he referred to Appleton's project as 'excessively audacious' and described her as 'a contributor, and an important contributor' to the authorship debates (lv).

Appleton's thesis is simple and quite elegant: Gabriel Harvey (1552/3–1631) was the true author of the Martin Marprelate tracts, and because of Edward de Vere's indirect attacks on Harvey, Martin Marprelate and the militant Puritan cause, the Earl of Oxford used the name 'William Shakespeare' and the London stage to continue his polemical campaign against the religious enthusiasts. The author of the second preface to Appleton's book some- what undermines the unity of this argument by supporting the first part of her thesis (Harvey as 'Martin Marprelate'), but characterizing the second part of her thesis ('William Shaksepeare' is Edward de Vere) as a 'particu- larly entertaining and compelling thesis' (Wright 2001: lxi). Can one have a thesis, an academic thesis, which is particularly *entertaining*? What would be the *other* of academia here? Perhaps that most entertaining of arts, the theatre? But then Shakespeare, author of plays, would always be the enter- taining other of academia, the impasse or resistance of academia. Appleton begins and ends with the belief that 'William Shakespeare' was the pseudo- nym of Edward de Vere, but also believes that there was a man from Stratford called William Shakespeare who went along with the strategy, the deception, the game, the theatre. There was William Shakespeare *and* there was the Earl of Oxford, 'the other Shakespeare'. There is always the other *of* Shakespeare.

What can we learn from these antiquarians working away on the works and the life and times of Shakespeare? While the Darwinian and Freudian heritage of the questioning of Shakespeare's authorship is immersed in problems of attribution, the current debate is also obviously fractured by a pathology of institutional attribution. Between the Regis Professor and the unaffiliated amateur is the comforting unassailable asymmetry that patient academic *research* can always be distinguished from the avid *search* for the hitherto concealed key to all mythologies. Between researching and search- ing there should be a difference of tempo. Research moves slowly, in a group, like a gaggle of turtles, asking questions, making hypotheses that will probably not be answered with any probability. The search, on the contrary, is a solitary affair, whether it is precipitous or dragged out for years, and can only begin by finding answers for a presupposed question.

Without casting dispersions on Michael Wood's fine documentary and book on Shakespeare's life, one could use this as an example of a search that begins with the *belief* or conviction or passionate hope that the answer to everything lay in Shakespeare's always hidden Catholicism. Every ques- tion, every clue, every scrap of evidence, every text will then somehow reveal what you are looking for: Harvey *therefore* de Vere. The sheer excitement and passion of an *original* discovery, the eureka moment of doing what no one has ever done before will lead to a bewildering confirmation of every-thing: the world has changed, all the pieces fit together and, as if one were naming a planet after me since I was the first to see it, *my name* will forever be associated with this discovery.

For at least the last 150 years Shakespeare scholarship has had continually to reaffirm this absolute difference between researching and searching. It has had to hold on to the idealized and impossible distinction between amateur enthusiasm and judicious reflection, as if all academics who work on Shakespeare were Kantians and all those outside of the academy were a cornucopia of the pathologies that Kant warned about – with such passion – in the three Critiques. William Shakespeare's identity as 'Shakespeare', author of the plays and poems, has had to rely on the fragile assurance that academia resists the blinding pleasure of eureka moments and the propen-sity only to find what you are *already* looking for. Faced with conspiracy theorists and bad scholars, the burden has been on academia to present itself, without faltering, as the epitome of reason, of a Lockean probability that resists all the traps of blind assurance. Those believers who are outside of the institution must be seen as religious enthusiasts and mad-hatter foot-notists whose judgement is impaired because they believe *too much*. And Shakespeare scholarship must hold the line: *we* must all be secularists when it comes to the questions of Shakespeare, author.

On the one hand, this battle for 'hearts and minds' has perhaps forced a certain rationality and secular reticence on the academic work on Shakespeare's biography. Some might shake their heads in quiet dismay when even the great Greenblatt has somehow gone over to the other side and fallen into the *mythos* of biography. On the other hand, the Baconists and Oxfordists or anti-Stratfordians have highlighted that any academic work on William Shakespeare and his works has an unavoidable proximity to the onto-theological injunctions that 'Shakespeare, author' must *either* be uniquely no one *or* someone unique. When it comes to Shakespeare, academia itself cannot avoid theology. If they were not already there, when it comes to Shakespeare, the gods are always sitting in the Academy, in Plato's garden, and their whispering, their siren songs, are irresistible: the *truth* of William Shakespeare, the truth of the genius of Shakespeare, the truth of the works of Shakespeare, the truth of that 'ocean of words', the truth of English literature, the truth of the literary itself, the truth of the *name*, or the name of the truth (the *etymon*) of Shakespeare is . . .

This is perhaps what the 'outsiders' have brought to the academy: an obsession with the truth of the name that puts a strain on the exclusive institutional claim to 'Mr. William Shakespeares Comedies, Histories, &

Tragedies'. The search for the truth of the name pulls us away from the institution. Can one resist the call of *etymon* when it comes to 'Shakespeare, author'? As Plato suggested long ago in the *Cratylus*, in hunting for the true name of things we also can never avoid Socrates mimicking the dizzying madness of the etymologist, of succumbing to the irresistible urge *to name* what Borges called the 'many and no one' (Plato 1892a). For Elizabeth Appleton, all the writers of the period such as Harvey, Nash and de Vere used pseudonyms (and she does not admit William Shakespeare of Stratford into this entertaining club), and if this obsession with finding the true name tells us anything, it tells us that we are always getting the *wrong name*, that we are always getting the *name wrong*.

In an article first published in the *Oxford Literary Review* in 1990, 'The distraction of "Freud": Literature, Psychoanalysis and the Bacon–Shakespeare controversy', Nicholas Royle has argued that when it comes to the onto-theological-academia created by turning to the problem of 'Shakespeare, author' we need to start with the *need* to name, with the *need* to find the name, with the resistance *of* naming. Prompted by Derrida's reading of Ponge in *Signéponge* (1988), Royle characterizes 'anti-Stratfordian discourse' as 'an engagement with the question and power of the proper name' (Derrida 1988; Royle 1990: 106). Such an engagement already includes the names of the would-be searchers for the *etymon* behind the plays and poems of Shakespeare, and what wonderful names they are: Looney, Silliman and Battey! (Royle 1990: 106). Searching for the true name, the truth of the name, the anti-Stratfordians repeat the onto-theological attempt to turn the work into a monument to the author, to ward off death and oblivion and to preserve the living name as the 'many and no one'.

For Derrida, as Joyce had first suggested, the proper *name* of Shakespeare has already lost its heading and been hidden and disseminated, as the sound of a signifier no longer tied to the signified of a concept, throughout the text. Royle argues that Derrida offers a way of refuting, or at least worrying, the anti-Stratfordians without returning to the unending passion of the Christ-like author or giving way to the 'dangers of literary psycho biography' (Royle 1990: 106). The 'name' of Shakespeare is *everywhere* in the works. The works are the 'abyssing of the signature' (119). The gaps *of* the name, the name *in* gaps are *moving* in the text: *shaking, spearing, hearing*. For Royle, '*Hamlet* can be read not only as a text signed, on the "inside", by Shakespeare, but also as a text which is specifically *about* the idea and act of signing' (111). Royle gives us researchers and searchers after 'Shakespeare, author' a startling countering imperative: in hunting for the anguish of the no one that is *always* becoming someone and the someone that is *always* becoming the no one, read the works, keep reading and re-reading the works. 'Who wrote Shakespeare?' Royle keeps asking (106). 'Mr. William Shakespeares Comedies, Histories, & Tragedies' *wrote* Shakespeare, and they are still writing Shakespeare today: they never stop writing.

For what it is worth, I *believe* – and here it seems we can only really talk about belief – that Shakespeare knew what he was doing. As Márquez has Bolivar say in *The General in his Labyrinth,* memoirs are 'nothing but dead men making trouble' (Márquez 1991: 201). Like Austen after him, perhaps Shakespeare made certain that the irresistible urge for the life to eclipse the works was checked by the destruction of his private papers. Destroy my papers, and I'll give you my second best bed. Who wrote Shakespeare? The historical impasse, the wounding of the biographical, the effacement of the autobiographical, the moving gap of and in the plays and poems that can be neither bridged, nor filled: Shakespeare wrote Shakespeare.

But one cannot leave the irresistible hunt for 'Shakespeare, author', or *Sa,* that easily: *Sa,* what Derrida calls in *Glas* (1974), the not yet of *savoir absolu,* the Hegelian search for absolute knowledge, for that moment at the end of things when all subjective and objective knowledge becomes self-evident (Derrida 1990b). Reading Nicholas Royle's essay, I noticed his own name, 'Nicholas Royle', at the top of each page, and I began to search for the inscriptions of this proper name in the work. In the revised version of the article in Royle's 1995 book, *After Derrida,* I noted that the author was born in 1957 (Royle 1995). In his essay, Royle had referred to 'Friedman's study of 1957' (Royle 1990: 106). Did he really need to mention that it had been published in 1957, the year when, for him, everything began? Perhaps there was not much in this small tug on the biographical imperative. But there was more. When, after speaking about *paronomasia,* 'to slightly alter in naming', Royle cited the *OED* definition for *prosonomasia,* as 'a calling by a name, a *nick*naming' (my emphasis) he was quoting and re-citing his *own* name, Nick, as 'a familiar, a humorous, or derogatory name added to replacing the proper name, place, etc' (Royle 1990: 128). How is one to understand this naming *as* a replacing of the proper name? Was I the *first* to discover this? Had Nicholas Royle himself seen this? Could he see this?

I couldn't help myself, the idea of the Nick-name as that which, humorously, replaces the proper *name* or *place,* led me on irresistibly. Suddenly, I remembered Nicholas Royle's e-mail address: *n.w.o.royle @sussex.ac.uk* and the opening lines of his essay 'Mole' (1997): '"after a mole-like progression": how am I [n.w.o.r] going to read this, eat or keep it, keep it by eating it?' (Royle 2003: 241). Who was this 'I [n.w.o.r]'? As a post-war baby,

I thought the 'w' must stand for 'Winston', and then realized that it *must* be
'William'.[2] The 'o' seemed much more elusive: 'Oliver' seemed the most
likely. Osbert seemed less likely. Why has he got so many names, I wondered? Why so many family names, so many ghosts, so many grandfathers of
Christmas past, stored away and preserved in this name?

Following Royle's startling imperative, what did I hear, *shakes-hear*, when
I turned to these four letters n.w.o.r . . . *nwoor*. Suddenly, it seemed as if the
proper name, hidden and disseminated in the text, was *not* an origin or first
principle, an *arkhè* to end or to start with, and that this proper name was,
already, has always been, where else, but in *Hamlet*: 'I am but mad *north-
north-west*' (Shakespeare 1997b: 2.2.361). I could hear it. A note in the
Norton Shakespeare helpfully explained these lines: 'the smallest compass
point away from true north, and thus not far from sane; *or* possibly, only
mad on occasions when the wind blows from the north-northwest' (my
emphasis). I decided that the 'or' in this note was perhaps its most instruc-
tive observation: 'the smallest compass point away from true *north*, and thus
not far from sane; *or* possibly, only mad on occasions when the wind blows
from the *north-north*west': n.w.o.r is a 'not far from sane *or* possibly only
mad on occasions' name. And it is certainly a shake-speared name: a nor'
nor' westr' name. And it is, of course, an auth*or*'s name, a north-west author:
an author always with an *or*.

It occurred to me, as I briefly came to my senses, that this irrepressible
hunt for the name was the melancholy duty of the archivist of the
Shakespeare authorship controversy: including all the names of those who
might be what Freud had called 'the author of Shakespeare's works'.
Rereading Royle's citation of what he calls Freud's 'simple but amazing'
1930 footnote to *The Interpretation of Dreams* ('Incidentally, I have in the
meantime ceased to believe [and note, it is a question of belief] that the
author of Shakespeare's works was the man from Stratford'), I was struck by
a small difference in his later citation of Freud's 1937 letter to Arnold
Zweig, where Freud again dismisses 'the man of Stratford' as the 'author of
Shakespeare's works' (Freud and Zweig 1970: 140). In 1930, Freud writes of
'the man *from* Stratford' (*der Mann aus Stratford*), but in 1937 he writes 'the
man *of* Stratford' (*dem Stratforder*) (Freud 1950: 183 n. 1; 1968: 150).
If Shakespeare is *from* Stratford, it suggests that he did not remain *in*
Stratford, that he might have gone to London and become an actor, a poet
and a playwright: 'Shakespeare, author' lived *in* London, but he was *from*
Stratford. But if Shakespeare is the man *of* Stratford it is possible that he
remained in Stratford, that he may have ventured out from his provincial
world, and even spent some time working in London, perhaps as an actor,

perhaps as a playwright of sorts, but never really managed to get beyond Stratford, and certainly not go far enough to write the plays and poems of 'William Shakespeare'.

From Stratford to *of* Stratford: over seven years in a single word Freud has used not the proper name, but the proper *place*, the *topos*, to invalidate the claims of Shakespeare, author. Moses was not *from* Egypt, but *of* Egypt. Freud was not *from* Austria, but *of* Austria. For all the displacements of psychoanalysis, Freud cannot escape what Derrida called a certain *géopsychanalyse* (Derrida 2007). And then, just for a moment, there was a half mad and hardly academic whisper: has anyone ever checked a concordance to see how Shakespeare shakes, spears and hears the name Stratford? Could this be the key? And then I found what I was looking for in the 'ocean of words'. Act 2 scene 4 of *Richard III* opens with the Cardinal saying, 'Last night, I hear, they lay them at Northampton. / At Stony Stratford they do rest tonight' (Shakespeare 1997c: 2.4.3–4). A note alerted me to a strange topographical displacement: in the *quarto*, Northampton comes before Stony Stratford (or 'Stonistratford'), but in the *Folio*, Stony Stratford comes before Northampton. One version accurately describes the historical movements of Prince Edward, the other is historically incorrect: it is a work of fiction and places 'Stonistratford' *first.*

And just for a moment, I wondered in wonder – as Royle has suggested – at what Shakesp*eare* might *hear* in this displacement, in this reversal of the proper order of places, in the lines 'I hear . . . they lay them . . . at Stonistratford'. What Medusa was at work in this Stonistratford, in this decapitation of the capital 'S' of Stratford? How are we to understand this *paronomasia* and *prosonomasia* of the name of the place? What would the 'anti-Stratfordians' say about this porous and impervious Stonistratford? And then, the moment was gone, as I saw that Stony Stratford was not Stratford-upon-Avon in Warwickshire, but a small town in Buckinghamshire that now proudly describes itself as part of Milton Keynes.

Notes

[1] J. Donne Wilson (1912) argued that the authorship was shared between John Penry, Job Throckmorton and Sir Roger Williams. Donald J. McGinn (1966) made the case for Penry, and Leland H. Carlson (1981) makes a strong argument for Throckmorton.

[2] As must the name of our editor, William Leahy, whom I would like to thank for his very kind invitation to participate in this project and for our illuminating conversations about Shakespeare studies.

Chapter 6

Shakespearean Selves

Graham Holderness

Are you the author of the plays of William Shakespeare?
Shakespeare in Love

(Madden 1998)

As kingfishers catch fire, dragonflies draw flame;
As tumbled over rim in roundy wells
Stones ring; like each tucked string tells, each hung bell's
Bow swung finds tongue to fling out broad its name;
Each mortal thing does one thing and the same:
Deals out that being indoors each one dwells;
Selves – goes its self; myself it speaks and spells,
Crying What I do is me: for that I came.

(Hopkins 1996: 115)

Hopkins's magnificent poem is the most extreme statement of identity as 'self': intrinsic, unique, irreplaceable selfhood. Every living creature has within it, 'indoors', its own essence, its 'being' ('being indoors each one dwells'). But 'being' is also doing, since each thing speaks its individuality by 'doing' itself, performing its being. Action expresses essential being: being functions in utterance, in speaking and spelling. Creation is an immense multiplicity of individualities, of differences that emanate from a great commonality, a great simplicity: each thing does 'one thing', which is also 'the same': being itself.

Though a contemporary of Marx, Darwin and Freud, Hopkins of course, inhabited a world of mediaeval philosophy and theology divorced from the great intellectual currents of the time. While the dominant modern thinkers were refashioning the self as socially constructed, naturally conditioned, internally self-divided and alone in a godless universe, Hopkins continued to speak from a much older agenda in which the self is interior, immanent, essential and god-given.

Literary biography is, however, largely based on such older notions of the self and of human being. What is the relationship between the writer and his work? Who was the man who wrote Shakespeare's plays and poems? The biographer seeks to offer a coherent 'account of Shakespeare's life, writings and afterlife' (Wells 2002: xviii). Here the author is sovereign, the originator and shaper of the writing, the driving imaginative force, the controlling artistic authority. The writer precedes the work, so the relationship is from writer to work, the writer signing and stamping the work with his/her own character. The writer is cause, writing the effect. Shakespeare must have possessed an intrinsic being that expressed itself in a unique voice. The work should 'speak' and 'spell' the intrinsic Shakespearean self, that 'being' that 'indoors each one dwells'; the writing should fling out broad the name of 'Shakespeare'; and the literary biography should be able to delineate the character of the man who invested the works with that distinctive and unique quality of being.

Most contemporary Shakespeare criticism and scholarship derives from Marx and Darwin and Freud (through Barthes and Foucault and Lacan) rather than from the pre-modern philosophy celebrated by Hopkins; which is why Shakespeare biography was of little interest to Shakespeare criticism of the 1980s. There the reading relationship was backwards, as it actually is in practice, from writing to writer. The work precedes the author: the writer is an effect of the writing. Barthes and Foucault had declared 'the death of the author': the 'author' was in reality a function of the text. Because the literary work is constructed in the act of reading, and in relation to the context in which it is read, 'authorship' is just one element of that process, and the primary link between the writer and the work is broken. What matters is not what the author meant by the words he/she wrote, but what we mean by them when we read them.

Quite a lot is known about Shakespeare's life: but never really enough, as the life as we know it does not adequately seem to explain the poetry. For modern Shakespeare criticism, that hardly seemed to matter. Twenty years ago my critical anthology *The Shakespeare Myth* addressed 'Shakespeare' not as an author, but as an institution or cultural apparatus. This was the position on 'authorship':

We cannot rely, when addressing the work of a Renaissance dramatist, on the apparent clarity and simplicity of a direct, controlling relationship between author and written text. These plays were made and mediated in the interaction of certain complex material conditions, of which the author was only one. When we deconstruct the Shakespeare myth what we discover is not a universal individual genius creating literary texts that remain a permanently valuable repository of human experience and wisdom; but a collaborative cultural process in which plays were made by writers, theatrical entrepreneurs, architects and craftsmen, actors and audience. (Holderness 1988: 13)

Much of this still stands. The production of literary drama is a collective and collaborative activity; the dramatic work, whether being performed in the theatre or reproduced through the printing house, is rarely if ever under the author's sole control; and above all, we cannot get outside our culture's recognition that writing turns into meaning not when it is under the control of the writer, but when it is activated by the reader. 'Shakespeare', I said in *The Shakespeare Myth*, in a much-quoted sentence, 'is, here, now, always, what is currently being made of him' (xvi). This approach has since been labelled 'presentism'. Our reading or viewing of the plays constructs the meaning of the work, between the horizons of our understanding, within the context of our experience, and answering to the deepest needs of our being; in which case the authority of the author inevitably diminishes in proportion to the empowerment of the reader. The Author is dead; long live the reader.

According to presentism, an interest in the Shakespeare biography is not a question about history, or reality or truth; but a question about contemporary preferences and priorities. It is about *what sort of man we would prefer Shakespeare to have been*. We go to the past to answer questions that are asked in the present; we seek our own reflections in the glass of history. Agnes Heller called this attitude to the past 'nostalgia'. Her image is that of a well, into which we peer, and to the surface of which we seek to draw the elusive shapes of the past. Nostalgia 'cannot resurrect the dead . . . but it makes the dead speak and act as if they were alive. Having been brought to the surface from the well, which mirrors our faces whenever we lean over it, these dead are everything we desire to be' (Heller 1993: 40). While we imagine that what becomes visible in that long, receding tunnel, that well, is the past itself; we find that in actuality we are engaged in a narcissistic contemplation of the reflection of our own wishes and desires in the surface of the water.

One of the most powerful voices of the 1980s wrote in very similar accents:

I began with the desire to speak with the dead . . . [but] I never believed that the dead could hear me . . . I knew that the dead could not speak . . . . It was true that I could hear only my own voice, but my own voice was the voice of the dead, for the dead had contrived to leave textual traces of themselves, and those textual traces make themselves heard in the voice of the living. (Greenblatt 1988: 5)

The opening of *Shakespearean Negotiations* of course. For Greenblatt both literature and history consisted of 'textual traces' from which the life has disappeared, but which remain capable of living expression. They are not however 'sources of numinous authority', but 'signs of contingent social practices' (5). Greenblatt states this as a paradox: he is interested in early modern texts, and frequents them to find out what they mean. At the same time he believes that there is no transhistorical human nature; that history is a contemporary narrative, a story we tell ourselves about the past; and that language is no transparent and unmediated window onto an objective and independent reality, but rather a closed system within which all our perceptions and interpretations – including those of history and human nature – are contained. A word or object from the past exists and has meaning only within the system and structure, the perpetual contemporaneity, of living language. The author is still here in this process, but assuming a diminished role; and the emphasis is resolutely 'presentist', since the voices of the dead can only be heard when mimed by the voices of the living.

But almost twenty years on, in 2004, Greenblatt published *Will in the World: How Shakespeare Became Shakespeare,* an attempt to bring those dead back to life. The reception of this biography is already a well-known story. The book is a formal biography, using the established facts and traditions, reading the plays and poems in the light of them, and producing potential explanations of how the life and the works might be interrelated. The book was alternately praised and criticized as a popular/academic crossover text. It was seen both as a fulfilment of Greenblatt's New Historicism, and as an act of 'apostasy' against it. It was celebrated for the quality, and castigated for the poverty, of its scholarship. Above all, it was attacked for investing more in speculation and invention than in historical evidence; and lauded for exactly the same thing. It is just a 'biographical fiction' said Colin Burrow (2005: 9). The book is 'entirely Greenblatt's fiction' said Richard Jenkyns (2004: 22), and indeed 'an improbable fiction'. Alistair Fowler, in one of the most hostile reviews received, suggested that Greenblatt might have been better off making 'a crossover into historical fiction' where he could freely have fomented conjecture with even less respect for evidence. This should not be the case in a literary biography: here the 'subject veers too much between Shakespeare's imagination and Stephen Greenblatt's own' (2005: 5).

On the other hand plenty of reviewers lined up to praise Greenblatt's imaginative and inventive approach to his subject. The book should be read as 'imaginative writing' (Aune 2006). Greenblatt's 'chief allegiance is to imagination', says Lois Potter (2005: 375), and the book rightly stresses 'the importance of imagination in our approach to this supremely imaginative writer'. Charles Marowitz calls the book an 'extended flight of fancy', but of a valid kind: 'a speculative leap into the murky life of Shakespeare, using one's knowledge of the period, hints from the collected works and a creative use of conjecture, is a perfectly legitimate endeavour' (Marowitz 2005).

Now apart from Samuel Schoenbaum's *Shakespeare: A Documentary Life* (1975) (which was a companion volume to the full-blown biography and mythography *Shakespeare's Lives* [1970]) there is no such thing as a speculation-free biography of Shakespeare. How could there be? Greenblatt's challenge to orthodoxy was to be much more overtly fictional or metafictional in his method, much more self-reflexive in declaring the conjectural and speculative character of his writing. The best-known example is the possible meeting Greenblatt provisionally stages between Shakespeare and Jesuit martyr Edmund Campion, which he invents as a possible event in Shakespeare's Lancastrian and recusant lost years. But the episode is clearly signalled as a piece of story-telling: 'Let us imagine the two of them sitting together' (Greenblatt 2004: 108). Are you sitting comfortably? If not, if you don't want to join the author in his flight of fancy, then don't bother.

Will in the World has two main methods: reading from documentary facts or recorded traditions towards the works; and reading back from the works in an attempt to bestow distinguishing features on the life. In short, Greenblatt uses the author and the writing as both cause and effect. He posits a Shakespearean 'self' that drove the writings: but he accepts that this 'self' is 'obscure' and impenetrable. He accepts that the channel of causation from self to work is hard to map; but presupposes that some such transference must have occurred:

> This book . . . aims to discover the actual person who wrote the most important body of literature of the last thousand years. Or rather, since the actual person is a matter of well-documented public record, it aims to tread the shadowy paths that lead from the life he lived into the literature he created. (12)

Some of these paths seem very shadowy indeed. Take the long chapter called 'Speaking with the Dead', which focuses on *Hamlet* and on the deaths of Shakespeare's son Hamnet and his father John. As Gary Taylor (2004: 9) points out, although this is all about Shakespeare's imagined attempts to speak with the dead, the phrase is the famous one used by Greenblatt himself in his earlier work: 'I began with the desire to speak with the dead'. So who's speaking here? And who's dead?

The biographical basis of the chapter rests in a few documentary facts. Shakespeare's 11-year old son Hamnet died in 1596. His father John Shakespeare died in 1601. Between these two deaths Shakespeare wrote *Hamlet.* The play is, of course, permeated by all sorts of emotions and questions a bereaved father might feel and ask. But the hero of the play, Hamlet, is haunted by the ghost of his dead father, not afflicted by the loss of a son.

Greenblatt tells a story (adumbrated earlier, of course, by James Joyce) that aspires to explain the play that lies between these two momentous departures. Shakespeare 'undoubtedly' returned to Stratford for Hamnet's funeral (312). There he heard the words of the burial service that echo eloquently in the play. But there, Greenblatt suggests, he became acutely aware of how much he and his family missed in being deprived of Catholic rituals for the dead: the Latin memorial prayers, the candles, bells and crosses, the alms-giving and requiem masses. Shakespeare wanted, Greenblatt suggests, to mourn his son in the traditional pattern of worship, and was unable to do so. 'What ceremony else?', he must have thought as he stood by the grave-side, unable to pray for his son's soul.

The Roman Catholic 'spiritual testament' signed by John Shakespeare and hidden in the rafters of his Stratford house requested those he leaves behind to 'vouchsafe to assist and succour me with their holy prayers and satisfactory works, especially with the holy Sacrifice of the Mass, as being the most effectual means to deliver souls from their torments and pains'. Greenblatt goes even further and suggests that John Shakespeare may have pleaded with William, 'appealed urgently to his son' (316) to have masses said for the soul of Hamnet. This is pure invention, but Greenblatt makes it sound convincing enough: 'The arguments, or pleading, or tears that may have accompanied such appeals are irrevocably lost' (316). This is, of course, the anguished pleading we also hear from the Ghost in *Hamlet,* who comes from Purgatory.

Greenblatt is drawing on historical work that assessed the impact of the Reformation on the relationship between the living and the dead, and which earlier formed the basis for his *Hamlet in Purgatory.* He also echoes his own earlier work in *Shakespearean Negotiations.* 'What mattered' he says in *Will in the World,* 'was whether the dead could continue to speak to the living, at least for a short time, whether the living could help the dead, whether a reciprocal bond remained' (315). But out of these diverse roots, Greenblatt creates imaginatively a vivid drama in which a father, perhaps nearing death, appeals to his son to maintain a practice of traditional piety;

and the son is perhaps unable or unwilling to do so. Now this is not just about Shakespeare.

In the 'Prologue' to *Hamlet in Purgatory* Greenblatt writes about *his* father, who died in 1983. Scarred by the painful death of his own father, Greenblatt Sr. lived in a perpetual denial of death. Yet, 'when we read his will', Greenblatt says,

> [W]e found that he had, after all, been thinking about his death. He had left a sum of money to an organisation that would say kaddish for him – kaddish being the Aramaic prayer for the dead, recited for eleven months after a person's death and then on certain annual occasions . . . the prayer is usually said by the deceased's immediate family and particularly by his sons . . . . Evidently my father did not trust either my older brother or me to recite the prayer for him. (Greenblatt 2001: 6–7)

Kaddish is a central Jewish prayer, praising the power and glory of God, one version of which is used as a memorial prayer for the dead. So all this talk of bereavement, and maimed rites, and fathers appealing for ancient observances, and speaking with the dead, is certainly about Shakespeare, and about *Hamlet*. But it is also about Stephen Greenblatt. John Shakespeare and other Catholics, he says, in requesting requiem masses 'were asking those who loved them to do something crucially important for them' (Greenblatt 2004: 317). Greenblatt's father did not ask him to say kaddish, and that in itself was clearly doubly painful for the son. But he says it anyway, 'in a blend of love and spite' (Greenblatt 2001: 7), and ends the preface to *Hamlet in Purgatory*: 'this practice then, which with a lightly ironic piety I, who scarcely know how to pray, undertook for my own father, is the personal starting point for what follows' (9).

'What purports to be an image of Shakespeare is only an idealised image of the biographer himself', says Gary Taylor, and Greenblatt has 'mined his own life to supply the emotional raw materials that energise this book' (2004: 9). So there is a 'personal starting point' for this exercise, as well as a starting point in the author, and innumerable others in the historical context. By the end of this chapter in *Will in the World* all these are merged together: 'Shakespeare drew upon the pity, confusion and dread of death in a world of damaged rituals (the world in which most of us continue to live) because he himself experienced those same emotions at the core of his being' (Greenblatt 2004: 321). The world of damaged rituals is that of Protestant early modernity, which killed off the old Catholic consolations of purgatory and efficacious prayer for the dead. But it is also the world of secular modernity, in which the son of a pious Jew involuntarily absorbs his culture's agnosticism and feels a consequential loss. Shakespeare lived in this world, *Hamlet* lives in that world, and so too does Greenblatt. All experience these fundamental emotions of irreparable loss, aching nostalgia and the desire to speak with the dead, 'at the core of . . . being'.

We have clearly reached a significant point here, the 'core of being', the 'heart of the matter'. Once Greenblatt would not have talked about the 'core of being'. It is a phrase that speaks to pre-modern ideas of human nature and essential being. In the universe of post-structuralist criticism and theory, identity is unstable and changeable (cp. *Renaissance Self-Fashioning*); the reality of human existence lies in the externalities of language and social context; literature is not about personal experience but about the circulation of social energy.

To return to the 'core of being' is to revert to much more traditional notions of the self, identity, existence and essence. But interestingly what lies at the core of being is not the isolated autonomous and disconnected individuality that Marxist theory attributes to bourgeois ideology. Instead what we find in those depths of human emotion and desire is – another. In Greenblatt it is the father; in Shakespeare the son; in *Hamlet* father and son. Greenblatt can admit that he has a core of being because someone else has, by his death, penetrated it so deeply. He reads and hears the self-same ache of painful love in *Hamlet*; and from there he speculates that it must have lain at the core of Shakespeare's being too.

Like all of Shakespeare's work, this is a story that cannot be proved (or disproved). It is a story woven between the pegs of certain documentary facts: the death of Hamnet, 1596; the death of John Shakespeare in 1601; the composition of the play *Hamlet,* first published in 1603; John Shakespeare's Spiritual Testament. But it is also a story mapped between certain poles of emotional truth: first what we read in the play – the anguish of the father, the grief of the son; and secondly Greenblatt's own sense of bereavement and obligation. These two points are then triangulated against a third that cannot be known in the same way, the condition of the author's heart and soul; what was passing in the core of the Shakespearean being.

Where does this leave us? We have got the author back from the dead. His emotional experience predicates the writing, causes it to be. But that remains an inferential relationship impossible to prove or demonstrate. So the critic has recourse to his imagination, and creates a narrative consistent with the documentary facts, and with the emotional truths embedded both in the writing, and in the heart of the critic. As one critic puts it, he 'lets his imagination loose in the fields of his knowledge' (Middlebrook 2006: 16).

No one disputes Greenblatt's knowledge: but for some readers the result remains unclear as to whether it is 'fact or fiction, criticism or history' (Fowler 2005: 3).

In trying to account for the effect great literature has on him then, the critic is to some extent making it up as he goes along. But this is not just a sort of opportunistic appropriation of the work, perverting it from its original meaning: since the motivation for doing it comes from a very deep source, what Greenblatt calls the 'core of being'. Literature touches us so deeply that we are driven to presuppose that the author must also have been touched in some comparable way, depth calling to depth.

Now this method can be challenged: we can say, as many readers have, that this is nothing to do with the author of Shakespeare's plays, and that the critic is just writing about himself. In defence of the method we could say that the documented facts of Shakespeare's life are so sparse that it is impossible to avoid filling the gaps they leave with invention. If the result is a consistent and plausible way of explaining the evidence: the poems, the facts, the traditions – then it will do, it is the nearest we ever really get to the truth.

But clearly this opens up other possibilities as well. If what happened at the core of Shakespeare's being to generate *Hamlet* was much the same as what happened at the core of Greenblatt's being at the death of his father, then there is nothing unique about the experience. Similar things obviously happen at the core of everybody's being. And if we reach out from our own being to complete a story that lies dormant among the tattered traces of historical fact, then there are many other stories that we could tell, stories that might equally convincingly, or even more convincingly, account for the evidence.

But did we not start with the 'self' as something individual, intrinsic, unique, irreplaceable? Let me return to G. M. Hopkins. In the second part of 'As kingfishers catch fire', all things, including human beings, are 'selves'. But in human beings there is something 'more'. For the individuality that occupies humanity is also an Other – the God who, as creator, indwells all human beings. Man can 'be' godlike, expressing a god-given grace, which for Hopkins means 'acting' out the nature of Christ. So individuality is now multiple, since human being is also sharing in the being of God through the human Christ; 'Christ plays in ten thousand places'. 'Plays' like a light, like an actor, like a child, human and divine at once. And since this is, of course, a poem of Trinitarian Christian theology, the grace that human beings can participate in is a grace given from 'the Father', and returned to the Father in the performance of Christ-like action, 'graces'. This is what we are here for. For that I came.

Intrinsic, unique, irreplaceable individuality turns out to be multiple, relational, a family affair. Inside the human self are God the father, God the son and God the Holy Spirit as well as the unique human self. Human beings are linked to one another through their common creation at the hands of the maker of all things. Action expresses being as interaction. The 'self' is after all a busy, crowded place. Biography is not intrinsic but relational.

> I say more: the just man justices;
> Keeps grace: that keeps all his goings graces;
> Acts in God's eye what in God's eye he is –
> Christ – for Christ plays in ten thousand places,
> Lovely in limbs, and lovely in eyes not his
> To the Father through the features of men's faces. (Hopkins 115)

Chapter 7

Shakinomics; or, the Shakespeare Authorship Question and the Undermining of Traditional Authority

William Leahy

For, among the very ones who state and repeat that we must 'stick to' the truths or the institutions of the past, this drive avows the contrary of what it believes it affirms. It displaces the question. It is based on a need where a reality would have to correspond to this need. An order is indispensable, they declare; the respect for 'values' is necessary for the proper functioning. . . . Nonetheless, the conviction is lacking. To act as if it already existed and because it is a source of national or individual profit is to replace veracity with utility. It is to suppose a conviction for the sole reason that a conviction is needed, to decide on a legitimacy because it preserves a power, to impose or feign confidence because of its profitability, to claim belief in the name of institutions whose survival becomes the first object of a politics.

(*Certeau 1997: 6*)

There is something weird about Shakespeare. Indeed, just about everything relating to Shakespeare is weird. Take his biography, for example. Little is straightforward when studying Shakespeare in comparison to any other writer of his period in history: or indeed, any period in history. With other writers there is always something certain, something unproblematic. With Shakespeare there is no such certainty. There seems only 'difficulty'. Let us consider a few examples:

1. It is often claimed he was born and died on the same date. This is strange enough. This date is 23 April, St. George's day. The English national poet being born and dying on the day commemorating the English national saint is, to say the least, coincidental.
2. The second record in existence mentioning Shakespeare – the first registered his baptism on 24 April 1564 – is in the Bishop of Worcester's

marriage record, granting a marriage license to Shakespeare and Anna Whateley on 27 November 1582. Recorded in the same register, *on the following day* (28 November 1582), we see Shakespeare marrying a different woman, Anne Hathaway. Strange, indeed.

3. Shakespeare next appears in London in 1592. This record sees him lending £7 to John Clayton. How did the young man from Stratford develop into a moneylender in the capital city just ten years later?

4. According to the orthodox narrative of his life, in the following years he became a full-time actor and a full-time playwright. There is some evidence for this, of course. Yet record after record also places him as a full-time *entrepreneur*. So, he has three careers running simultaneously in two geographical locations a great distance apart (London and Stratford).

5. The only universally acknowledged portrait of Shakespeare, the Droeshout engraving from the *First Folio* of 1623 is, well, *strange*. It is terribly drawn and lacks any sense of proportion. The head is too large, the shoulders too narrow and, it seems, the body is possibly back to front. Not only that, there is much uncertainty regarding the identity of the artist responsible for it.

6. When the *First Folio* was published, 17 of the 36 plays contained therein had not been previously published. Of those which had been published, many had not featured the author's name on the title page.

In many ways, these are all relatively superficial discrepancies, explained away by pointing to the fact that Shakespeare lived a long time ago and in a period so foreign to our own that such problems and 'gaps' are inevitable. There is a great deal of truth in such a claim; records, if kept in the first place have a habit of disappearing over time. Whether explanations exist or not, there is still a great deal of strangeness when it comes to examining Shakespeare's biography. Furthermore, given that we are discussing the most celebrated (and researched) artist in the history of western civilization in whom all sorts of ideologies and authorities are invested, 'explaining away' is not really appropriate; we need to understand and accept what we know and what we do not know. In order to pursue this idea, it is worth outlining some of the deeper difficulties that are inherent in an orthodox narrative of Shakespeare's life:

1. Nothing exists in Shakespeare's hand except six signatures, three of which appear on the same document, his will; no plays, no poems, no letters.

2. No books, plays or poems are mentioned in his will (which does survive); nothing implying a literary career of any kind.

3. The plays demonstrate a profound knowledge of classical literature, a familiarity with a number of languages and the likelihood that the author travelled widely within Europe (especially Italy). Shakespeare had, at best a limited education (he did not attend university) and there is no record of his travelling abroad.
4. No record exists of Shakespeare receiving payment for any of his writing. This is unusual for a working playwright.
5. There is no 'literary' mention of his death in 1616.

These are profound lacunae in the biography of western civilization's greatest writer and produce enormous difficulties when attempting a coherent narrative tracing the life and work of this individual. Or, at least one would think so. This is not the case however, as is shown by the number of orthodox biographies which continue to appear at regular intervals. Biographies telling and re-telling essentially the same story are published annually, at least. Since 2003, for example, there have been extensive biographies by Michael Wood (2003), Stephen Greenblatt (2004), Peter Ackroyd (2005), James Shapiro (2005), René Weis (2007), Bill Bryson (2007), Charles Nicholl (2007) and Jonathan Bate (2007). While not all of these texts are full biographies, they all argue the same point – that Shakespeare, the man/actor/entrepreneur from Stratford-upon-Avon wrote all the plays and poems traditionally attributed to him. Some of the books attempt to deal with certain problems regarding this attribution in various ways, but all conclude that such lacunae described above do not undermine the notion of Shakespeare being responsible for all the works attributed to him. These conventional biographies essentially tell and re-tell the same story of a single, romantic, mythical hero, a story in which all difficulties disappear in a surrender to that which is beyond understanding; Shakespeare's genius.

In contrast to this (and perhaps surprisingly), it is the narratives which attempt to address these lacunae that are generally regarded as problematic, greeted with derision and thought to be the works of poor scholars with some kind of axe to grind (or alternative hero to worship) (Anderson 2005; Greenwood 1908; Hoffman 1955; Ogburn 1984; Price 2001). Analysis which holds that such attribution issues impact enormously on the idea that Shakespeare wrote all the plays and poems attributed to him is usually ridiculed and dismissed out of hand (Bate 1997: 65–100; Bryson 2007: 179–95; Schoenbaum 1970; 1991: 386–451). Perhaps the clearest example of the tenor of these kinds of dismissals of, let's call it for convenience 'oppositional biography', is that which appears on the website of the Shakespeare Birthplace Trust:

> The phenomenon of disbelief in Shakespeare's authorship is a psychological aberration of considerable interest ... causes include ignorance; poor sense of logic; refusal, wilful or otherwise, to accept evidence; folly; the desire for publicity; and even certifiable madness (as in the sad case of Delia Bacon, who hoped to open Shakespeare's grave in 1856). (www. shakespeare.org.uk/content/view/15/15/)

This situation is, as always with Shakespeare, strange; it is weird. Given that there are, as shown above significant historical problems with orthodox attribution, with the traditional narrative of Shakespeare, it is surprising that any investigation of these difficulties is received with such scepticism. Indeed, to a very great extent these difficulties are simply denied. Yet, there are 'alternative biographies', alternative authors and alternative scenarios out there. The cases put forward for alternative authors are, it must be said no stronger in theoretical terms than the orthodoxy (indeed, they are generally weaker), but they do exist and they are believed by many (Anderson 2005; Bacon 1857; Dawkins 2004; James and Rubinstein 2005; Looney 1920; Ogburn 1984; Saunders 2007; Williams 2006). The case put for an alternative biography and/or scenario is much stronger and, in my view, seriously challenges the orthodox biography (Greenwood 1908; Price 2001). Given this situation what, we need to ask ourselves, determines that which can be regarded as legitimate in this field of study, and, alternatively what can be regarded as illegitimate? Rather than being dependent upon the 'truth' as such, or indeed historical accuracy, is this question of legitimacy dependent merely upon authority of one kind or another?

Conventional Shakespearean biography is a profitable yet highly un-nuanced genre, in the sense that the starting point for each biography seems to be a desire to avoid controversy and replicate as closely as possible the biographies that preceded the latest one. Strangely (this is Shakespeare, however), the desire of the biographer seems to be to find nothing new and merely reproduce in a personalized prose that which has been said over and over again. The many biographies which appeared between 2003 and 2008 which I listed above, in essence tell us no more than Sir Sidney Lee did in 1898. There is a tinkering around the edges, a prioritization of a personal style and an articulation of personal 'issues'. But there is nothing 'new'. In contrast then to the biography of any other writer, indeed any other human being, the apotheosis of the Shakespearean biography is the reiteration of what is already there; it is to tell us what we already know. If this is an accurate representation of the state of conventional Shakespearean biography, it is an interesting and, one would say, a troubling phenomenon.

In a famous maxim, Walter Benjamin said that 'In every era the attempt must be made anew to wrest tradition away from a conformism that is about to overpower it' (Benjamin 1992: 247). It is, I suppose, the duty of historians, biographers and literary analysts to ensure that such a process happens. We are, as researchers, duty bound, are we not, to question the past, to confront received knowledge and regard accepted wisdom sceptically. To a very great extent, one must say that this seems to have singularly failed to happen in the genre of orthodox Shakespearean biography, the same story and the same myths continually being replayed and recycled. Perhaps it is true to go as far as to say that such, indeed is the reality for the whole of orthodox Shakespeare studies, where deep analysis is displaced rather on to investigations of identity, sexuality, gender, psychology and so on. As Marjorie Garber writes, '[Shakespeare is] a scenario of desire that has to be repeated with exactitude for every generation . . . [and] stand[s] for a kind of "humanness", which purport[s] to be inclusive of race, class and gender . . .' (Garber 2008: 118).

Returning to the 'single story' that defines conventional Shakespearean biography, it is true to say that this narrative tells a significant 'truth' to our culture; it produces an important 'knowledge' which underpins concepts of great importance to us. Yet, if we consider this single story with 'cautious detachment' (Benjamin 1992: 248); if we begin to ask certain questions – what does this orthodoxy consist of?; what are its constituent parts?; what is this knowledge and where did it come from?; what is this conformism?; why does it exist and why has it been so convincing? – we come to realize that there exist what Foucault has termed 'carefully protected identities' here and that the single story has been 'fabricated in a piecemeal fashion' (Foucault 1987: 78). For if we truly give time to these questions we find a revealing truth, a theological truth and, as Michel de Certeau called it, a *theoretical truth* at the very heart of orthodox Shakespeare biography (Certeau 2002: 183).

Given the paucity of facts that are known about Shakespeare of Stratford's life and the need for biographers to essentially invent much of what they write, it is appropriate to state that those who are certain that Shakespeare of Stratford wrote all of the plays and poems attributed to him – the vast majority of people – are involved in a system of belief. They are convinced that they are right in their view and can point to significant and important evidence – the author's name on some plays, Francis Meres' famous citation (1598; 1938: 281v–282r), Ben Jonson's celebration of the writer in the *First Folio*, indeed, the very existence of the *First Folio* itself and so on and so forth – which gives this view substance. I do not now wish to say they are wrong or mistaken in their view. Indeed, I would stress that it is currently the case that proponents for any and all alternative authors of the works attributed to Shakespeare are in exactly the same position and, that of all candidates Shakespeare is the strongest. I merely wish to say that what supporters of Shakespeare (and any of the other candidates) hold in this respect is a belief, irrespective of how convinced they are of its truth. The evidence that exists for Shakespeare (and some other alternatives) as the author is enough to build a belief upon but is not enough to build knowledge upon. As far as Shakespeare is concerned, there is simply too much uncertainty. While there is much mileage in the idea of the religious nature of Shakespeare studies (with Shakespeare replacing god in this secular religion), I am not trying to make a wider point about such theological resonances here. I merely wish to state that it is only possible for anyone to say 'I *believe* Shakespeare of Stratford wrote the plays;' it is not possible – or at least not legitimate – to say 'I *know* Shakespeare of Stratford wrote the plays' (and as stated, I extend this to any and all other proposed candidates for the authorship of the plays and poems).

In one sense, of course none of this is particularly profound. So, the vast majority of the inhabitants of the world who have an opinion about the matter believe rather than know that Shakespeare of Stratford wrote the plays attributed to him. That is no big deal. However, the *effects* of this not particularly profound reality are, as we know, more than profound; they are decisive. They determine the very 'realms of truth' of this entire field of investigation; they define what it is possible or not possible to say; they confer authority on some and deny authority to others; further, they enable individual researchers to be regarded as inspirational and others as idiotic; in short, this belief determines the truth. Given this, it is perhaps worthwhile contemplating the power of this belief and how it has become so convincing.

Considering this matter, it is useful to turn to the work of Michel de Certeau, who wrote at length on the question of what makes any belief credible and legitimate. According to Graham Ward, Certeau felt that 'it is impossible for we human beings to live without believing; to believe is an anthropological *a priori*. We believe because we desire and we desire because we lack fulfilment, the *jouissance*, that forever we search out' (Ward 2000: 6). For Certeau, belief in the modern world is something rather different to what we would regard as the norm, in that (he writes) 'I define "belief" not as the object of believing (a dogma, a program, etc) but as the subject's investment in a proposition, the *act* of saying it and considering it as true.'

(Certeau 2002: 178). Thus belief for Certeau consists of iteration rather than mere content, in the power of saying something and the transactional value this involves. But, he continues, it is not in the mere saying that belief consists, it is in 'narrated reality' (186), in iteration *and* reiteration, in the constant and continual saying and repeating that something is true, rather than in the actual object of truth itself. The final part of this whole 'anthropology of credibility' is constituted by the fact that, according to Certeau, 'we defer the truth about the object to other experts, whom we have never met nor can substantiate, [who] enable us to accept as credible that which *we are told* is true' (Ward 7). Belief therefore consists much more in the idea of believing in something because other people do than in any individual adherence to a dogma or truth. For Certeau, this 'anthropology of credibility' is crucial, as the 'capacity for believing' supports the 'functioning of authority' and indeed 'the will to "make people believe" ("*faire-croire*") . . . gives life to institutions' (Certeau 2002: 178). This last point regarding authority is necessarily important in the context of this essay, but I will continue in this vein a little longer in order to tease out the implications of what Certeau is saying. It is worth stating clearly that Certeau was interested in and spent much time theorizing the totality of society's compunction to believe. My interest is much more local, in the way that it can be applied to the specific subject of the Shakespeare authorship question.

Certeau believed that 'our society has become a recited society, in three senses; it is defined by *stories* (*récits*) . . . by *citations* of stories, and by the interminable *recitation* of stories' (186). In such a recited society, what people believe in is founded in citing the authority of others. Because we defer the truth about the object of belief to experts unknown to us, a recited society is populated by any number of pseudo-believers placing their faith in what they have been told (again and again) is true. The narrations of these experts have the power of 'fabricating realities out of appearances' (186) and thus 'fiction defines the field, the status, and the objects of vision' (187). And so the original story – that, for example, of Shakespeare of Stratford as the single, romantic genius-author – is *told*, this story is continually *cited* as the true and single story, and this story is constantly *recited* as the true and single story. Thus belief resides in the telling – citing and reciting – rather than in any original object such as the reality of, for example, Shakespeare's youth or his relationships and so on. And this belief is promulgated and propagated by experts who continually cite and recite it as truth. We are convinced and we believe.

Certeau then concludes that 'citation appears to be the ultimate weapon for making people believe' (188), particularly citation by experts – we believe because the expert believes and the expert knows. Authority is located within these experts, these proponents of the single story of Shakespeare of Stratford, not because they are providing a true story, but because they keep telling the same story over and over again. This is the case despite the fact that many believers may well feel the story to be false (or, at least, problematic):

> Vis-à-vis the stories of images, which are now no more than 'fictions', visible and legible productions, the spectator-observer *knows* that they are merely 'semblances', the results of manipulations – '*I know perfectly well that it's so much hogwash'* – *but all the same* he assumes that these simulations have the status of the real: a belief survives the refutation that everything we know about their fabrication makes available to him. (187–8)

Thus Stephen Greenblatt can begin his (orthodox) biography of Shakespeare 'Let us imagine . . .' (2004: 23) and then proceed to state, as though fact, all sorts of elaborate fictions. And Jonathan Bate can call his first chapter 'A life of anecdote' (1997: 4) while then proceeding to construct a 400 page thesis on the genius of Shakespeare. Certeau almost seems to have had them in mind when he writes that 'fiction defines the field' (187); knowing fiction, what is more.

This authority of the experts has another and highly pertinent consequence in this current context. To cite, Certeau says, is 'also to designate the "anarchists" or "deviants" (to cite them before the tribunal of public opinion); it is to condemn to the aggressivity of the public those who assert through their acts that they do not believe in it' (189). Thus many interested in the Shakespeare authorship question are demonized and ridiculed in public, in the media; because they do not believe, do not succumb to the power of citation and do not accept the authority invested in those who cite. Schoenbaum famously entitled the section of his book which examined the authorship question 'Deviations' (383–451), the Shakespeare Birthplace Trust regards anyone interested in the authorship question as suffering from a 'psychological aberration' and Stephen Greenblatt famously compared non-Stratfordians to creationists and Holocaust deniers. In response to an article in the *New York Times* on the Shakespeare authorship question, Greenblatt wrote a letter to the editor:

> The idea that William Shakespeare's authorship of his plays and poems is a matter of conjecture and the idea that the 'authorship controversy' be taught in the classroom are the exact equivalent of current arguments

that 'intelligent design' be taught alongside evolution. In both cases an overwhelming scholarly consensus, based on a serious assessment of hard evidence, is challenged by passionately held fantasies whose adherents demand equal time. The demand seems harmless enough until one reflects on its implications. Should claims that the Holocaust did not occur also be made part of the standard curriculum? *(New York Times* 4 September 2005)

As stated, this comes from the author of a biography of Shakespeare, the first one hundred pages (at least) of which are pure conjecture.

It is clear, therefore that facts play only a bit part in this whole field of inquiry. There are, as already stated a very limited number of such facts and no true object of belief. Rather, there is a constant and continual assertion that Shakespeare of Stratford wrote all of the plays and poems traditionally attributed to him, assertions made by experts and figures of authority, who make their claims based upon those of other figures of authority, other experts, based upon other experts and so on and on. Thus, rather than a legitimization by an appeal to facts, we get, as Certeau says, 'legitimisation by means of ethical values, by a theoretical truth, or by appealing to a roll call of martyrs . . .' (183). The field of orthodox Shakespearean biography can be said to be constituted by such a theoretical truth, and this 'legitimisation by appealing to a roll call of martyrs' is well established, from Rowe (1709) through Alexander Pope (1725), Dr Johnson (1765), Edmund Malone (1790) and into the modern era with Sidney Lee (1898), Chambers (1930) Schoenbaum (1970; 1991), Bate (1997), Greenblatt (2004), Shapiro (2005) and on and so forth. The fields of Shakespeare biography and the Shakespeare authorship question would seem to be constituted by Certeau's 'acts of saying' then, the realms of truth defined and administered by those experts to whom society defers; tenured academics.

The orthodox story is seductive because it promotes the notion of a single, romantic genius, but does seem to be delineated by its existence as this 'theoretical truth'. This is, naturally enough, problematic. However, there is a further reason why the orthodox story is problematic now, at this moment in time, and which is founded in that most significant development of the modern world, the internet. There has been a questioning of the orthodox biography and, indeed a Shakespeare authorship question for hundreds of years, existent on the margins of Shakespeare studies, maligned and shunned. It has existed in small groups and occasional publications and could only really have minimal impact. There were limited opportunities to disseminate the message and the controllers of such dissemination – authority figures such as academics – worked to resist the very *raison d'être* of the subject. The internet has, of course, effectively blown apart the ability to control the Shakespeare authorship controversy and it has blossomed and matured in this new environment. Not only that, like the internet itself, it has effectively undermined the power of traditional figures of cultural authority. There is no policing in terms of orthodoxy and the alternatives are free to be discussed and to flourish. Indeed, there is no appeal to authority; one can view what one wishes to view. While a hierarchy of authority still exists, there has been an enormous impact on the ability of experts to control the field because the avenues for iteration and reiteration, for citing and reciting have multiplied and alternative beliefs are as easy to disseminate as orthodox beliefs. Such a realization is perhaps evident in the vituperative claims made by the likes of Greenblatt and the Shakespeare Birthplace Trust when considering these alternatives. The loosening of traditional authority is difficult for those in authority to negotiate and this anxiety can manifest itself in a form of stubbornness – 'they are wrong and will always be wrong'. There is clearly a great interest in the subject of the Shakespeare authorship question outside of academia, and the continued refusal by academics to regard this as a legitimate subject of study will only exacerbate academia's separation from the world around it. This is particularly the case if it is seen to continue to promulgate a 'theoretical truth' and refuses to consider what many regard as legitimate alternatives. But a solution is at hand, one that can enable both the academic and non-academic parties. This solution I term 'Shakinomics'.

In chapter one of their book, *Wikinomics: How Mass Collaboration Changes Everything*, Tapscott and Williams delineate a practical example of their thesis, evident in the subtitle of their text. This example concerns a failing gold-mining firm, Goldcorp Inc, and how the new CEO of this company, Rob McEwen turned around its fortunes. Goldcorp's problems lay in the fact that it was experiencing great difficulty pinpointing new reserves of gold and was wasting enormous amounts of its resources in attempting to locate such reserves. McEwen had had his experts working hard in order to find new deposits and he was spending millions of dollars in the process. Unable to come up with a solution, McEwen decided he needed a break and he attended a 'MIT conference for young presidents' (8). At this conference,

[T]he subject of Linux came up and McEwen listened to the remarkable story of how Linus Torvalds and a loose volunteer brigade of software developers had assembled the world-class computing operating system

over the Internet. The lecturer explained how Torvalds revealed his code
to the world, allowing thousands of anonymous programmers to vet it
and make contributions of their own. (8)

According to Tapscott and Williams, 'McEwen had an epiphany' (8) and
realized that if his own experts could not find the needed gold reserves,
then perhaps somebody else not employed by his company could. McEwen
therefore decided to 'open source' the exploration process in the same way
Torvalds had Linux. In doing this, McEwen was challenging his entire
industry. The mining industry is a most secretive one – indeed, most indus-
tries are – and to reveal every 'scrap of information (some four hundred
megabytes worth)' (9) was to attack '"a fundamental assumption; you
simply don't give away proprietary data"' (8–9). This open sourcing encouraged any number of individual 'experts' not in the employ of Goldcorp to
contribute to the search for deposits, with the result that 'an astounding
eight million ounces of gold have been found. McEwen estimates the collaborative process shaved two to three years off their exploration time' (9).
Tapscott and Williams sum up the importance of this anecdote:

> [McEwen] realized the uniquely qualified minds to make new discoveries
> were probably outside the boundaries of his organization, and by sharing
> some intellectual property he could harness the power of collective gen-
> ius and capability. In doing so he stumbled successfully into the future of
> innovation, business, and how wealth and just about everything else will
> be created. Welcome to the new world of wikinomics where collaboration
> on a mass scale is set to change every institution in society. (10)

There are Shakespeare experts all over the world, both inside and outside
of academia. The conventional narrative of Shakespeare's life is, I hope
I have shown, both unsatisfactory and somehow 'stuck'; no new deposits are
being found and the subject is, on its own scholarly terms, failing. It is perhaps time to 'open source' Shakespeare's biography, time for those experts
who have little or no authority to be mobilized in order to reveal hidden
deposits, new areas of research, new fields of gold. It is time for academics
to liberate themselves from the limits of their own authority and consider
the wonderful richness of that which they have not, or will not contemplate.
It is time to jump into the world of mass collaboration and find wealth and
knowledge wherever it manifests itself. It is time to enter the world of
'Shakinomics'.

Chapter 8

Fighting over Shakespeare's Authorship: Identity, Power and Academic Debate

Sandra G. L. Schruijer

For many years the authorship of the Shakespeare canon has been debated (Auchter 1998; Michell 2000). Although more than seventy candidates have been presented over time, people that explicitly identify themselves as Stratfordians, Oxfordians, Marlovians, Baconians or others, seem not to get any closer. Converts to the non-Stratfordian camp are to be found mainly among actors, writers, practitioners and people from other academic disciplines rather than from those with an academic career in English literature. Among the wider audience many are not aware that there even is an authorship question and are likely to accept the man from Stratford-upon-Avon as the real author. The debate among the factions supporting different authors, insofar as it is held, is vehement but more often aggressive. Constructive communication between different groups of people is very difficult.

In this chapter I will not propose a new candidate for the authorship, nor will I present new evidence aimed to convince the reader about one side or the other. I am not an expert in English literature and neither do I claim to have an outstanding knowledge of Shakespeare. What I will offer is a different perspective, namely one coming from a social psychologist who has spent most of her academic and professional life understanding conflict between parties, such as groups and organizations, and facilitating collaboration. In other words, I will try to understand the psychological dynamics that create and maintain the intensity of the Shakespeare authorship debate, its painful elements and the lack of progress in terms of factions coming closer.

In what follows, I will describe my first naïve footsteps in the Shakespeare authorship minefield after which I will adopt a social–psychological perspective to make sense of what I encountered. Concepts such as social identity, task and relational conflict are key to my understanding. In the second part I will situate the Shakespeare authorship debate in a larger ideological context, needed to get a better insight into some of its peculiarities. Throughout the text I will illustrate my arguments with some of my own experiences at the front. I will also include examples from the domains of art and history which illustrate comparable dynamics to the ones characterizing the Shakespeare authorship debate. A final source of information involves a survey among people involved in the Shakespeare authorship question that taps their perceptions regarding the debate and their arguments pro and contra various candidates.

Some years ago Oxfordian Jan Scheffer from the Netherlands very enthusiastically introduced me to the Shakespeare authorship question. I started reading and it quickly became clear to me what I know from my own work, namely, that it is hard to communicate across group boundaries. I was eager to share my new discoveries concerning the authorship with a dear English friend and colleague and told him what I had picked up from the website www.shakespeare-oxford.com. His pejorative reaction was one I was not prepared for at the time: 'Oh come on, that's nonsense, one can find anything on the internet!' I realized I had touched something. While reading more, I was surprised by the fierceness of the debate, with those contesting the common assumption that the man from Stratford-upon-Avon was the author of the Shakespeare canon being ridiculed – 'mainstream scholars as well as eccentrics' – or even demonized; 'you deny the reality of Shakespeare one moment, you can deny the reality of the Holocaust the next' (Bate 2002). Generally, non-Stratfordian work is dismissed as non-scientific by the academic establishment that almost uniquely consists of Stratfordians: as I learned personally when sharing some thoughts from a psychological perspective on the matter on one of the authorship discussion websites. A staunch Stratfordian immediately rejected what I said, ending his comment with something like 'surely there must be academic standards even in her field?'

Then I read Diana Price's *Shakespeare's Unorthodox Biography: New Evidence of an Authorship Problem* (2001). It convinced me that the Bard could not be Shakespeare. Although, again, I am not a scholar in English literature, I thought of Price's book as fully convincing and her line of reasoning thorough and scientific. However, such an opinion was not shared by key voices belonging to the Stratfordian camp. Prof. Alan Nelson accused Price of not being able 'to put an argument together', of being unwilling to 'accept evidence, so she must find a way to discredit it', of engaging in 'the selective demolition of evidence' and 'untrammeled speculation' ending his personal authorship debate with a 'Closing note: Fully acquainted with the fact that no anti-Stratfordian will ever let a traditional academic have the last word, and unable ever to convince an opponent who prefers the preposterous to the probable, I hereby declare that for this website, in respect to Diana Price's book, the rest is silence' (Nelson 2003).[1]

Why then is it so difficult to engage in a meaningful, open and constructive debate in which differences of opinion are seen as fruitful as they may aid in gaining a deeper understanding of, in this case, the authorship and its mysteries? Innovation and creativity are unthinkable without such 'task conflict'. Indeed, the development of science is based on principles of task conflict. Unfortunately, a confrontation with diversity may result in feelings of threat. Task conflict can easily result in relational conflict where proving one's point at the expense of others, or, winning the argument and beating the opponent, become the goals rather than gaining a deeper insight (Schruijer 2002). In science, many examples of task conflict that have eroded into relational ones can be found. Relational conflicts go together with negative stereotyping and win–lose dynamics. The Shakespeare authorship debate appears to be no exception. A social–psychological perspective can help to understand some of its dynamics.

The social psychology of intergroup relations aims at understanding the causes, triggers and processes of intergroup conflict. Why do intergroup competition, win–lose dynamics, prejudice and stereotyping occur? How come that people belonging to different groups see the same world so differently and engage in what is called 'group-serving' biases in which one's own group is put in a positive light vis-à-vis another group? Many theories have been formulated to explain these phenomena but I will focus here on the predominant ones (for more see Schruijer 1990, 2008). The Realistic Conflict Theory (Sherif 1967) locates the cause of intergroup conflict in the incompatibility of groups' goals, for example, in competing for scarce resources. In the case of the Shakespeare authorship question: finding out – or rather demonstrating, who the real author of the Shakespeare canon is (and most assume there can only be one). Groups that are in conflict become focused on winning. Between groups communication decreases while stereotyping and selective listening and other group serving biases appear.

Stereotyping is part and parcel of the Shakespeare authorship debate. Stratfordians see Oxfordians as conspiracy theorists or a bunch of amateurs, while Oxfordians regard Stratfordians as being stupid. Both parties do not find it really necessary to listen to each other's arguments as they already 'know' who the real author is. Critical remarks by Stratfordians on Oxfordian work are easily interpreted by Oxfordians as rude while critical remarks by Oxfordians on Stratfordian work are seen (by Oxfordians) as respectful and justified, with the Stratfordians being a little too sensitive. And the same applies the other way around. A super ordinate goal could solve the inter-group conflict from a Realistic Conflict Theory perspective. Yet is there no super ordinate goal, namely, finding out more about who the author of the Shakespeare canon really was?

There is more at stake; namely, people's identities. Social Identity Theory (Tajfel and Turner 1979) can be seen as a complementary theory to the Realistic Conflict Theory. It emphasizes the role of people's social identity in understanding intergroup conflict and group-serving biases. The premise is that individuals strive towards a positive self-concept. One source that may contribute to a positive self-concept is one's group membership(s). Social identity has been defined as 'that part of the individuals' self-concept which derives from their knowledge of their membership of a social group (or groups) together with the value and emotional significance of that membership' (Tajfel 1981: 225). People involved in the Shakespeare author-ship question identify, to a larger or smaller extent, with the cause of unearthing the truth regarding the real author. The more they identify with the cause – from which they can derive a positive social identity – the more the earlier mentioned group-serving biases are likely.

By comparing one's own group on a relevant dimension with a relevant comparison group, for instance, Oxfordians comparing themselves with Stratfordians regarding who knows best who the real author is, group mem-bers discover whether their group membership provides them with a positive distinctiveness vis-à-vis (what psychologists call) the outgroup. Stereotyping (of other groups but also of one's own group) can thus be understood as an expression of the need to create a meaningful social identity. Differences sometimes are created so as to arrive at a positive distinctiveness vis-à-vis another group.

If through comparing one's group with a relevant other on a particular dimension a negative distinctiveness is obtained (the other group has bet-ter evidence for example, or has all academic authority), group members experience a negative social identity. This can be overcome by various strat-egies. One can change group membership (physically or psychologically): Stratfordians can become Oxfordians or vice versa. Alternatively, group members can change the comparison dimension. Stratfordians may decide, 'Ok, Oxfordians have good points but in terms of academic authority we are better off'. Oxfordians may say, 'we have not won the argument (yet), but we have the true spirit, we care for the truth'. Group members can also change comparison group. Stratfordians, for example, assuming they do find the Shakespeare authorship question relevant and do feel challenged, can start comparing the scope of their knowledge regarding the true author not with Oxfordians but with the larger public; while Oxfordians may decide to compare themselves with, let's say, Baconians. Further, one can change the evaluation of the negative distinctiveness. 'All right', Stratfordians might say, 'we have less convincing evidence, but it is irrelevant as the truth is so self-evident'. Oxfordians might say 'we are worse off academically, but that is good – it keeps us alert to find even better evidence'.

Finally, group members can directly confront the comparison group on that comparison dimension which resulted in a negative distinctiveness. This strategy most likely leads to intergroup conflict; 'We Oxfordians will show Stratfordians that we know better'. Which strategy will be chosen is largely a function of how stable and/or legitimate the current status quo is perceived to be. A direct confrontation is especially likely when the group experiencing a negative social identity does not consider the current state of affairs as legitimate and furthermore can conceive of feasible alternatives. The latter case seems to apply to the Oxfordians as they have been increasing in number over the last decades and enlarged their public support, maybe more so than they realize themselves, as illustrated in a note by Charles Berney in a recent *De Vere Society Newsletter*. He recounts the story that he visited an old study friend whom he had not seen for more than fifty years, and who shares his interest in the Shakespeare authorship question. The friend's wife then remarks: 'I thought that had been settled'. Upon which Charles asks: 'Which way?' And she replies: 'It was the rich guy – the lord' (2008: 27).

It is important to realize finally that group members not only experience a psychological need to be superior to other parties on a particular dimension, but also a need for validation of their self-perceived superiority from important others (Rijsman 1997). In other words, Oxfordians want to hear the Stratfordians say that the Oxfordians are right regarding the true authorship, and vice versa, the Stratfordians wanting the Oxfordians to publicly acknowledge the superiority of Stratfordian thinking.

The Shakespeare authorship debate is hardly of a task conflictual nature. Sadly, it is predominantly characterized by relational conflicts between Stratfordians, Marlovians, Oxfordians, Baconians and many other non-Stratfordians. Such relational conflicts are expressed in negative stereotyping, selective listening, the use of downgrading language, and attributing the differences in point of view to a lack of intelligence. Such group-serving biases are not restricted to Stratfordians. All factions are characterized by these to a smaller or greater extent. Interestingly, non-Stratfordian work is referred to as anti-Stratfordian, both by Stratfordians as well as by many non-Stratfordians, as if having a different opinion equals being against those who think differently. The different factions fight for who is right; a 'real' conflict as being right is a scarce resource. The debate is constructed such that only one can be right (it is the Stratford man, or Oxford, or Marlowe, etc., no doubts are involved and no compromises seem possible apart from the allowance for collaborative authorship), although the conclusive piece of evidence does not exist.

Overall then, Stratfordians and non-Stratfordians compete on the same dimension, namely, who knows best who the author of the Shakespeare canon was, and pursue validation from their respective comparison group. Getting acceptance from one's opponent in this case would be the Stratfordians saying to Oxfordians or Marlovians for that matter: 'you are right, we were wrong all along'. Simply put, this is not going to happen.

The Survey

I would now like to present some of the findings of a survey that was administered among Oxfordians and some other non-Stratfordians. Its aim was to gain further insight into how different factions proposing different individuals as the real author of the Shakespeare canon perceive each other, each other's arguments and the authorship debate as a whole. I tried to have the survey distributed among Stratfordians but two attempts failed. Nevertheless, the distribution of the survey through different channels resulted in a response of 5 Stratfordians, 76 Oxfordians and 9 others. The lack of responsiveness of Stratfordians was amply compensated for by the enthusiasm of Oxfordians who provided me with an abundance of information. In what follows I focus on the responses of the Oxfordians (36 from the USA, 26 from the United Kingdom and 10 from continental Europe) and the handful of Stratfordians.

In one section of the survey a question asked what, in the eyes of the respondents, the strongest arguments in favour of the Stratfordian claim to authorship were and what the weakest. Likewise the strongest and weakest arguments for the Oxfordian claim were solicited. Oxfordians see tradition as the main argument that makes the Stratfordian claim to authorship strong. Tradition or orthodoxy was mentioned by one third of the participating Oxfordians. For example, one Oxfordian stated: 'Many thousands of "academics/experts" have invested their reputations over hundreds of years. It must be very difficult for opinion-makers to let their colleagues, friends, and literary tradition down'. And another one: 'Orthodoxy and clinging to an emotional and heroic devotion to continuing a longstanding academic tradition based on a belief for 400 plus years'.

The second most frequently mentioned argument, in favour of the Stratford man, and mentioned by 25 per cent of the Oxfordians, pertained to the name of William Shakespeare on the *First Folio* or on other works. Only 5 per cent referred to references to the Stratford man in contemporary sources. Two of the five Stratfordians however did mention that latter argument, besides others. To be precise, their responses comprised the following: 'The references to Shakespeare by Ben Jonson in his tribute and the correlation of Shakespeare's life (birth date, leaving London, retiring date, death date) to the plays'. Another one: 'The contemporary documentation of Shakespeare's authorship (dozens of references, name on publications) as well as his growing wealth (his buying of real estate in Stratford and London)'. A third stated that 'All evidence points to him, hence conspiracy theorists attack the evidence rather than being influenced by evidence'. One person, who called himself a doubtful Stratfordian, was more modest. He stated: 'The evidence, though not very strong, is stronger than for any other candidate'.

Oxfordians list many weak arguments of the Stratfordian case. Thirty-three per cent mention the illiteracy of the Stratford man, Shakspere,[2] and his family. For example: 'His signatures are the incompetent, inconsistent efforts of an illiterate attempting to copy example signatures as "marks"; Will is the product of a provincial grain merchant. It has none of the style one would expect of "Shakespeare"'. And another one, given the punctuation, seemed to exclaim: 'No recorded or discovered relationship to a pen. There is no "weak" argument. There is *no* argument'. Other less-often mentioned weak arguments pertain to his character or the lack of a match between his biography and the works. Also the lack of a paper trail was mentioned by 25 per cent of Oxfordians. And in descending order: his poor education, the conjectures (the 'must haves'), Shakspere's lack of travel abroad, the fact that people at the time were apparently unaware of a great playwright living among them, the fact that 'genius' would explain all, and 'how good the grammar school was' according to the Stratfordians. One Oxfordian explained it as follows:

Nearly everything about his life is a supposition. To those who say his life experiences do not matter, I ask: what about Twain, Faulkner, and Hemingway, whose every Mississippi River trek, evidence of southern heritage, or African hunting trip is of great moment in multiple biographies? Of course the life of an author is fair (and important) game in the study of literary history. To suppose that the Stratford man attended a grammar school (where he learned a little Latin and Greek), listened to tales of the sea in a local pub, gleaned the intricacies of court politics from conversations with the 3rd Earl of Southampton, and came to an appreciation of all things Italian by staring at the stars is to suppose that 900 monkeys typing on 900 typewriters for 900 years could produce *Hamlet.*

The disagreements between Oxfordians and Stratfordians and the incompatibilities of their viewpoints are obvious. The same applies when it concerns the weak and strong arguments for Edward de Vere as the author of the Shakespeare canon. Oxfordians see mostly strong arguments, the strongest being the parallels between the works on the one hand and the life of Edward de Vere on the other. Thirty per cent in this context refer to his education for example, life experiences, travel and his aristocratic background. Another often-mentioned argument refers to de Vere's reputation as a playwright at the time. For example: 'The author of the plays etc. obviously had deep knowledge of languages, foreign countries, history, heraldry, law, falconry, ancient untranslated texts, court gossip, the bible, was bad with money, ancient family etc; all of which De Vere had/was and the Stratford man *did/was not*'. Or, 'Oxford's life was like Mozart's, another genius, in that he was totally inconsiderate. Frustration, like Marcel Proust, paired with intelligence and knowledge, produces such literature. Oxford is the elected enemy of the Stratfordians. The others are small fry'. Another one sees the work of Stratfordian Alan Nelson, who has written a book on Edward de Vere (2003) as the strongest argument: 'Can there be a stronger argument than that of a scholar, who makes an effort to write a book of 800 pages, which shows that his subject is a "nobody" whom one should forget as soon as possible, because he is of no importance? But Prof. Nelson wants to show his fall by committing character assassination. Why? His fall is his rise'. And finally: 'His life experiences are replete throughout the poetry and plays. Frankly, I am stunned that any person with a brain who looks at the evidence objectively could come to a conclusion other than that Oxford wrote this canon'. In comparison, two Stratfordians see no arguments in favour of Oxford whatsoever; one mentions his travel as the strongest argument, one his poems, while the doubtful Stratfordian points to biographical similarities.

The weakest argument for Oxford as seen by the Oxfordians, pertains to the question why secrecy was so persistent (mentioned by 17 per cent) as well as his early death or the dating of the plays (also mentioned by 17 per cent), and then thirdly, the fact that there exists no play in his own name (8 per cent). The Stratfordians present as the weakest argument a difficult chronology, lack of contemporary evidence and an unfit character, or, in the words of one Stratfordian; 'He died too soon. He lived too profligately. Most likely would not have had the temperament to produce such a monumental opus. Also, his own poems and letters don't "smack of" Shakespeare'.

National Identities and Interests

The Shakespeare authorship debate however, is not only about a difference of opinion regarding who the author of the Shakespeare canon was. More is at stake. Apart from identities that are derived from one's membership of the Stratfordian, Oxfordian or Marlovian factions, other identities are involved too; national identities and interests. The bard is a national symbol of England; the bard, who was a genius coming from nowhere, a country-boy who became the world's most famous writer, without having the aristocratic background and thus making it without hereditary privileges. It is the English version of the American newspaper boy who worked his way up and became a millionaire. Shakespeare is a hero; he was a genius and did not need an elite education in order to exhibit his talents; a version of reality that appeals to a majority that will never receive an elite education and feel confined within their class but who still aspire to the top. All children learn about Shakespeare; their parents go to Shakespeare plays or act in one themselves (and I imagine that a large majority of English households contain one or more books with Shakespeare's plays or sonnets). Moreover, tourists flock to the country searching for Shakespeare trails. As one respondent of the survey remarked; 'Well, I think that Shakespeare is an institution. Every Englishman has visited Stratford, and very few have not seen a Shakespeare play. Shakespeare is who he is, and Stratford-upon-Avon will not let go of him lightly'. People in England live with Shakespeare and do not want their national symbol tampered with.

The latter is exemplified by my friend (Englishman, academic, psychologist), who I referred to earlier. I asked him to answer a few questions on the Shakespeare authorship debate after I'd sent him Price's book. I asked him how nationality is related to the authorship question. My friend: 'The English/British have an unshakeable belief in their country's greatness and its cultural, sporting, moral, political, technological, scientific, military and, of course, literary superiority. Shakespeare is a big part of all that. The other day, my son in discussion with me suddenly raised the question "why is

Britain best?" So it's not just my generation'. One of the questions I asked my friend was how he felt about some of Price's arguments supporting her view that the man from Stratford cannot have been the author of the Shakespeare canon. He found many arguments compelling. He felt shocked by the little evidence there is to support the traditional view. He had hoped 'that there was a stronger case for the traditional William than appears to be the case'. He continued with:

> The genius who comes from nowhere has a huge appeal, in whatever sphere of endeavor. And geniuses do sometimes come from nowhere, and have undistinguished educational careers. The idea that an aristocratic background is a prerequisite of poetic and literary genius is not one that endears itself to your average Brit. And what's wrong with going to the local grammar school? Accepting De Vere as Shakespeare certainly diminishes the character and achievement of the second greatest ever Englishman [as voted in a recent poll]. I don't want it to be true. In the same way I suspect that the greatest ever Englishman, Winston Churchill, was voted into that position partly because he had a decidedly undistinguished school career, did not go to University, was essentially self-educated, and for much of his life was spurned by the establishment. The successful underdog has great appeal.

The same issue was commented upon by one respondent of the survey. This person stated that: 'I believe that much of today's liberal academic community defends the man from Stratford not only because of tradition, but because he represents the "common man", who through diligence and hard work raised himself up to be the greatest writer in the history of the English language. Politics does have a bearing'.

Coming back to my friend, some doubt was instilled: 'Price has severely damaged my faith in the Stratford assumption, and now I have an open mind.' Then I met together with his family at his house. I continued the conversation on the Shakespeare authorship question with his next of kin present, naively thinking that we could continue where we had left off. However, he was firmly back in the Stratfordian position. Later we reflected on this evening and its events. Being a psychologist himself, he recognized and acknowledged that his firm beliefs, with which all children are raised, namely that Shakespeare is Shakspere, needed some defending at the time with his family present.

Let us furthermore not forget that the Shakespeare cult serves economic interests with Stratford-upon-Avon being one of the most popular towns for tourists to visit. One survey item revealed that Oxfordians believe that economic interests (namely, the attraction of Stratford-upon-Avon) prevent the truth coming out. Or as one Oxfordian stated: 'The truth about Shakespeare will not come from the UK, because the Stratfordian mafia have the power to stifle it, and will delay it, to safeguard their economic interests'. By the way, Charlie Chaplin, who was eager to get a glimpse of the great man's past, made an interesting observation regarding Stratford-upon-Avon:

> [T]hat such a mind ever dwelt or had its beginnings there, seems incredible. It is easy to imagine a farmer's boy emigrating to London and becoming a successful actor and theatre-owner; but for him to have become the great poet and dramatist, and to have had such knowledge of foreign courts, cardinals and kings, is inconceivable to me. I am not concerned with who wrote the works of Shakespeare, whether Bacon, Southampton or Richmond, but I can hardly think it was the Stratford boy. Whoever wrote them had an aristocratic attitude. His utter disregard for grammar could only have been the attitude of a princely, gifted mind. And after seeing the cottage and hearing the scant bits of local information concerning his desultory boyhood, his indifferent school record, his poaching and his country bumpkin point of view, I cannot believe he went through such a mental metamorphosis as to become the greatest of all poets. In the work of the greatest of geniuses humble beginnings will reveal themselves somewhere – but one cannot trace the slightest sign of them in Shakespeare. (Chaplin 2003: 358–59)

In addition to all of this, there are academic identities and interests at stake. It seems that Stratfordian academic identities are challenged by the non-Stratfordians who do not occupy chairs in departments of English Literature, or positions lower in the academic hierarchy for that matter. The non-Stratfordians are generally independent researchers, combining their research interest in Shakespeare with a professional career outside academia, or an academic career but not in the domain of English literature. Non-Stratfordians, then, in the eyes of the Stratfordian academics, do not have the appropriate background or status to challenge the knowledge the Stratfordians have been working with all their academic lives (Chandler 2003). The independent researchers are labelled 'amateurs' and the academics from different disciplines 'tourists', as I was once called by a devoted Stratfordian. The latter snapped at me that I had no right to make any comments on the Shakespeare authorship question as 'I was only a tourist in his discipline'. I replied by saying that looking at the way people communicate is very much my discipline. Moreover, creativity often results from multidisciplinary encounters.

The closed question in the survey shows that Oxfordians do not see non-Stratfordians as a bunch of amateurs and are strongly convinced that 'if non-Stratfordians had academic power equal to the Stratfordians, the true author (not the conventional Shakespeare) would be embraced'. Further, they feel that 'non-Stratfordians have a harder time to get promoted at departments of English literature even though their research might be unrelated to the authorship debate'. The opinions of the handful of participating Stratfordians clearly do not differ. One respondent, an American Professor Emeritus commented that 'As an active member of the organization of English Department Heads, I can testify to the bias existing toward any heretical views challenging Stratfordian orthodoxy on most campuses.'

Stratfordians then, have positions of power, universities being filled with academics supporting the Stratfordian claim. They state that the majority of Shakespeare scholars support the Stratfordian view but that may be largely passively, because they may have never questioned the authorship explicitly. Most Stratfordians ignore the non-Stratfordians. It is especially the non-Stratfordians that want to be heard and taken seriously by academia. In other words, the non-Stratfordians without much academic power want recognition from those with academic power who happen to be Stratfordians. This is an almost impossible situation. Given the asymmetric power relations, with Stratfordians outnumbering non-Stratfordians both in academia and in society – and as the larger population is largely unaware of the fact that there is a debate in the first place – Stratfordians are unlikely to change allegiance and non-Stratfordians are likely to remain frustrated.

It reminds me of the story of Vulfolaic who was a devoted Christian living in the early Middle Ages. At that time bishops tried to increase the support for the Christian faith while also strengthening their own power base, for example, by construing a distinction between the Christian faith and superstition and between saints and imposters (Brown 1982). The church realized that people living in a violent society had a strong need to witness miracles and were ready to believe in them. Bishops helped in creating a desirable new identity, being Christian, by promising people that a better world was waiting for them. Bishops positioned themselves as the sole patentees of identifying 'real' relics, and carefully eliminated potential competitors. The devoted Christian Vulfolaic once witnessed a miracle, inspiring him to start preaching (Geary 1988). He did so while being seated on a column on which he had endured a cold winter. Many followers gathered around him. The local bishops felt threatened by Vulfolaic. Only they could witness and interpret miracles properly, and could exclusively identify saints and relics. Vulfolaic in their eyes had not received the proper training to preach, a task solely reserved for bishops. During his absence, they destroyed Vulfolaic's column. Bishops' sense-making activities were given priority over those of others. As such the definition of reality and the construction of identity are power-based (Smircich and Morgan 1982).

The question here seems to be wider than just about who knows best who Shakespeare was; the underlying issue is, who has a patent on the truth? Academics are the ones who practice science; they create and nurture knowledge. And knowledge is power. Hence, academics' identities and academia as an institution may be under threat. What if non-academics gain equal access to information and gain as much knowledge as academics, or even more? Distinctions are called for: between the 'real academics' (those working at the university) and the 'amateurs' (independent researchers); between the 'specialists' (the English literarians) and the 'tourists' (academics without a background in English literature) – so as to preserve the reputation of academics and the trust the larger public has in universities.

An interesting parallel can be found in the vicissitudes of Bouwe Jans, who dared to challenge the Van Gogh museum, the dominant elite when it concerns authentication of Van Gogh paintings. Jans acquired a painting in 1993 that was signed 'Vincent'. After 15 years of research he has been able to convincingly demonstrate that it is an authentic Van Gogh (2001 and 2003; see also www.artquakes.com). The Van Gogh Museum, however, continues to reject Jans' painting even though Jans has been able to refute all of their reasons why his painting cannot be a genuine Van Gogh and despite the fact that various independent Van Gogh experts who researched the painting validated it as authentic and a complete provenance is available. Jans feels humiliated and frustrated by 'the establishment' that ignores the outcomes of his own research and that of the independent scholars and that conceives of him and these scholars as 'amateurs'. Furthermore, the Van Gogh museum excludes the possibility of doubt. Its verdict can only be 'yes, it is a Van Gogh', or, 'no, it is not a Van Gogh'. Such exclusion of doubt not only frustrates the owner's feelings of distributive and procedural justice, it may also serve to reduce the uncertainty or anxiety on the part of the museum. If one would allow a 'maybe', others may come forward with unknown, potential authentic Van Gogh paintings, while the authenticity of paintings that were earlier attributed to Van Gogh with a firm 'yes' (in possession of the museum) can then be doubted. And Van Gogh is big business, the Van Gogh museum being the most popular museum in The Netherlands. Reputations and professional identities are threatened here by an amateur. Society has granted the museum a patent on the truth regarding the authenticity of Van Gogh paintings, and given the increase in paintings' monetary value when an authenticity label has been provided. Truth appears to be closely linked to power, identity and certain interests.

As such, the Shakespeare authorship debate does not occur in an ideological and socio-structural vacuum. Non-Stratfordians form a minority with little power. Yet their deviance is threatening as the fierceness of the debate illustrates. Classical social–psychological research shows what happens to a group member that goes against the opinion of a majority (Schachter 1951). First the deviant is confronted with rational arguments, subsequently put under emotional pressure, after which he or she is ignored and finally is evicted from the group. A group member with a deviant opinion quickly gets labelled as 'difficult', is blamed for 'resisting' or depicted as 'not loyal'. He or she is often marked as a rebel and rejection or even denunciation follows. The problem that gave rise to the divisiveness thus gets individualized, exactly the function of a scapegoat. A deviant can be created so as to preserve the beliefs of the majority.

That deviants are threatening can be derived from the treatment of whistle blowers. Many lose their jobs after they have been declared psychologically unstable, despite protective legislation (Alford 2001). The power of the system needs enforcing even if it means killing deviants. I recently learned about the fate of the English soldier Henry Farr who fought in the First World War (Mak 2006). He was sent home with shell shock. At some point he was ordered to return to the front though he was not cured. He refused and was subsequently executed because of cowardice, by his own peers. The allowance of his wife and daughter was terminated instantly. His daughter only learned the inside story when middle-aged. His granddaughter fought for rehabilitation which only now, almost a century later, materialized. Many other English soldiers shared the fate of Henry Farr and his family.

Heretics can be conceived of as deviant insiders, as 'close enough to be threatening but distant enough to be considered in error' (Kurtz 1983: 1087). Non-Stratfordians can be seen as heretics as they challenge the establishment and the establishment feels threatened. The following bizarre conversation I had with an English woman in The Netherlands can serve as an illustration of the threat involved. The lady was sitting next to me at a gathering where Stephen Greenblatt was to present his new book (2004), when she said to me:

Woman: 'I am not so sure about his [Greenblatt's] approach'.
Me: 'Me neither'.
Woman: 'Oh?'

Me: 'I question Shakespeare's identity. I think someone else wrote the plays and sonnets'.

Woman: 'Oh that is so insipid'.

Me: 'Why?'

Woman: 'There is so little known about sixteenth-century writers'.

Me: 'But there is much more known about his contemporaries' [referring to Price].

Woman: 'Are you saying then that he was not married to Anne Hathaway?'

Me: 'No. There was a man from Stratford called Shakspere – he was married to Anne Hathaway. I think Shakspere was a different person than 'Shakespeare'.

Woman: 'Oh, but spelling was so inconsistent at the time'.

Me: 'Sure, but Shakspere's name was never spelled as 'Shakespeare'.

Woman: 'Oh, but then he must have changed his name to Shakespeare when he went to London. I hope you will not be offended with what I am going to say'.

Me: 'That depends on what you are going to say'.

Woman: 'Saying that Shakespeare did not write the plays and sonnets is like saying there is no relationship between HIV and Aids'.

Doubting Shakespeare's identity is thus stupid, dangerous and immoral.

Heresy is a problem of authority. Heresy questions 'the authority of an institutional hierarchy to dictate interpretation of what is truth and what is not' (Kurtz 1983: 1094). Organizing heresy hunts function to relieve anxiety on the part of the dominant institution. Heresy has a divisive effect as it threatens the current power distribution, but it also strengthens the elite as it can now rally support to fight the common enemy. As a consequence, the conflict escalates, making it more and more difficult to reach a compromise or to mix positions. Non-Stratfordians are insiders to the extent that they love Shakespeare too. Their deviance consists of them pointing to a different author. By doing so they threaten popular beliefs, established truths and the authority of academics to define what the truth is. Resistance is formed, resistance that is inherent in giving up a powerful and familiar idea. Parties polarize, fight their enemy and dig themselves in by committing to earlier convictions and allegiances, and by engaging in face-saving strategies. Yet the dominant institution on the one hand and the heretics on the other, are interdependent in developing and articulating their respective belief systems. It implies that at one level Stratfordians need non-Stratfordians to further their own thinking and vice versa.

The long-standing debate over the question 'who was the real author of the Shakespeare canon?' pertains to more than just different groups of people who have different ideas on the matter. Something that is basically a task conflict has developed into a relational conflict, where winning one's case has become a dominant drive, accompanied by ridiculing those who adhere to a different point of view. The debate, then, is an example of social competition in which positive social identities are constructed through one's adherence to one of the various factions supporting different authors: Stratfordian, Marlovian, Oxfordian, etc. However other social identities are involved too, especially academic ones and also national ones. English people do not like their Shakespeare to be messed with. And Stratfordian academics with a background in English literature (a pleonasm) distance themselves from those in the debate that are either independent researchers or academics with a different disciplinary background (unless, I assume, they support the Stratfordian view).

Thus, the Shakespeare authorship controversy needs to be placed in a larger socio-structural and ideological context. In order to understand the dynamics one needs to consider the (academic) power differences between the Stratfordians and the non-Stratfordians, national and academic identities, and the economic interests in maintaining a Stratford cult. Non-Stratfordians are largely treated as heretics by Stratfordians. This implies however, that they feel that their academic authority is challenged. In other words, they feel threatened exactly because the non-Stratfordians have something valuable to say.

I hope that the nature of this psychological perspective has helped in understanding the fierceness of the debate. The survey, although being only a preliminary study and lacking a strong Stratfordian participation, illustrates the incompatible points of view and the role identities play. A logical question at this point might be: how further? Millions of people, all over the world, do not know about the controversy; if informed they trust the official, that is the Stratfordian point of view, while almost all Stratfordians deny that there is an issue in the first place. Yet, as philosopher Bertrand Russell has remarked, 'If fifty million people say it is a foolish thing, it is still a foolish thing.' The recent creation of an MA in Shakespeare Authorship Studies at Brunel University by William Leahy is a giant leap forward in generating awareness that there is an issue and legitimizing it in the academic world; to be more precise, among departments of English Literature. I suggest involving other disciplines also, such as History or the Social Sciences that may be more open to the debate, especially outside the United Kingdom.

And finally there are the young people. The survey shows that the average age when respondents were exposed to the authorship question was 46. Taking up the authorship question during high school, as part of the formal curriculum, may be difficult inside the United Kingdom now but may be less so elsewhere. For example, for three consecutive years I have introduced the Shakespeare authorship question to a school in the south of the Netherlands, the Odulphus Lyceum. The idea is that pupils think for themselves and make up their own minds. Thus far, pupils have involved their whole class in a mock jury in order to decide who, in their view, the real author is. Some have written an essay on the authorship question, based on their own research, while last year they made a film on the matter. The pupils as well as their teachers have been very enthusiastic. A new era may be near. After all, '. . . one generation's heresy is frequently the next generation's orthodoxy' (Kurtz 1983: 1089).

Notes

[1] Nelson's comments were posted on the internet at www.socrates.berkeley.edu/~ahnelson. This site is no longer accessible, however. Nelson's comments (and Price's responses) can be viewed on Diana Price's site at http://www.shakespeare-authorship.com/responses/nelson.

[2] Oxfordians denote the Stratford man as Shakspere, to distinguish him from the name published on the plays 'Shake-speare' or 'Shakespeare'; Shakspere is the name with which the Stratford man was baptized and that he and others used, with some variations.

Chapter 9

Mark Rylance (Former Artistic Director, Globe Theatre, London)

Interviewed by William Leahy[1]

William Leahy: Where do you stand in terms of the Shakespeare authorship question and how did you reach this view?

Mark Rylance: Well, of course I was a Stratfordian for 28 years of my life, though I cannot remember when I was first told in school that a man from Stratford wrote the plays. My first encounter with Shakespeare was being taken to the theatre and hearing him. I particularly remember being taken to the RSC in Stratford-upon-Avon in the 1970s by my parents. I very much enjoyed visiting the town and imagining where he lived and worked. I played Hamlet at 16 in school, but I don't remember talking about the authorship at all. I remember it was the play that mattered and we felt we didn't need to talk about authorship as there wasn't anything really there that was revealing. That lasted right through Drama school and my first full season as an actor at the RSC between 1982 and 1984. I recently read Mark Twain's wonderful book of 1909, *Is Shakespeare Dead?* and wondered how it had escaped my attention in the American high school I attended, where Twain was taught almost every year.

Much later, the second time I was in Stratford (playing Hamlet and Romeo at the same time), I met some friends and they had some very interesting things to say about Romeo, talking very beautifully about the alchemical imagery in Romeo's language. I was struggling at this time; we were in early previews and it was a great help to hear these descriptions of lead, silver and gold in the verse and what they might be indicating about Romeo's psychological state and the changes that were happening in the course of the play. When you first preview a big part like this you have so many choices that you have explored in rehearsal and then you are bombarded with opinions from the audience, and you really have to make some decisions about how to calibrate the whole thing on many levels. Anyway, I asked these friends where they had met with these ideas and they told me that they had heard them at the Sir Francis Bacon Research Trust in Alderminster, a village just outside Stratford. As luck would have it, there was a meeting the following morning and I went along. It was a really fascinating talk and I started to go regularly on Sundays, not because I was interested in the authorship at all but because what I heard was really useful for the playing of parts and particularly playing Hamlet. I had done a hundred performances on tour and I was now playing in Stratford. I knew that on certain evenings it went remarkably well and other evenings it went well but not remarkably well and, of course, I was fascinated as to why that was the case.

I learned a lot of things from the Francis Bacon Research Trust that I had never heard in rehearsal rooms or read in Stratfordian footnotes; about mythical cycles and internal psychological patterns of change from European classical traditions; Greek, Roman, Judaic and Celtic. These traditions of storytelling and wisdom, the Hermetic tradition as Ted Hughes has called them, were an underground influential culture in Shakespeare's day, much as an interest in Communism and Socialism were underground and influential in Hollywood during the last century. I found this thinking very helpful playing Hamlet. It helped me to understand when to keep my cards to my chest and when to reveal my hand. Aspects of the text, which were previously just decoration or theatrical filler in a Stratfordian interpretation, became clues to underlying meaning. References to metals, the elements, the Greek gods, all became conscious and useful from the hand of a widely read and widely experienced author. The movement between desire, thought and action was now rounded with a stillness, a source. I learnt a lot about stillness. The soliloquies became much more vital turning points. You see, that kind of learning can be problematic to an editor who believes the actor from Stratford wrote the plays. Why bring it up and increase the gap between your author and his plays? Why is Bacon so rarely mentioned in footnotes of Shakespeare editions, though he wrote about many of the same matters, often employing parallel language?

So I went along a lot and to my utter surprise gradually became aware that the author of the plays seemed more like this man Francis Bacon than the man from Stratford. It was a very gradual change for me, but once that change had occurred then the additional force entered my playing imagination: these plays were a passionate revelation of a secret personal history, not just a commercial theatre writer's imagination. The potential for truthful human nature in the plays was greater and therefore the responsibility to be truthful in one's service of the plays greater. The humility of the author's mask was also thought provoking.

At that time, I didn't know about the Earl of Oxford or Mary Sidney. Now, of course, the whole question is exploding; there are so many candidates coming forward with interesting arguments. This is the situation at present. Each good piece of biographical research opens a window into the plays, so why not enjoy having a few biographical windows rather than just one. I don't know that I would be very upset if it was proved categorically that Francis Bacon had nothing to do with the plays. Oxford's case is very compelling. Francis would always remain a host or guide who led me to a deeper truth that I experience in the plays, whether he actually wrote them or not. William Shakspar also has a place as a guide or host during my younger years before I started to look more closely at the evidence. I certainly understand what it feels like to be attached to one candidate, but I feel right now I am very interested in and benefit from a number of different windows, particularly Baconian and Oxfordian research and research into the links between Mary Sidney and, for example John Webster.

William Leahy: When you look back at the time when you began to doubt that Shakespeare from Stratford was the author, how did it impact upon your profession, upon how you read and acted the plays?

Mark Rylance: I began to understand that there was a real human need behind the writing. There was a life that had been lived and that had been experienced and that someone was speaking from the heart. A voice of experience is so strong and my work changed with this realization. I started to be less ready to think that 'this is a bad bit of writing here' and 'this is a bit that I could muck about with' and change. Rather, I started to think that if I don't understand it and someone of the life experience and the learning of say, Oxford or Bacon or someone like that wrote it, then I have got some distance to go in terms of understanding it. So, I thought that maybe I cannot use this bit of text right now but I should not write it off. Earlier, I would have just cut it right away and maybe that was a healthy thing as a young person but later on I had much more respect and wonder. It just opened up the possibility for a lot more experience and book-learning behind the plays for me to draw on. I think it also encouraged me to be as bold as the author had been and to try to observe nature as well as the author had. These were not fantasy characters; they were drawn from real people around the author's life. They demonstrate huge knowledge and close observation, as well as imagination.

William Leahy: Are there specific works or acts or scenes or poems that you can remember changing with this realization? When you had this epiphany, if you like?

Mark Rylance: One example along that line is the end of *Tempest*. It is left for you as an actor to determine what happens between Prospero and his brother Antonio because Antonio does not speak; he can hit Prospero, he can leave the stage, he can embrace Prospero, he can cry, he can laugh. The author's attitude is perhaps informative in making such a choice. Should Fortinbras, at the end of *Hamlet*, machine gun Horatio or should he come on very sorrowfully and cry over Hamlet, or just really listen to every word Horatio has to say? There is a wide range of desperate and hopeful endings employed in productions. Are great liberties taken with Shakespeare's plays because the orthodox author is such a cipher? Perhaps that was the intention, of course! The play in the theatre should reflect the life outside the theatre at any given time. The acting company is ultimate author.

Some interpretations yield more, I feel. *Measure for Measure* is a classic case. It's a comedy but nowadays mostly played as a tragedy. Can Isabella love the Duke and, anyway what is he up to? What the hell is he up to in the whole play really? Now from my understanding of Bacon's imagination and concerns, it is unlikely that the Duke is just a sinister character who is there to patronize and viciously abuse society and Isabella. My interpretation is influenced by Bacon's writing about philanthropy and the difficulty of mercy and justice in society and the use of disguise and simulation to teach people through experience. The fifth act for me, playing the Duke, became a necessary public display of mercy by Isabella. Yes, it is very cruel to have her believe that her brother has been executed. But it was necessary to show the people how forgiving she could be, even in the suffering of that wrong. Isabella plays the fifth act in front of the whole of society – this relates to the problem that the Duke was having at the beginning; too much law has not worked and too much liberality has not worked. Having this woman who has been so clearly wronged by the judge come out in front of society and forgive this judge is the gamble that the Duke takes. He is not certain at all that she will forgive. But he knows that if she does it will achieve more than any law or any education programme. Thus, a public act of mercy is an incredible thing to do; not a staged, fake one but an actual one; the equivalent, though opposite effect of a public execution. I am not sure I would have come to that kind of interpretation without understanding Bacon and indeed I had an argument with the brilliant Simon McBurney, of Theatre de Complicite, who interpreted the play completely differently in the National Theatre and could not believe that Isabella could possibly have fallen in love or that the Duke could not be anything but a vicious tyrant – and for good reason from his point of view. But my authorship studies led me to a different view based on my understanding of Bacon's concerns for society and the text of the play. Both are viable. Obviously for me, the broadly philosophic one is closer to my understanding and closer to the author's description of the play as a comedy, in the classical sense.

William Leahy: How did this change in your views impact upon your career? You were the Artistic Director of the Globe for ten years, so how did your everyday Shakespearean life go ahead?

Mark Rylance: I had to do a lot of talking, a lot of trying to understand why people were occasionally so upset. I think that has become almost as fascinating as the authorship question itself. I had to proceed very patiently, make wider circles of understanding that embraced other views as well as my own view. It was good for me. If I had come in and said 'right I am not a Stratfordian and I am not going to have any Stratfordian directors here and all the busts are going to go from the front of the theatre', then it would have been outrageous. I would have got the sack and rightly so. By the way, James Shapiro has said in the *New Yorker* that I should never have been given the job because of my authorship doubts, despite his high respect for my work as an artist. It was frustrating to witness the kind of abuse and censorship allowed Stratfordians, while being suspected without warrant of such behaviour oneself. Even being careful, I experienced warnings from management, comments from staff that my views were inappropriate to my position and outright anger from academics. From the public I remember only curiosity and encouragement. I was conscious from the start that my role as Artistic Director made my words and actions more powerful in the community. I really didn't want to make anyone feel stupid or wrong because they held a different view on the authorship than I did. But I wanted the minority included. I wanted the individual welcomed and I wanted a spirit of enquiry and discussion at the Globe. That was the community I wanted to represent as Artistic Director.

Of course we are always revising our views on the character of an author like Shakespeare in little ways, that's part of the fun of it; a new portrait. But when you first change your mind away from the actor's story, towards a hidden author, there is a great river of justice you can jump into and it will carry you along in the swirling currents of emotion about the injustice that has been done to the true unrecognized author! When I first changed my mind in Stratford I invited the whole RSC acting company to the Swan Theatre and had my new friend Peter Dawkins from the Francis Bacon Research Trust come and talk to them. I thought it was so obvious and that everyone would change their minds. But, of course many were dreadfully upset. Some walked out of the meeting.

I encountered something that Shakespeare has embedded in us so deeply – our own image of who the author is. I know post-modern literary theory has tried to kill that image. Actually they seem to have released ever wilder enjoyment of that image by trying to kill it. I had to realize back at the RSC that many people who love Shakespeare have been personally touched, and affected by the words and stories. They feel they have been spoken to directly, have been in some way reflected; they have discovered something about themselves in the mirror of the plays. To be told that the mirror is two-way and a very conscious author is standing on the other side of the mirror rather than there being just an anonymous glass and silver manufacturer is part of the problem, part of the upset.

William Leahy: As well as the Shakespearean world that you inhabit you also inhabit this other world of quite popular culture acting with some of the big Hollywood stars. Have you ever discussed the authorship question with those sorts of actors?

Mark Rylance: No, I don't bring it up unless asked now. I do find a lot of actors actually very relaxed and open about it if the subject comes up, but I suppose the uptight ones avoid the subject with me. I don't know many Hollywood stars. Unfortunately, now, many will assume I know more about it than they do and they may be shy to raise the subject. I don't think it is all that important actually, but I think it's rather a wonderful subject. Because of the emotion and high profile but low danger of hurt other than to established patterns of thought, it makes a very useful model of change in a field of study. It is useful in observing what happens when orthodoxy gets embedded and doesn't move with the facts; any orthodoxy. We are facing so many orthodox views in so many fields of human endeavour that have fallen behind facts and need to revise their ground plans – economics and the limited resources of the earth, for example. I like hearing people's individual views and enthusiasm. I like opening any doorway into the plays. I love mystery too, and discovery.

William Leahy: Do you have a feeling that there might be more actors sympathetic to the authorship question out there, who just need to be prompted as it were?

Mark Rylance: I think a lot of people have not actually looked into it. They have other things to do. A lot of people have not read or heard the plays! That's all right. I think many more would be sympathetic to the authorship question if they looked into it, yes. I cannot see how anyone who has read Diana Price's *Shakespeare's Unorthodox Biography: New Evidence of an Authorship Problem* (2001) could not feel there is reason for doubt. It does not propose another candidate but rather sums up why there is a question about the Stratford man. Evidence that doesn't support his supposed life as a writer. She is particularly interesting on the *First Folio*, without the publication of which we wouldn't have 17 of the plays; 17 of the plays were not published in any form until the *Folio*! The main point that Diana Price makes so very well is that until the *Folio* appeared and people like Ben Jonson and Leonard Digges mentioned the Stratford monument in the preface, there was no direct connection between the name of the author Shakespeare and the actor from Stratford. Now that in itself might seem a slight thing but then when you look at the fact that he leaves no literary trail in his life, the *Folio* then becomes an incredibly important piece of evidence for the authorship of the man from Stratford. Without it, what would we have? Just to make this clear to you; the man from Stratford leaves no evidence of education; he leaves no record of correspondence especially concerning literary matters; he leaves no evidence of having been paid to write; he leaves no evidence of a direct relationship with a patron; he leaves no evidences of an original manuscript; he leaves no hand written inscriptions, receipts, letters and so on touching on literary matters; he leaves no commendatory verses or epigrams, either contributed or received; he leaves no miscellaneous records, for example, referred to personally as a writer in his lifetime; he is never referred to personally as a writer; he leaves no evidence of books owned, written in, borrowed or given and he leaves no notice at his death. Now 25 other writers of this period [noted in Diana Price's book] leave evidence in some or all of those categories; he is the only one who leaves no evidence in any. That's a very curious fact. So there's an incredible silence about him during his lifetime. Ben Jonson writes about all kinds of people for 18 years, but does not mention the man from Stratford. Jonson makes fun of someone who is *like* the man from Stratford in his satires, but he doesn't really come forward as this great champion of the author until the *Folio* and he leaves us two Shakespeares really; the author and the man.

Allied to this is another question. Why, I am often asked, was the true authorship kept a secret? Why is there no written evidence remaining to link the writers of these plays with their authorship? And how was it kept secret? Well, President Kennedy had affairs with women wherever he went. A lot of people knew about that but the press never talked about it, did they? He was the president, so you didn't do that. But, he was in the public eye all the time and yet it was a secret. Bacon did not even want his name on his scientific works initially; he was going to publish all his works under a mask as he loved disguise. There are also records at the time saying that there were many noble men at court who hid their writing or wrote under another name. It was a military age, a pressurized age, a secretive age. So there are a number of different reasons for such secrecy. Why and how it remained secret after all the characters had passed away is a good question. After Kennedy was no longer President, so to speak. My attention turns to Alexander Pope and David Garrick for that one, those who created the Stratford Festival and left us the strange Westminster monument.

Note

[1] This interview took place at the Globe Theatre, London on 1 November 2007.

Chapter 10

Dominic Dromgoole (Artistic Director, Globe Theatre, London)

Interviewed by William Leahy[1]

William Leahy: In your book *Will & Me: How Shakespeare Took Over My Life* (Dromgoole 2007), you are quite damming about Stratford-upon-Avon, about what it is and what it represents. What is your problem with Stratford?

Dominic Dromgoole: My first experience of Stratford was a hugely magical one. I went there with my Mother for a two-day visit to see a number of shows and I fell in love with the place. But with hindsight I realized that I thought it was magical only because I was eight or nine and, like every-body, there is a willingness to accept rubbish when you are so young. This feeling is great, of course, but as one gets older one sort of loses it forever. At that age a gift shop is full of extraordinary items that are magical and full of references to history. Anne Hathaway's cottage, which is obviously bogus as an adult, seemed like Doctor Who's Tardis and the Shakespeare Birthplace Trust seemed like the very centre of learning. And so on that first trip I obsessively combined Stratford with a time in my life which was magical. Later in my life, we would go to Stratford on school trips. We would arrive in Stratford car park and the teacher would stand up and make a speech about us being ambassadors for our school, that we should behave, be as good as possible, not to disgrace our school, to be there on time for the play and so on. We would say 'yes sir, yes sir' and then shoot straight past him to the pub and get drunk in the hour before we went in to see the show and then turn up and, more or less disrupt the whole thing. And, in response we would be seen as disrespectful to the very idea of Shakespeare. And this relates to my problem with Stratford. Yes, the plays are full of wise and intellectual language but they are also full of language that is very direct and funny and rude and alive. I felt that this distance between the two extremes was improper and felt that a lot of this was centred in Stratford at that time. I don't think it has always been the case for Stratford at all; I just think at that particular moment when I was experiencing it, it was.

William Leahy: In the book you are also fairly sceptical about academia and particularly about how literary theory is applied to Shakespeare. You have said that you feel academia 'builds walls'. What do you mean?

Dominic Dromgoole: I remember reading G. Wilson Knight when I was young and being hugely taken with his ideas. I was young, so I know this made him much more important for me, more alive for me. Then one gets to a certain age and one discovers that there is a sort of language and a sort of critical theory that is so deliberately obtuse that one really wonders who it is for. There is a wonderful book that came out in the 1980s called *Political Shakespeare* by Dollimore and Sinfield. Being the 1980s, the book was left wing and there were some fantastic thoughts in it, some fantastic shafts of wisdom. But often it was written in this language in which each of the authors strained to write in the most painfully tortured prose. The conscious use of such esoteric language seemed to revel in shutting out the less educated. It felt like bullying. Instant migraines followed on from trying to draw up its meaning as, for instance, this sentence: 'If we only talk of power producing the discourse of subversion we not only hypostatise power but also efface the cultural differences – and context – which the very process of containment presupposes' (Dollimore 1985: 12). That sentence should be shot for cruelty to the English language.

William Leahy: I believe that is Jonathan Dollimore.

Dominic Dromgoole: Hmm, yes.

William Leahy: Another problem that you articulate in your book is what you call 'the cultural arrogance which poisons Shakespeare and indeed much classical theatre' (Dromgoole 111). You seem to object to, shall we call it a 'bourgeois use' of Shakespeare. By that I mean the way Stratford uses him, the way academics use him. You seem to place those institutions very much in the middle classes where you feel they are doing something unjust, something wrong with Shakespeare.

Dominic Dromgoole: It is hard with Shakespeare because he was such a shape-shifter in the course of his own lifetime and his story is a funny one; it moves; it changes. His father was obviously socially ambitious and keen for position and money. His mother had connections to a high Catholic family. So there was social growth in the course of his own lifetime and then, for reasons we don't know or understand there was a sudden crash and his father lost his position. So he went from being, I imagine, not very well off to being quite grand and I have a personal image of his father in robes pushing Shakespeare in front of the Guildhall when Leicester's men or whoever came to play there. Then suddenly all of that was stripped away and you get this strange movement in Shakespeare's life. He came to London, and as far as we know he had very little money then and it is very hard to deny the fact that he was a greedy bastard; he liked money, he went after money. He bought land, often in dodgy circumstances, he bought big houses; he became very wealthy and it was obviously important to him. The amazing thing about Shakespeare in a way is how that story, the father-falling story, is such a classic paradigm for writers and especially for playwrights. It is a stunningly similar story to Chekov; his father was a rather busy, greedy shopkeeper and he rose socially and then he had a sort of collapse, a sort of nervous breakdown. It is the same story as Arthur Miller, whose father was a very wealthy man in New York and a proud patriot; and then he crashed with the depression and Arthur had to take over family responsibilities. It is the same story with Tom Stoppard. In some way the son acquires that entrepreneurial energy and acquires a desire to look after the family and to tend to it and in some ways that entrepreneurial energy is transformed into a desire to make plays. So I do think it is very difficult to nail Shakespeare down to a particular class. People want him to be one particular thing; they will say he was a working class hero and wrote from that perspective or that he was greedy for money and he fell in with aristocrats and became an aristocrat himself. But then somebody with those sympathies could never have written *Timon of Athens* or *King Lear*. So he was very liquid in his sensibility and too fast-moving for anyone to categorize him.

William Leahy: Is that why you call him an 'instinctive, impulsive creative animal'? (240).

Dominic Dromgoole: Yes he was; he was a playwright. Playwrights like writing, they like writing fast, they like creating plays, they like making drama. First and foremost Shakespeare is a playwright and a poet but he sat there and he wrote plays. My conviction is that he wrote them fast. The best playwrights do write plays fast. What he brought to his plays, why they were so extraordinary, why they are so head and shoulders and full body above everything else is because of a peculiar inheritance in them of a variety of factors; personal factors, political factors, historical factors that combine at that moment to sort of give him the ability to write this extraordinary stuff. He had this amazing ear; he could hear a variety of things and it all came to him and he kept it. He was a sponge in that way. You can romanticize it by saying that he is an automatic writer but it is not quite that easy; it is never easy but he was certainly an instinctive writer rather than a deliberate writer.

William Leahy: In the book you do not really deal with the Shakespeare authorship question in any real sense but there is one paragraph that refers to you visiting Stratford at the age of ten:

> The historical mysteries of Stratford were fuel for that fantasy. The lack of clues about Shakespeare, and the different versions of what his life may have been, impressed themselves on me. His tantalising presence, so immanent and so evanescent at the same time, was a gripping, unsolved crime. It is the same detective story which still impels legions of eccentric academics to propose that Shakespeare was not Shakespeare at all, but a conglomeration of any other notable Elizabethans – Frances Bacon, the Earl of Oxford, Christopher Marlowe – who can be dragooned in to cover their blinkered embarrassment that the greatest genius of our species was the son of an illiterate glover. I knew nothing of the authorship question at the time, but could see the lack of real clues required the diligent attention of a master sleuth. I was on the case. Beyond every corner we turned, beneath every table we sat at, behind every bush in the gardens, there may be some little historical memento which could sharpen this blurry image. (45)

You seem to acknowledge in this passage that there is some kind of problem matching what we know of Shakespeare and the plays. Do you recognize some sort of problem here?

Dominic Dromgoole: No, I don't think there is any problem in matching Shakespeare and the plays. I think there is a rich and fantastic series of connections between Shakespeare and the plays which I find ever more rewarding the more I work on them. I completely agree that Shakespeare is elusive and that he will always be elusive. I went to a terrific exhibition at the National Portrait Gallery to see the collection of different portraits of him and yet still came out not quite knowing what he looked like or who he was or whether he was a bank manager, a poet or a lover; it seemed Shakespeare sort of evanesced before your eyes while you were there. Whenever you do try and get a fix on him and say 'that's what he was', 'that's what he felt', 'that's what he thought'; you are always deluding yourself if you say it with too much conviction because he will trip you up. So to lock him down and give him a rigorous biography, which I think certain biographers do – this happened, that happened, it's exactly like this, it's exactly like that – one just thinks, 'well come on, you know there is room for doubt there, there are questions there'. I think in some ways Shakespeare wanted that, I think he wanted to be elusive. I don't think, if he was around today he would be at premieres, be giving television interviews, be writing articles for the newspapers about the meaning of his plays. I think he liked to push his stuff out and let it live rather than saying 'look at me, I'm a writer'. He was more 'look at the play'. So Shakespeare as a man will always be elusive and always has been. If you go looking for him you are never going to find him.

William Leahy: You have been Artistic Director of the Globe for over three years. Has the authorship question surfaced in any of your dealings? If it has, how have you dealt with it, how have you negotiated it?

Dominic Dromgoole: There was this phony war between me and Mark [Rylance] because people were always picking on Mark about his views. Mark and I sat down and had a very wonderful, civilized, delightful series of conversations and set out our differences and sort of understood where we disagreed and where we agreed and where we thought it was interesting. So, you know, the existence of the relationship between the Shakespearean Authorship Trust[2] and the Globe has come up occasionally, and we have to keep rehashing it and so on, but I am delighted that the questions are still out there, for the search to go on and for people to find some kind of understanding. To shut it out and say it is wrong to even think about it – which is what you get from Stratford to some extent – is a shame, because whether you agree with it or disagree, it is a form of historical inquiry; it does throw fresh light on the period, a fresh light on the plays and it is worthwhile just for that. As I said, Shakespeare, the Stratford Shakespeare will always remain elusive and will always remain strange and always remain mysterious and I think it is a healthy line of enquiry to try and find out more about him. I enjoy the sort of weird forensic detail of, for example *The Lodger* (2007), the Charles Nicholl book which is a great re-creation of that moment in London. It is obsessive about re-creating the texture of that life. It is important to dig as hard as one can but one has to acknowledge the fact that Shakespeare is never going to be there and he is never going to be there in a way that you want him to be there. In that sense, I share Mark's opinion; there is nothing wrong with digging because it throws up an immense amount of historical insight about that time and one can see the plays through the prism of that inquiry whether one agrees with it or not.

William Leahy: So you do not get any actors coming up to you and saying 'you know, listen, I think we need to think about this authorship question thing'?

Dominic Dromgoole: No; in three years, one hundred and twenty actors a year, three hundred and sixty actors – not one. It just does not occur.

William Leahy: The Shakespeare canon is an enormous and multifaceted beast. Do you have doubts yourself about any of the works? Do you have doubts about certain sections of certain works?

Dominic Dromgoole: Oh yes. There is a lot of *Timon of Athens*, for example which looks very hybrid and very mixed and there is the sort of visceral, satirical and silly knock about energy in that which is much more Middleton than it is Shakespeare. Then if you look at 'The Scottish Play', it has a burst of Middleton in the middle of it. If you look at the earlier works one gets a sense of 'you do this bit, he does that bit'; a feeling that sections are portioned out to different people. So there is certainly a degree of collaboration.

William Leahy: But there are no plays you feel are the work of a different author?

Dominic Dromgoole: Entirely, no. I think you see the presence of Shakespeare rippling through *Timon of Athens*, because you can see the slight, impressionistic sketch for *Lear* and there is a relationship between the two. There is a dialogue between the two and you can see shades of Shakespeare here and there. So I do not think there are any plays that are entirely by someone else.

William Leahy: I am sure that you have heard of the theory that whoever wrote the plays must have visited Italy because so much of Italy appears in the plays. What is your feeling about that?

Dominic Dromgoole: I find it very tempting and very hard to deny. I am tempted by the idea that he either had an extraordinary understanding of people he knew or encountered or he had been on a trip and set something of this in his imagination. Because it is not like other places in the plays where you can see that he has read something or cobbled together a bit of knowledge from here, there and wherever; there is this sort of obsession with that small triangle of Italy, that is true. So, I find it very hard to deny that he probably did have some personal knowledge of Italy because of his degree of obsession with the place and his knowledge of it. That said, I don't think he went to every single place he wrote about. He wrote in a spirit of imagination rather than in a spirit of reportage.

William Leahy: Why do you think so many people believe that someone other than Shakespeare wrote the plays; what drives them to think in that way?

Dominic Dromgoole: I think there are a variety of reasons. I think the moment that something becomes that big and has that much orthodoxy attached to it there is a hunger and desire to question it. Shakespeare has that importance and thus will attract such criticism. I like active enquiry,

I applaud it; I think it is great. The only thing I do have a problem with is the stuff that you can get thrown at you which is, quite frequently along the lines of, 'he could never have written those plays because of the family he came from, because he was not from a certain class and because he was not a member of court; how could he understand politics, how could he understand how people in such circles spoke?' and so on. That line of argument I do have a problem with because it runs counter to my own understanding of writing and my own understanding of writers. It runs counter to all my own instincts regarding art and artists. If you go back through the history of playwrighting, there have not actually been that many aristocratic playwrights; the number is very small. So when I hear that, I do have a resistance to it. If people say let's throw this up in the air and question it I think that is fine, that is good.

William Leahy: In the final section of your book you describe walking from Stratford to London, with various people. In this section, your conceptualization of Shakespeare comes through very clearly in that you see him as an artist immersed in the natural environment, the English landscape, tied to ordinary people and expressing a kind of earthy Englishness. What is it that provides you with that conceptualization? Is it the works, is it what you know of Shakespeare's life or is it a mixture of the two? And going on from that, do you think that if a number of the works were not written by this man it would impinge upon that conceptualization that you have?

Dominic Dromgoole: It is the works and it is what I know of the life; we all make our own Shakespeares, don't we? We all conceive our own Shakespeares which are, funnily enough quite close to us and funnily enough quite close to our image of ourselves. In the book, I quote the end of Anthony Burgess' book, which I still think is one of the best biographies about Shakespeare. One of his final paragraphs is an exquisite bit of writing about how when we look at Shakespeare we are looking at ourselves and we have to face up to that. So as well as the work and as well as the life there is what I have taken from Shakespeare, how it has affected me and how it has made me. So inevitably it is deeply subjective. I think the natural thing just comes from that walk and it just comes from that landscape. There is something about that landscape that is hugely affecting and very engaging and very, for want of a better word, human in that it is not grand like the Highlands, the Himalayas or the Rocky Mountains. It is not overpowering or awesome, so that you feel you are a tiny part of this massive creation. There is something about those hills, those curves, those bends and those twists and little churches, small villages and the little places to stop where the human relates to those landscapes. You can walk for a day or two days and find a hill and you can look back and see a house you started out from. You constantly see people working the earth and you can see people defined against a stream or a tree or whatever and there's a relationship between them not being dwarfed by it; they are in some sort of dynamic relationship with the landscape. That, for me, Shakespeare grew up in and I think it did affect him and I think he has got dirty fingers and his body can be found in the soil. One way or another he is not disconnected to the natural world. So that idea of Shakespeare, which to a large extent was already three quarters formed in my head was reinforced by trudging through that landscape.

Notes

[1] This interview took place at the Globe Theatre, London on 26 November 2008.
[2] From the website of this organization at www.shakespeareanauthorshiptrust.org; 'Our objective is the advancement of learning with particular reference to the social, political, and literary history of England in the 16th and 17th centuries and the authorship of the literary works that appeared under the name of William Shakespeare'. Mark Rylance is Chairman of this organization, which does not argue for any particular candidate but recognizes a problem with Shakespeare as the author.

Bibliography

Ackroyd, P. (2005), *Shakespeare: The Biography*. London: Chatto & Windus.

'Actors question Bard's authorship'. (9 September 2007), http://news.bbc.co.uk/go/pr/-/1/hi/6985917.stm. Accessed 23 April 2009.

Alford, C. F. (2001), *Whistleblowers: Broken Lives and Organizational Power*. Ithaca, London: Cornell University Press.

Anderson, M. (2005), *Shakespeare by Another Name: The Life of Edward De Vere, Earl of Oxford, the Man who was Shakespeare*. New York: Gotham Books.

Appleton, E. (2001), *Anatomy of the Marprelate Controversy 1588–1596: Retracing Shakespeare's Identity and that of Martin Marprelate*. Lewiston: Edwin Mellon Press.

Asquith, C. (2003), 'Oxford University and *Love's Labour's Lost*', in *Shakespeare and the Culture of Christianity in Early Modern Europe*, eds Dennis Taylor and David N. Beauregard. New York: Fordham University Press, pp. 80–102.

—(2005), *Shadowplay: The Hidden Beliefs and Coded Politics of William Shakespeare*. New York: Public Affairs.

Aubrey, J. (1958), *Aubrey's Brief Lives*, ed. Oliver Lawson Dick. London: Secker and Warburg.

Auchter, D. (1998), 'Did Shakespeare write Shakespeare? A bibliography of the authorship controversy', *Bulletin of Bibliography*, 55, 63–72.

Aune, M. G. (2006), 'Crossing the border: Shakespeare biography, academic celebrity, and the reception of *Will in the World*', *Borrowers and Lenders*, 2(2), n.p.

Bacon, D. (1856), 'William Shakespeare and his plays: An inquiry concerning them', *Putnam's Monthly Magazine*, 7(37), 1–19.

—(1857), *The Philosophy of the Plays of Shakspere Unfolded*. London: Groombridge & Sons.

Barthes, R. (1988; 1997), 'The death of the author', in *Twentieth-Century Literary Theory*, ed. K. Newton. London: Macmillan.

Bate, J. (1986), *Shakespeare and the English Romantic Imagination*. Clarendon: Oxford.

—(1997), *The Genius of Shakespeare*. London: Picador.

—(1998), *The Genius of Shakespeare*. London: Picador.

—(2002), 'An interview with Jonathan Bate', *Frontline: Much Ado about Something*. Available at: www.pbs.org/wgbh/pages/frontline/shows/muchado/forum/bate.html.

—(2007), *Soul of the Age: A Biography of the Mind of William Shakespeare*. London: Random House.

Baxendale, S. (2004), 'Memories aren't made of this: Amnesia at the movies', *British Medical Journal*, 329, 1480–83.

Belsey, C. (2009), 'The death of the reader', *Textual Practice*, 23(2), 201–14.

—(1985), *The Subject of Tragedy: Identity and Difference in Renaissance Drama*. London: Methuen.

Benjamin, W. (1992), 'Theses on the Philosophy of History', in *Illuminations*, ed. Hannah Arendt, trans. Harry Zohn. London: Fontana Press, pp. 245–55.

Bennett, A. (1995), *Keats, Narrative and Audience: The Posthumous Life of Writing*. Cambridge: Cambridge University Press.

—(2005), *The Author*. London: Routledge.

Berney, C. (2008), *De Vere Society Newsletter*, 15(3).

Blakemore, E. G. (ed.) (1974), *The Riverside Shakespeare*. Boston: Houghton Mifflin.

Borch-Jacobsen, M. (1989a), *The Freudian Subject*, trans. Catherine Porter, London: Macmillan.

—(1989b), 'Hypnosis in psychoanalysis', trans. Angela Brewer, *Representations*, 27 (Summer 1989), 92–110.

—(1990), 'Talking cure', *Oxford Literary Review*, 12, 31–55.

Borges, J. L. (1985), 'Everything and nothing', in *Labyrinths*, trans. James E. Irby. London: Penguin, 284–85.

Brink, J. R. (1997), 'Appropriating the author of *The Faerie Queene*. The attribution of the *View of the Present State of Ireland* and *A Brief Note of Ireland* to Edmund Spenser', in *Soundings of Things Done: Essays in Early Modern Literature in Honor of S. K. Heninger Jr* eds P. E. Medine and J. Wittreich. London: Associated University Presses, pp. 93–136.

—(1994), 'Constructing the *View of the Present State of Ireland*', *Spenser Studies*, 11, 203–28.

Brooke, A. (1562; 1978), *Brooke's 'Romeus and Juliet,' Being the Original of Shakespeare's 'Romeo and Juliet'*, ed. J. J. Munro. London: Chatto and Windus.

Brown, P. (1982), *Society and the Holy in Late Antiquity*. London: Faber and Faber.

Bryson, B. (2007), *Shakespeare*. London: Atlas Books.

Burgess, A. (1972), *Shakespeare*. Harmondsworth: Penguin Books

Burrow, C. (2005), 'Who wouldn't buy it?', Review of *Will in the World*, by Stephen Greenblatt. *London Review of Books*, 27(2), 20 January, 9–11.

Carlson, L. H. (1981), *Martin Marprelate, Gentleman: Master Job Throckmorton Laid Open in his Colours*. San Marino: Huntington.

Certeau, M. De. (1997), *Culture in the Plural*. trans. Tom Conley. Minneapolis: University of Minnesota Press.

—(2002), *The Practice of Everyday Life* (new edition). Berkeley, CA: University of California Press.

Chambers, E. K. (1930), *William Shakespeare: A Study of Facts and Problems*. 2 vols. Oxford: Oxford University Press.

Chandler, D. (2003), 'Historicizing difference: Anti-Stratfordians and the academy', *Elizabethan Review*. Available at: www.jmucci.com/ER/articles/chandler.htm.

Chaplin, C. (2003), *My Autobiography*. London: Penguin.

Chillington, C. A. (1980), 'Playwrights at work: Henslowe's, not Shakespeare's *Book of Sir Thomas More*', *English Literary Renaissance*. 10(3), (Fall 1980), 439–79.

Crawford, R. (2005), 'The Bard: Ossian, Burns, and the shaping of Shakespeare', in *Shakespeare and Scotland*, eds. W. Maley and A. Murphy. Manchester: Manchester University Press, pp. 124–40.

Coleridge, S. T. (1956–1973), *Collected Letters of Samuel Taylor Coleridge*, ed. Earl Leslie
    Griggs, 6 vols. Oxford: Oxford University Press.
—(1957–2002), *The Notebooks of Samuel Taylor Coleridge*, 5 vols., ed. Kathleen Coburn.
    London: Routledge and Kegan Paul.
—(1969), *The Friend*, ed. Barbara E. Rooke. London: Routledge and Kegan
    Paul.
—(1983), *Biographia Literaria*, ed. James Engell and W. Jackson Bate. London:
    Routledge and Kegan Paul.
—(1987), *Lectures on Literature 1808–1819*, 2 vols., ed. R. A. Foakes. London:
    Routledge and Kegan Paul.
Collinson, P. (2004), 'Job Throckmorton', in *Oxford Dictionary of National Biography*,
    ed. H. C. G. Matthew and Brian Harrison. Oxford: Oxford University Press,
    pp. 54, 691–92.
Crinkley, R. (1985), 'New perspectives on the authorship question', *Shakespeare
    Quarterly*, 36(4), 515–22.
Cross, C. (2004), 'John Udall', in *Oxford Dictionary of National Biography*, ed. H. C. G.
    Matthew and Brian Harrison. Oxford: Oxford University Press, pp. 55, 849–50.
Dalby, A. (2006), *Rediscovering Homer: Inside the Origins of the Epic*. New York:
    Norton.
Darwin, C. (1998), *The Origin of Species*, ed. Gillian Beer. Oxford: Oxford University
    Press.
Dawkins, P. (2004), *The Shakespeare Enigma: Unravelling the Story of the Two Poets*.
    London: Polair Publishing.
DeLillo, D. (1999), *Underworld*. London: Picador.
Derrida, J. (1977), 'Limited Inc', trans. Samuel Weber, in *Glyph*, 2, 162–254.
—(1979), *Spurs: Nietzsche's Styles / Eperons: Les Styles de Nietzsche*, trans. Barbara
    Harlow. Chicago: University of Chicago Press.
—(1981), 'Plato's Pharmacy', *Dissemination*, trans. Barbara Johnson. Chicago:
    University of Chicago Press, pp. 61–171.
—(1982), 'Signature event context', *Margins of Philosophy*, trans. Alan Bass. Chicago:
    University of Chicago Press, pp. 307–30.
—(1984a), *Signéponge / Signsponge*, trans. Richard Rand. New York: Columbia
    University Press.
—(1984b), 'No Apocalypse, not now (full speed ahead, seven missiles, seven mis-
    sives)', trans. Catherine Porter and Philip Lewis, *Diacritics*, 14(2), (Summer
    1984), 20–31.
—(1984c), 'My Chances / *Mes Chances*: A Rendezvous with Some Epicurean
    Stereophonies', eds, Joseph H. Smith and William Kerrigan, *Taking Chances:
    Derrida, Psychoanalysis, and Literature*. London: Johns Hopkins University Press,
    pp. 1–32.
—(1985), *The Ear of the Other: Otobiography, Transference, Translation*, trans. Peggy
    Kamuf. New York: Schocken Books.
—(1986a), *Mémoires: for Paul de Man*, trans, Cecile Lindsay, Jonathan Culler and
    Eduardo Cadava. New York: Columbia University Press.
—(1986b), 'Shibboleth', trans. Joshua Wilner, *Midrash and Literature*, eds
    Geoffrey H. Hartman and Sanford Budick. New Haven: Yale University Press,
    pp. 307–47.

—(1986c), *Glas*, trans. John P. Leavey Jr, and Richard Rand. London: University of Nebraska Press.

—(1987), *The Post Card: From Socrates to Freud and Beyond*, trans. Alan Bass. London: Chicago University Press.

—(1988), 'Telepathy', trans. Nicholas Royle, *Oxford Literary Review*, 10, 3–41.

—(1988), *Signéponge / Signsponge*, trans. Richard Rand. New York: Columbia University Press.

—(1990a), *Of Grammatology*, trans. Gayatri Chakravorty Spivak. Baltimore: Johns Hopkins University Press.

—(1990b), *Glas*, trans. John P. Leavey Jr. and Richard Rand. Lincoln: University of Nebraska Press.

—(2005), 'Justices,' trans. Peggy Kamuf, *Critical Inquiry* 31, 689–721.

—(2007), 'Geopsychoanalysis: "and the rest of the world"', in *Psyche: Inventions of the Other, Volume I*, trans. Peggy Kamuf, ed. Peggy Kamuf and Elizabeth Rottenberg. Stanford: Stanford University Press, pp. 318–43.

—(1992), 'Aphorism Countertime', trans. Nicholas Royle, *Derrida on Literature*, ed. Derek Attridge. New York: Routledge, pp. 414–34.

—(1992a), '"This strange institution called Literature": An interview with Jacques Derrida', in *Acts of Literature*, ed. D. Attridge. London: Routledge, pp. 33–75.

—(1992b), 'Aphorism countertime', in *Acts of Literature*, ed. D. Attridge. London: Routledge, pp. 416–33.

—(1993), *Specters of Marx: The State of the Debt, the Work of Mourning, and the New International*, trans. P. Kamuf. London, Routledge.

—(1995a), *The Gift of Death*, trans. D. Wills. Chicago and London: University of Chicago Press.

—(1995b), *Points . . . Interviews, 1974–1994*, trans. P. Kamuf, ed. E. Weber. Stanford: Stanford University Press.

—(1998), *Monolingualism of the Other; or, The Prosthesis of Origin*, trans. P. Mensah. Stanford: Stanford University Press.

Dobson, M. (1992), *The Making of the National Poet: Shakespeare, Adaptation and Authorship, 1660–1769*. Oxford: Clarendon Press.

Dobson, M. and Wells, S. (2001), *The Oxford Companion to Shakespeare*. Oxford: Oxford University Press.

Dollimore, J. (1985), 'Introduction: Shakespeare, cultural materialism and the new historicism', in *Political Shakespeare: New Essays in Cultural Materialism*, eds Dollimore, Jonathan and Sinfield, Alan. Manchester: Manchester University Press.

Donadio, R. (2005), 'Who owns Shakespeare?', *The New York Times*, 23 January 2005. Available at: http://query.nytimes.com/gst/fullpage.html?res=9C07EFD81738F 930A15752C0A9639C8B63&sec=&spon=&pagewanted=all. Accessed 29 April 2009.

Dromgoole, D. (2007), *Will & Me: How Shakespeare Took Over My Life*. London: Penguin Books Ltd.

Duncan-Jones, K. (2004), 'Will-o'-the wisp forever', Review of *Will in the World*, by Stephen Greenblatt. *The Spectator*, 9 October, 54.

Eccles, M. (1944), 'Elizabethan Edmund Spensers', *Modern Language Quarterly*, 5(4), 413–27.

Eco, U. (1989), *Foucault's Pendulum*, trans. William Weaver. London: Secker and Warburg.

Edwards, Rev. F. (2001), 'Preface', in Elizabeth Appleton, *Anatomy of the Marprelate Controversy 1588–1596: Retracing Shakespeare's Identity and that of Martin Marprelate.* Lewiston: Edwin Mellon Press, xliii–lvii.

Felperin, H. (1991), 'Bardolatry Then and Now', Jean I. Marsden, ed., *The Appropriation of Shakespeare: Post-Renaissance Reconstructions of the Works and the Myth.* New York: Harvester Wheatsheaf, pp. 129–44.

Forrest, H. T. S. (1920), *The Five Authors of Shakespeare's Sonnets.* London: Chapman & Dodd.

Foster, D. W. (2002), 'In the name of the author', *New Literary History*, 33, 375–96.

Foucault, M. (1980). 'What is an author?', in *Textual Strategies: Perspectives in Post-Structuralist Criticism*, ed. J. Harari. London: Methuen, pp. 141–60.

—(1977), *Language, Counter-Memory, Practice: Selected Essays and Interviews*, ed. D. F. Bouchard, trans. D. F. Bouchard and S. Simon. Ithaca, NY: Cornell University Press.

—(1987), 'Nietzsche, genealogy, history', *The Foucault Reader.* Ed. Paul Rabinow. Harmondsworth: Penguin Books, pp. 76–100.

Fowler, A. (2005), 'Enter speed', Review of *Will in the World*, by Stephen Greenblatt. *Times Literary Supplement*, 4 February, 3–5.

Freud, E. L. (ed.) (1961), *Letters of Sigmund Freud 1873–1939*, trans. Tania and James Stem. London: Hogarth Press.

Freud, S. and Zweig, A. (1968), *Briefweschel.* Frankfurt am Main: S. Fischer Verlag.

—(1970), *The Letters of Sigmund Freud and Arnold Zweig*, ed. Ernest L. Freud, trans. Professor and Mrs. W. D. Robson-Scott. London: Hogarth.

—(ed.) (1970), *The Letters of Sigmund Freud & Arnold Zweig*, trans. Prof. and Mrs. W. D. Robson-Scott. London: Hogarth Press and the Institute of Psycho-Analysis.

Freud, S. (1950), *Die Traumdeutung.* Wien: Franz Detiche.

—(1973–1786), *The Pelican Freud Library*, trans. James Strachey, Alix Strachey, Alan Tyson, eds. James Strachey, Angela Richards, Alan Tyson, Albert Dickson. 15 vols. Harmondsworth: Penguin.

—(1982), *The Interpretation of Dreams*, trans. James Strachey. London: George Allen and Unwin.

Friedman, W. F. and Friedman, E. S. (1957), *The Shakespearean Ciphers Examined: An Analysis of Cryptographic Systems Used as Evidence that Some Author Other than William Shakespeare Wrote the Plays Commonly Attributed to Him.* Cambridge: Cambridge University Press.

Garber, M. (1987), *Shakespeare's Ghost Writers: Literature as Uncanny Causality.* London: Methuen.

—(2008), *Profiling Shakespeare.* New York and London: Routledge.

Gaston, S. (2007a), 'Enter TIME', in *Starting With Derrida: Plato, Aristotle and Hegel.* London: Continuum, pp. 60–80.

—(2007b), 'Herodotus: Almost pre-Socratic', in *Starting With Derrida: Plato, Aristotle and Hegel.* London: Continuum, pp. 25–37.

—(2007c), 'Starting with Plato', in *Starting With Derrida: Plato, Aristotle and Hegel.* London: Continuum, pp. 3–24.

Geary, P. J. (1988), *Before France and Germany: The Creation and Transformation of the Merovingian World*. New York and Oxford: Oxford University Press.

Good, J. M. (1981), 'William Taylor, Robert Southey and the word autobiography'. *The Wordsworth Circle* 12, (2), 125–7.

Grazia, M. De. (1991), *Shakespeare Verbatim: The Reproduction of Authenticity and the 1790 Apparatus*. Oxford: Clarendon Press.

Graziosi, B. (2002), *Inventing Homer: The Early Reception of Epic*. Cambridge: Cambridge University Press.

Greenblatt, S. (1973), *Sir Walter Ralegh: The Renaissance Man and his Roles*. New Haven: Yale University Press.

—(1980), *Renaissance Self-Fashioning: From More to Shakespeare*. Chicago: University of Chicago Press.

—(1985), 'Shakespeare and the Exorcists', in *Shakespeare and the Question of Theory*, eds P. Parker and G. Hartman. London: Methuen, pp. 163–87.

—(1988), *Shakespearean Negotiations*. Oxford: Clarendon.

—(1994), '"Intensifying the surprise as well as the school": Stephen Greenblatt interviewed by Noel King'. *Textual Practice*, 8(1), 114–27.

—(2001), *Hamlet in Purgatory*. Princeton: Princeton University Press.

—(2004), *Will in the World: How Shakespeare Became Shakespeare*. New York: Norton.

—(4 Sept 2005) 'Letters', *New York Times*.

Greene, R. (1592), *Greene's Groats-worth of Wit*. Transcribed by Risa S. Bear, *Renascence Editions*, August 2000, from the text of the Wright edition of 1592 (S.T.C. No.12245)

Greengrass, Paul. (2004), dir., *The Bourne Supremacy*. USA; Universal.

—(2007), dir., *The Bourne Ultimatum*. USA; Universal.

Greenwood, Sir G. (1908), *The Shakespeare Problem Restated*. London: John Lane.

Grillo, E. (1949), *Shakespeare and Italy*. Glasgow: Glasgow University Press.

Grivelet, M. (1985), 'A Portrait of the Artist as Proteus', Kenneth Muir, ed., *Interpretations of Shakespeare: British Academy Shakespeare Lectures*. Oxford: Clarendon, pp. 27–46.

Grossman, M. (2009), 'Whose life is it anyway? Shakespeare's prick', *Textual Practice*, 23(2), 229–46.

Han, Y. (2001), *Romantic Shakespeare: From Stage to Page*. Madison: Farleigh Dickinson.

Hazlitt, W. (1998), 'On Genius and Common Sense: The Same Subject Continued', *Table Talk* (1821), in Duncan Wu, ed., *The Selected Writings of William Hazlitt*, 9 vols. London: Pickering and Chatto, 1998), vol. 6, pp. 36–43.

Heller, A. (1993), *A Philosophy of History in Fragments*. Chichester: Blackwell.

Herford, C. H. and Simpson, P. (eds) (1925–1952), *Ben Jonson*. Oxford: Oxford University Press.

Hoffman, C. (1955), *The Murder of the Man Who Was Shakespeare*. London: Max Parrish.

Holderness, G. (ed.) (1988), *The Shakespeare Myth*. Manchester: Manchester University Press.

—(2001), *Cultural Shakespeare: Essays in the Shakespeare Myth*. Hatfield: University of Hertfordshire Press.

Honan, P. (1998), *Shakespeare: A Life*. Oxford: Oxford University Press.

Honigmann, E. J. A. (1998), *Shakespeare: The 'Lost' Years.* Manchester: Manchester University Press.

Hopkins, G. M. (1996), *Selected Poetry*, ed. Catherine Phillips. Oxford: Oxford University Press.

Hume, R. D. (1997), 'Before the Bard: "Shakespeare" in early eighteenth-century London', *English Literary History*, 64(1), 41–75.

James, B. and Rubinstein, W. (2005), *The Truth Will Out: Unmasking the Real Shakespeare.* London: Pearson Longman.

Jans, B. (2001), *Artquakes and Vincent Van Gogh.* Weybridge: Pillar Publications.

—(2003), *Artquakes – Aftermath.* Weybridge: Pillar Publications.

Jenkyns, R. (2004), 'Bad will hunting', Review of *Will in the World*, by Stephen Greenblatt. *The New Republic*, 22 November, 21–4.

Johnson, S. (ed.) (1765), *The Plays of William Shakespeare in Eight Volumes.* London: J. & R. Tonson

Johnson, H. (1910) *Did the Jesuits Write Shakespeare?* Chicago

Jones, E. (1957) *Sigmund Freud: Life and Work.* vol. 3, London: Hogarth Press.

Jonson, B. (1875), *The Works of Ben Jonson*, ed. William Gifford. 9 vols, London: Bickers and Son.

Joyce, J. (1969), *A Portrait of the Artist as a Young Man.* Harmondsworth: Penguin.

—(1974), *Ulysses.* Harmondsworth: Penguin.

Joyce, J. (1992), *Ulysses*, Introduction. Declan Kiberd. London: Penguin.

Keats, J. (1958), *The Letters of John Keats*, ed. Hyder Edward Rollins, 2 vols. Cambridge [MA]: Harvard University Press.

Knapp, J. (2005), 'What is a co-author?', *Representations*, 89, 180–99.

Kurtz, L. (1983), 'The politics of heresy', *The American Journal of Sociology*, 88, 1085–115.

Lacan, J. (1977a), 'Desire and the interpretation of desire in *Hamlet*', trans. James Hulbert, *Yale French Studies*, 55/56, 11–52.

—(1977b), in *The Four Fundamental Concepts of Psycho-Analysis*, ed. Miller Jacques-Alain. trans. Alan Sheridan. London: Hogarth Press.

Lake, P. and Questier, M. (2002), *The Antichrist's Lewd Hat: Protestants, Papists and Players in Post-Reformation England.* New Haven: Yale University Press.

LaPorte, C. (2007), 'The Bard, the Bible, and the Victorian Shakespeare question', *English Literary History*, 74, 609–28.

Lee, S. (1898), *A Life of William Shakespeare.* London: Spottiswood.

Lehmann, C. (2001), 'Strictly Shakespeare? Dead letters, ghostly fathers, and the cultural pathology of authorship in Baz Luhrmann's *William Shakespeare's Romeo + Juliet*'. *Shakespeare Quarterly*, 52(2), 189–221.

Liman, Doug (2002), dir., *The Bourne Identity.* USA: Universal.

Lohman, F. Louise W. M. Buisman-de Savornin (1963), *Wie was Shakespeare.* H. J. Paris.

Looney, J. T. (1920), *'Shakespeare' Identified in Edward de Vere, 17th Earl of Oxford.* London: Cecil Palmer.

Lukacher, N. (1986), *Primal Scenes: Literature, Philosophy, Psychoanalysis.* Ithaca, NY: Cornell University Press.

Madden, J. (1998), dir., *Shakespeare In Love.* USA. Miramax.

Mak, G. (2006), *In Europa.* Amsterdam: Atlas.

Maley, W. (1995), 'Britannia major: Writing and Unionist identity', in *Contemporary Writing and National Identity*, eds T. Hill and W. Hughes. Bath: Sulis Press, 46–53.

—(1999), 'Spectres of Engels', in *Ghosts: Deconstruction, Psychoanalysis, History*, eds P. Buse and A. Stott. London: Macmillan, pp. 23–49.

Malim, R. (ed.) (2004), *Great Oxford: Essays on the Life and Work of Edward De Vere, 17th Earl of Oxford.* Tunbridge Wells: Parapress Ltd.

Malone, E. (ed.) (1790), *William Shakespeare: Plays and Poems.* London: J. Rivington & Sons.

Márquez, G. G. (1991), *The General in his Labryinth*, trans. Edith Grossman. London: Johnathan Cape.

Marowitz, C. (2005), 'Stephen Greenblatt's *Will in the World*'. *Swans Commentary*, 25 April.

Meres, F. (1598; 1938), *Palladis Tamia*, ed. Don Cameron Allen. New York: Scholars' Facsimiles and Reprints.

McGinn, D. J. (1966), *John Penry and the Marprelate Controversy.* New Brunswick: Rutgers University Press.

Michell, J. (2000), *Who wrote Shakespeare?* London: Thames and Hudson.

Middlebrook, D. (2006), 'The role of the narrator in literary biography', *South Central Review*, 23.3: 5–18.

Miller, J.-A. (ed.) (1977), *The Four Fundamental Concepts of Psycho-Analysis*, trans. Alan Sheridan. London: Hogarth Press.

Miller, J. H. (1963), *The Disappearance of God: Five Nineteenth Century Writers.* Cambridge: Belknap.

Miller, P. N. (2007), ed., *Momigliano and Antiquarianism: Foundations of the Modern Cultural Sciences.* Toronto: Toronto University Press.

Momigliano, A. (1966), 'Ancient history and the antiquarian', in *Studies in Historiography.* New York: Harper, pp. 1–39.

—(1971), *The Development of Greek Biography.* Cambridge, MA: Harvard University Press.

Nelson, A. (2003), *Monstrous Adversary: The Life of Edward De Vere, 17th Earl of Oxford.* Liverpool: Liverpool University Press.

—(2004), 'Stratford si! Essex no! (An open and shut case)', lecture delivered at the University of Tennessee debate on the Shakespeare authorship question (unpublished and unpaginated).

Nicholl, Charles. (2007), *The Lodger: Shakespeare on Silver Street.* London: Allen Lane.

Nietzsche, F. (1968), 'Beyond good and evil', in *Basic Writings of Nietzsche*, trans. Walter Kaufman. New York: Modern Library.

Ogburn, C. (1984), *The Mysterious William Shakespeare.* New York: Dodd, Mead & Company.

Orwell, G. (1946), 'Benefit of clergy: Some notes on Salvador Dali', in *Critical Essays.* London: Secker and Warburg, pp. 120–9.

Pierce, W. (1911), ed., *The Marprelate Tracts 1588, 1589.* London: James Clarke.

Plato (1892a), 'Cratylus', in *The Dialogues of Plato*, trans. Benjamin Jowett, 5 vols. Oxford: Clarendon Press, I.

—(1892b), 'Parmenides', in *The Dialogues of Plato*, trans. Benjamin Jowett, 5 vols, Oxford: Clarendon Press, IV.

Pope, A. (ed.) (1725), *The Works of Shakespeare in Six Volumes.* London: Jacob Tonson

Potter, D. (1996), *Karaoke and Cold Lazarus.* London: Faber and Faber.

Potter, L. (2005), Review of *Will in the World,* by Stephen Greenblatt. *Shakespeare Quarterly,* 56(3): 34–76.

Price, D. (2001), *Shakespeare's Unorthodox Biography: New Evidence of an Authorship Problem.* Westport, CT: Greenwood Press.

Proper, I. S. (1953), *Our Elusive Willy: A Slice of Concealed Elizabethan History.* Dingo Editions.

Proust, M. (1989), *In Search of Lost Time: I,* trans. C. K. Scott Moncrieff and Terence Kilmartin. London: Penguin.

Rand, R. (1982), 'O'er brimm'd', *Oxford Literary Review,* 5, 53–5.

—(1984), 'Greenwood', in Jacques Derrida, *Signéponge / Signsponge,* trans. Richard Rand. New York: Columbia Universitry Press.

Reiman, D. H. and Powers, S. B. (1977), eds, *Shelley's Poetry and Prose.* New York: Norton.

Rijsman, J. (1997), 'Social diversity: A social psychological analysis and some implications for groups and organizations', *European Journal of Work and Organizational Psychology,* 6, 139–52.

Rollins, H. E. (1958), ed., *The Letters of John Keats,* 2 vols. Cambridge, MA: Harvard University Press.

Rowe, N. (1709), *The Works of Mr William Shakspear.* (6 vols). London: Jacob Tonson.

Royle, N. (1988), 'Telepathy: From Jane Austen and Henry James', *Oxford Literary Review,* 10, 43–60.

—(1990a), 'The Distraction of "Freud": Literature, Psychoanalysis and the Bacon–Shakespeare Controversy', *Oxford Literary Review,* 12, 101–38.

—(1990b), 'Nuclear *Pieqe: Mémoires of Hamlet* and the time to come', *Diacritics,* 20(1) (Spring 1990), 39–55.

—(1995), *After Derrida.* Manchester: Manchester University Press.

—(2003), 'Mole', in *The Uncanny.* Manchester: Manchester University Press, pp. 241–55.

Saunders, A. W. L. (2007), *The Master of Shakespeare: Volume One; The Sonnets.* Tortola: MoS Publishing.

Savage, R. (ed.) (1929), *Minutes and Accounts of the Corporation of Stratford-upon-Avon and Other Records 1553–1620.* Vol 4. London: Oxford University Press.

Schachter, S. (1951), 'Deviance, rejection and communication', *Journal of Abnormal and Social Psychology,* 46, 190–208.

Schoenbaum, S. (1970), *Shakespeare's Lives.* Oxford: Clarendon Press.

—(1975), *Shakespeare: A Documentary Life.* Oxford: Clarendon Press

—(1991), *Shakespeare's Lives* (revised edn). Oxford: Oxford University Press.

—(1966), *Internal Evidence and Elizabethan Dramatic Authorship: An Essay in Literary History and Method.* Evanston: Northwestern University Press.

Schlegel, A. W. von. (1997), 'Lectures on Dramatic Art and Literature (1808–11)', Jonathan Bate, ed., *The Romantics on Shakespeare.* London: Penguin, pp. 88–110.

Schruijer, S. (1990), *Norm Violation, Attribution and Attitudes in Intergroup Relations.* Tilburg: Tilburg University Press.

—(2002), 'Delen en helen: Over conflict en samenwerking tussen groepen', Inaugural address, Tilburg University.

—(2008), 'The psychology of interorganizational relations', in *The Oxford Handbook of Interorganizational Relations*, eds S. Cropper, M. Ebers, C. Huxham and P. Smith Ring. New York: Oxford University Press, pp. 417–40.

Shakespeare Birthplace Trust, (www.shakespeare.org.uk/content/view/15/15/).

Shakespeare, W. (1997a), *The Most Lamentable Tragedy of Titus Andronicus*, in *The Norton Shakespeare, Based on the Oxford Edition*, ed. Stephen Greenblatt. New York: Norton.

—(1997b), *The Tragedy of Hamlet, Prince of Denmark*, in *The Norton Shakespeare, Based on the Oxford Edition*, ed. Stephen Greenblatt. New York: Norton.

—(1997c), *The Tragedy of Richard the Third*, in *The Norton Shakespeare, Based on the Oxford Edition*, ed. Stephen Greenblatt. New York: Norton.

Shakespeare, W. (2005), *Romeo and Juliet*, ed. T. J. B. Spencer. London: Penguin.

Shakespeare, W. (1979), *The Tempest*, ed. Frank Kermode (revised edn). London: Methuen.

Shakespeare, W. (1980), *Romeo and Juliet*, ed. Brian Gibbons. London: Methuen.

Shakespeare, W. (1981), *Antony and Cleopatra*, ed. M. R. Ridley (revised edn). London: Methuen.

Shakespeare, W. (1982), *Hamlet*, ed. Harold Jenkins. London: Methuen.

Shakespeare, W. (1983), *Antony and Cleopatra*, ed. John Ingledew. Harlow, Essex: Longman.

Shapiro, James. (2006), 'Shakespeare's professional world', in *Searching for Shakespeare*. ed. Tanya Cooper. London: Yale University Press, pp. 23–31.

—(2005), *1599: A Year in the Life of Shakespeare*. London: Faber & Faber.

Sherif, M. (1967), *Group Conflict and Cooperation*. London: Routledge and Kegan Paul.

Slater, G. (1931) *Seven Shakespeares*. London: C. Palmer.

Smircich, L. and Morgan, G. (1982), 'Leadership: The management of meaning', *Journal of Applied Behavioral Science*, 18, 257–73.

Smith, J. H. and Kerrigan, W. (eds) (1984), *Taking Chances: Derrida, Psychoanalysis, and Literature*. London: Johns Hopkins University Press.

Smith, R. M. (1946), 'Irish names in *The Faerie Queene*', *Modern Language Notes*, 61, 27–38.

Staunton, H. (1864), *Memorials of Shakespeare*. London.

Stewart, A. (2009), 'Early modern lives in facsimile', *Textual Practice*, 23(2), 289–305.

Stritmatter, R. (2006), 'What's in a name? Everything, apparently . . .'. *Rocky Mountain Review of Language and Literature*, 60(2), 37–49.

Tajfel, H. (1981), *Human Groups and Social Categories: Studies in Social Psychology*. Cambridge: Cambridge University Press.

Tajfel, H. and Turner, J. (1979), 'An integrative theory of intergroup conflict', in *The Social Psychology of Intergroup Relations*, eds W. Austin and S. Worchel. Monterey, CA: Brooks/Cole.

Tapscott, D. and Williams, A. D. (2006), *Wikinomics: How Mass Collaboration Changes Everything*. London: Atlantic Books.

Taylor, G. (1989), 'The date and auspices of the additions to *Sir Thomas More*', in *Shakespeare and Sir Thomas More: Essays on the Play and its Shakespearean Interests*, ed, T. H. Howard-Hill. Cambridge: Cambridge University Press, pp. 101–30.

—(1990), *Reinventing Shakespeare: A Cultural History from the Restoration to the Present*. London: Hogarth.

—(2004), 'Stephen, Will, and Gary too', Review of *Will in the World*, by Stephen Greenblatt. *The Guardian*, 9 October, 9.

Trosman, H. (1965), 'Freud and the controversy over Shakespearean authorship', in the *Journal of the American Psychoanalytic Association*, 13(3), July, 475–98.

Twain, M. (1909), *Is Shakespeare Dead? From My Autobiography*. New York and London: Harpers and Brothers.

Usher, P. (2002), 'Shakespeare's support for the new astronomy', *The Oxfordian*, 5, 132–46.

Vickers, B. (2007), 'Incomplete Shakespeare: Or, denying co-authorship in *1 Henry VI*'. *Shakespeare Quarterly*, 58(3), 311–52.

Vickers, B. (1974–81), ed., *Shakespeare: The Critical Heritage*, 6 vols. London: Routledge and Kegan Paul.

Ward, G. (ed.) (2000), 'Introduction', *The Certeau Reader*, Oxford: Blackwell, 1–14.

Weis, R. (2007), *Shakespeare Revealed: A Biography*. London: John Murray.—(2009), 'Was there a real Shakespeare?', *Textual Practice*, 23(2), 215–28.

—(2007), *Shakespeare Unbound: Decoding a Hidden Life*. New York: Henry Holt.

Wells, S. (2002), *Shakespeare: For all Time*. London: Macmillan.

Welply, W. H. (1932), 'Edmund Spenser: Being an account of some recent researches into his life and lineage, with some notice of his family and descendants', *Notes and Queries*, 162, 128–32.

White, R. S. (1996), ed., *Hazlitt's Criticism of Shakespeare: A Selection*. Lewison: The Edwin Mellen Press.

Williams, R. (2006), *Sweet Swan of Avon: Did a Woman Write Shakespeare?* Berkeley, CA: Peachpit Press.

Wilson, J. D. (1912), *Martin Marprelate and Shakespeare's Fluellen*. London: Alexander Morgan.

Wood, M. (2003), *In Search of Shakespeare*. London: BBC Books.

—(2003), *Shakespeare*. New York: Basic Books.

Wordsworth, W. (1992), '*Lyrical Ballads' and Other Poems, 1797–1800*, ed. James Butler and Karen Green. Ithaca: Cornell University Press.

Wright, D. (2001), 'Preface', in Elizabeth Appleton, *Anatomy of the Marprelate Controversy 1588–1596: Retracing Shakespeare's Identity and that of Martin Marprelate*. Lewiston: Edwin Mellon Press, lix–lxi.

Woolf, V. (1929; 1992), *A Room of One's Own*. ed. Morag Shiach. Oxford: Oxford University Press.

Young, E. (1759), *Conjectures on Original Composition in a Letter to the Author of Sir Charles Grandison*. London: A. Millar and J. Dodsley.

Index